Landing On Your Feet

Patrick –
All the Best
to you & your
Sales Team!

Landing On Your Feet

An Amazing Story of Business Mistakes, Survival, and Success

Michael G. Kerrison

BROADVIEW PRESS

NEW YORK • MINNEAPOLIS

Landing On Your Feet
An Amazing Story of Business Mistakes, Survival, and Success
By Michael G. Kerrison

Published by
Broadview Press, Inc.
7760 France Avenue South
Suite #1119
Bloomington, MN 55435 U.S.A.
Orders@BroadviewPressInc.com
http://BroadviewPressInc.com

Unattributed quotations are by Michael G. Kerrison

Design by Hugh Bennewitz

Copyright 2003 by Michael G. Kerrison

First Printing: 2003

Certain names and situations have been changed to provide confidentiality. Any perceived slight to any person was unintentional.

Publisher's Cataloging-in-Publication
(Provided by Quality Books, Inc.)

Kerrison, Michael G.
    Landing on your feet : a story of business mistakes, survival, and success / by Michael G. Kerrison.
    p. cm.
    Includes index.
    LCCN 2003090358
    ISBN 0-9728566-9-2

1. New business enterprises. 2. Entrepreneurship.
3. Success in business.   I. Title.

HD62.5.K47 2003   658.1'1
                           QBI03-200125

To my dearest ones-
Chad, Cammy, Madelyn, and Chelsea

"Success is never ending. Failure is never final."
-Robert Schuller

Table of Contents

Foreword   xiii
Introduction xv

Part One   *Filling In The Blanks*

1. AFew Notches Above Poverty 5
2. Bless Me, Father, for I Have Sinned 19
3. A Rough Start 27
4. Adversity Taught Me Well 35
5. Rowing My Own Boat 45

Part Two   *The Business Years*

6. Everything Happens for a Reason 61
7. Drifting 77
8. Flying Solo 87
9. Riding the Series/1 109
10. Going a Little Crazy 115
11. The Meltdown 125
12. The Turning Point 143
13. Saved by Sorbus 153
14. Tubby's Tutorial 159
15. Rebuilding the Business 173
16. More Ups than Downs 189
17. Leading NCC 201
18. Putting it all Together 209
In Closing 221

Part Three   *The Toolkit*

Selling Tools 225
Planning Tools 265
Management Tools 281

Index 291

Foreword

By Larry Wilson, founder of Wilson Learning Corporation

In 1975, I watched a young man glide down a long aisle smooth and straight before flying up a stairs to an awaiting stage. Earsplitting music pulsated in the room, while strobe lights danced on the walls. I was at the annual IBM Hundred Percent Club, and I had just finished my keynote address to over one-thousand salespeople. As the man approached us, the MC revealed his remarkable credentials and accomplishments. I observed with interest and admiration. At 232 percent of quota, this person at age twenty-three had set a new level of performance at IBM, earning him the coveted award of "Rookie-of-the-Year." He was the best of the best. His name was Mike Kerrison.

I have spent my life's work trying to help people grasp the significance of their lives and to use their courage and creativity to face challenges, handle adversity, and grow as individuals. I have written five books and given countless speeches with these intentions in mind. Mike had been one of my students, and now, years later, I could be one of his. I have gotten to know Mike and his remarkable story. He has come a long way since that day in 1975. This book, *Landing On Your Feet* is one of the most authentic portrayals of what's really involved to start and build a business that I have ever read. Not only will it deliver powerful tools to help you run your business, but it will show you how to run your life with passion, meaning, and purpose.

We live in confusing and turbulent times. The trust and confidence we once had for America's corporations has been weakened. Many of our greatest companies are floating in a sea of red ink, now bobbing in the wreckage of their own greed. As a result, entrepreneurs are on the rise, seeking to fulfill their own dreams, no longer willing to be vulnerable to the whims of big business. But big or little, these companies all need help.

Paradoxically, we also live in a time of great opportunity. Mike Kerrison understands this. So he wrote this book for us, showing us how to succeed by learning from our mistakes, accepting our shortcomings, appreciating our gifts, and teaching us to never give up. He proves to each of us that we can accomplish whatever we put our mind to. His ideas are simply presented, easy to use, and can make a profound difference in our businesses and in our lives. For some of us, Mike's story could be life changing.

I am excited about this book and the influence it will have on thousands of readers. It represents the distillation of twenty-five years of work by one of our finest entrepreneur's. You will laugh out loud, cry in private, and rejoice in the fact that the average person can have true success and fulfillment in life. *Landing On Your Feet* will help you achieve both. Read, learn, apply, and enjoy. God bless!

Larry Wilson
Boca Grande, Florida
May 2003

Introduction

When people ask me how I started my business, I don't launch into a lecture on business planning or raising capital. I just tell them what happened. Not long into the story, they usually request that I back up and fill in some of the blanks-you know, jobs, childhood, where I grew up, things like that. In other words, where did this all begin? They gather and sort through the information, as if searching for clues, drawing parallels between the events of my life and their own.

Their expressions seem to ask, "Should I start a business?" or, "Do I have what it takes to do this, too?" They wonder if there is some magic to it all, some mystical formula, but starting a business requires no magic. It's done every day by average people who do extraordinary things because they are tired of being average. That is why I wrote this book-because despite what you may think, you are not average, and you can start a business, too.

I am hardly alone in this endeavor. Much has been written on this subject. Bookstores are jammed with success stories, many of which sit on my own shelf. I call them "business cookbooks"-recipes for success. A *dollop* of this and a *pinch* of that is often all that separates them-the author of each a specialty chef, spicing up the same old recipe. I have read all of them, and-as with any good cookbook-when I grab them off the shelf, my favorites have broken bindings, loose pages, dog-eared corners, coffee stains, and lots of notes. They provide a ready index of recipes to help me run my business, to be sure. But they are all missing a major ingredient. I feel underfed. You see, I rarely find a personal story, just the mechanics-which is never enough. I want to know these entrepreneurs and what really happened inside their business. Often these books tend to glorify the successes and shun the failures. That's where the real story gets lost. Our longing for victors over goats conceals the truth.

I want the truth. All the "desperate bits"-the authors' mistakes, their pain, their passion, their drive, their loneliness, their despair, their meltdowns, their recoveries, their fears, their families, the people who helped them, the people who hurt them. I'm trying to find someone out there like me! Someone who is going through the same things I am. I, too, am searching for clues, comparing notes. Don't misunderstand me; I enjoy reading books about Bill Gates, Lee Iaccoca, Sam Walton, and Jack Welsh. I admire them and their remarkable stories greatly. But I have trouble relating to them. The comparisons are too vague, the applications too abstract.

Whenever I shared my story with family and friends, I got a consistent reaction: "Mike, you should write this down-all of it." That always seemed to be a heady proposition, because I didn't seek to gratify my own vanity through my story since most people dislike vanity in others. That said, though, I have decided to yield to the weakness so natural to most entrepreneurs to tell you about myself and the good fortune I've had in business.

Yes, this is a rags-to-riches story. No, it is not unprecedented (I'm not Bill Gates). But I can tell you that all three of my technology companies prospered, reached multimillion-dollar levels, received statewide and national recognition, and eventually produced several millionaires. They sprang forth for different reasons and at different times, falling into each other like dominoes. What I find most exciting is that they serve as incontestable proof of my original premise: The average person can do extraordinary things. My story is one you can relate to-and one you can apply. It's a compass for you to follow so that one day you will have your own story.

I am going to take you on a journey that will uncover the "desperate bits." I will tell you without censorship what I did and how I did it. I will not try to be glib or clever, and I will not load you up with a bunch of popular business philosophy. Instead, I will give you the truth about myself and the straightforward, no-nonsense answers that work in business (and in life)-answers that have always worked but have been buried in a deluge of en vogue business theory.

This is not an autobiography or an instruction manual for business start-ups. Instead, it's an extended *curriculum vitae*, showing how one entrepreneur was formed. It's an opportunity for you to compare notes, with an inside look at how my childhood, ambition, desire, luck, and some talent all played a part in starting and building a business-which built a life.

As I reflect on all of this, if given the choice I would have no issue with going back and correcting many of the decisions of my life-no differently than an author correcting in a second draft the faults of the first. While you may find things that you deem fit to be imitated should you find yourself in similar circumstances, I believe the real learning will occur by examining the mistakes that I made along the way, because our success teaches us little. That's just the way we keep score. So in that spirit I will give you the whole, uncut version, beginning with snapshots of my formative years, with all their color and turmoil, followed by the business years, with all the ups and downs. I then wrap up with my *toolkit*-a bunch of rusty old tools that have always worked for me. I want you to have them, and use them to build your business.

Finally, this book strives to jar you to the recognition that you, too, can fulfill your dreams, however you define them. Do not think of yourself as average, suffering the label of having "great potential" when you instead can be labeled a "great achiever." I aim this book directly at you, the so-called average person just like me, who has a yearning to start a business and be extraordinary at something. It is also for the existing business owner wanting to revitalize his or her company and take it to the next level. The "blue-chip" executive can benefit, too-the one struggling to restore some of the energy and trust so often lost in a giant corporation. This book has something for all of you.

So if it's agreeable, I would like to start the journey. I must warn you, though, it was not always pretty. I made a lot of mistakes-some serious. But in the end it worked out better than I ever dreamed possible.

Landing On Your Feet

PART ONE

Filling In The Blanks

Chapter 1

A Few Notches Above Poverty

"This stinks! We're never gonna make any money doin' this!" I said, slamming my folded arms to my chest and slumping into my lawn chair.

"Yeah," Joey agreed sleepily.

We craned our necks up and down the road, praying for anyone to drive by. All we could see were barns, cows, cornfields, and a whole lot of dusty Ohio farmland.

"We'll never get enough money to go to Ohl's sittin' here. This is a terrible spot." I slumped even farther down into my chair and stared at the sky.

"Yeah . . . I was really lookin' forward to gettin' some candy," Joey said.

"Me, too."

Ohl's was a little country store three miles up the road. On our recent seventh birthday (only days apart), my best friend, Joey Devine, and I had each been granted the privilege of riding our bikes to Ohl's to spend our lemonade-stand profits. We now sat with our knees pulled to our chin, daydreaming about Ohl's, and Cracker Jacks, and bubblegum, and grape soda pop.

It was a perfect July afternoon in Valley City, Ohio, in 1958. My mother had promised us that an enterprise like a lemonade stand would be a dependable way for two seven-year-old boys to make money. She had been our first banker, extending credit in the form of two packets of Kool-Aid, three Lipton's tea bags, sugar, plenty of ice, and two plastic pitchers of water. The rest was up to us.

But after an enthusiastic start and three hours of scorching sun, Joey and I began consuming our inventory and lamenting our paltry income.

My mother appeared at the screen door with her hands on her hips. "You boys rich and famous yet?" she yelled.

"Mom, this is stupid. We've been sittin' out here for hours. All we got is a measly thirty cents. Can't you just give us some money, Mom? Pleeeeze?"

"Hey, quit your griping. Thirty cents is more than you started with. Besides, you know my policy on that," she said. "Anyway, you need to wrap up soon. Dinner's going on the table. And don't forget. You owe me for that Kool-Aid." Her voice trailed off as she disappeared into the house.

Joey and I abandoned our lawn chairs in favor of the lawn itself. Lying on our backs, we stared into the blue sky and harmonized tunes through a blade of grass. We had all but given up. I glanced over at my best friend. We did everything together.

Joey was one of nine kids, with seven brothers and one sister-his parents had obviously done their part in putting the "boom" in baby boomers. He was puny with a chubby face, and he wore glasses with thick, round lenses that made his eyes look too big. His hands were always searching the pockets of his bib overalls, and his hair, which was too long, hung stick straight to the top of his glasses. He wore brown sandals, the kind with crisscrosses on the toes, and his T-shirt had wide horizontal stripes. He looked like a character from the *Little Rascals*.

I had a more conventional look. During the summer Mom kept me in shorts and butch haircuts, with an occasional attempt at a flattop-always unsuccessful. The only things darker than my suntan were my knees, which were mostly covered with dirt, and when Mom wasn't rinsing them off with the garden hose she was basting me with calamine lotion since I had poison ivy most every summer. But my dirty knees, poison ivy, and bald spots (from the flattop attempts) didn't show much, thanks to my deep suntan, which helped me win an occasional battle at bath time.

Joey and I-now comfortable and dreamlike-continued to stare into the sky. Moments later I heard a loud rumbling noise coming from the railroad tracks.

"Hey, Joey, look!" I yelped, sitting straight up.

"What?" he asked, stringing a blade of grass between his fingers.

"Look what's coming!"

Joey rolled his head to the right. "Wow!" he shouted, and sprang to his feet.

Two huge fire trucks were creeping straight at us-no sirens, no bells. They were returning to the Valley City station. My dad had been a volunteer fireman on weekends, and I knew all these guys.

Joey and I ran into the middle of the road and waved our arms to slow them down.

"If these guys ain't thirsty, nobody is," I said.

Joey agreed.

We guided them to the edge of the road, where they obediently lumbered to a stop. The air brakes screeched, and the hot diesel engines quieted to a clinking idle. A fireman with a grimy face leaned out the window. "Whatcha' got there, boys?" he asked.

Joey and I ran to our table and held up two pitchers. "Lemonade and iced tea-only a nickel a glass," I said. We were proud of our presentation.

"There's plenty of ice, too," Joey added.

"Ooo-eee! That sounds mighty good, don't it boys?" the fireman said, yelling toward the back of the truck. Turning back to us, he said, "We'll take all ya' got." He opened the large, red door and swung his legs around. "Ya think five bucks oughta cover it?"

Joey and I looked at each other, wide-eyed. My heart was pounding like a baby bird's, and I figured Joey's was, too. We could hardly pour, our hands were shaking so hard. The men on top of the trucks hurled themselves to the ground, and the fire chief slid out of the cab. Their faces were streaked with soot.

"Say, ain't you George Kerrison's kid?" the chief asked me.

"Yes, sir, I am." My face was filled with determination as I continued to pour.

The firemen gathered around the small folding table. "Name's Mike, right?" the chief asked.

"Yes, sir.

He winked. "Thought so. Tell your dad we missed him today. Just got done puttin' out a barn fire." He pulled his suspenders from his shoulders. "Took us four hours, so we're real thirsty." He slapped his trousers in search of his wallet. "I'd say you boys were in the right place at the right time," the chief said as he handed me a five spot.

My hands trembled as I took the bill and placed it under the rock on the table. *This will last the rest of the summer*, I thought.

"I'll say. And thank you, sir. Thank you very much."

"Thank *you*," he said, raising his paper cup to propose a toast. "Well, boys, here's to another successful day for the Valley City Fire Department." He chugged down his drink, winced at its sweetness, and said, "Ahhh, that's mighty good stuff."

We raced to refill his cup.

"Well, boys, I'd say we're gettin' our money's worth. There must be five dollars' worth of sugar in here."

The firemen glanced at each other and sipped cautiously.

Suddenly my mother called me from somewhere inside the house. "Michael! Dinner! Time to come in!"

I glanced back at the house. We lived in a tiny ranch that had an overall squatty look to it, as if the builder had run out of wood and decided to quit. The front of the house had a large picture window that gobbled up most of the wall, and to the right was a concrete stoop that rose to the front door, which proudly displayed a large *K* for Kerrison. On either side of the stoop were two decorative wagon wheels, a reasonable attempt to add charm on a low budget. We never worried about "keeping up with the Joneses." Most of our neighbors had less than we did.

"Mom, I can't!" I shouted over my shoulder. "I got customers!"

Joey and I continued pouring.

"You get in here right now, young man!" my mother persisted. "Food's getting cold. Joseph Devine, your mother called. It's time for you to go home, too."

I gave a low growl. "Mom, we *can't*," I said, trying to keep control of the situation.

The firemen snickered. They sensed a showdown coming.

My mother finally appeared at the door, this time ranting and raving. "Michael Kerrison, don't you dare tell me you-*Holy cow!*" She stood gaping at two shiny fire trucks and seven firemen standing in her front yard. "When did all this happen?"

"That's what Mike's been trying to tell ya, Mrs. Kerrison. We got *customers*," my best friend said, smiling proudly.

Now, grinning, my mother nodded her head and folded her arms. "You sure do, Joey. You sure do."

It never occurred to me as a young lemonade salesman that I would one day own a sixty-million-dollar business. But looking back over all these years, that is where it all began. Half the formula for success is just showing up. It's a numbers game. At age seven I was learning the four P's of good marketing: product, price, place, and promotion. I guess there's a fifth P: patience.

My experience on that hot July afternoon, combined with my dad's advice, was the first layer of a solid foundation. Dad used to say,

"Mike, I want you to remember two things: One, always have a buck in your pocket, and, two, if you got a tongue in your head, you're never lost, and you're never broke." This was good business advice coming from a blue collar guy, which I suppose is one reason that I started my career as a salesman. But I'm getting ahead of myself.

Joey and I quickly cleaned up our stand and headed to our respective houses for dinner. With my arms full, I started the long stretch to the house. Clunking along, I idly noted our front yard "landscaping," which consisted of a few scrawny arborvitaes that provided inadequate camouflage for the concrete-block foundation. The yard itself had been reduced to dust by scorching summers, allowing for only a few haphazard green patches of grass. The long dirt driveway was lined with the annual plantings of our Christmas trees-Dad, a product of the Depression, enjoyed the economy of killing two birds with one stone. I can still picture my father wrestling the yearly tree into the house with its large root ball wrapped in burlap. This allowed for efficient planting after the holiday-but not without making a mess of Mom's floor. (In a recent visit to my old stomping grounds, I was astonished to see these "old friends" standing over fifty feet high, like monuments marking the time. I smiled at them, remembering the days when Dad brought them home.)

The front screen door slammed behind me as I entered our small living room, which had a Silvertone television set with a large, round screen, a high fidelity phonograph, a two-piece turquoise couch that looked like something Barbie and Ken sat on, and Dad's worn-out recliner. I would often find him there, stretched out, eyes closed, happily rubbing his feet together while listening to John Gary records. Dad was a quiet man. He preferred the calm of his records to the chatter of the Silvertone-though it did host his favorites like *Playhouse 90*, *The Honeymooners*, and *I Love Lucy*.

"Wash your hands," Mom said firmly. "And hurry up now."

"I'm comin', I'm comin'. Jeez."

"Hey, buster, watch that tone," she said.

Dad had been working the day shift that week and was home for dinner. He loved my report about the firemen and our successful sales day. He smiled and said, "Well, thereya go, Mike. Always have that buck in your pocket. You and Joey are rich." He was right. We were.

After dinner I headed for my bedroom.

Under my bedroom window was a silver propane gas tank sitting on four legs that looked like something out of a *Flash Gordon* movie. It was a primitive utility by today's standards but a fantastic ride to the moon for a seven-year-old with an overactive imagination. Rumblings from the gas man often woke me in the morning as he brought me fuel for my journey. I'd crawl from my window, hop on the tank, and blast off for a morning ride.

Most of our neighbors were farmers. Their houses and barns were old, gray, and spooky looking. I remember having an occasional nightmare where the outbuildings-usually in disrepair and badly in need of paint-would come alive and start eating my flesh. But the rabbits in one of the outbuildings helped to quiet such imaginings. I could kill an entire morning pulling them from their cages and gathering each one into my lap to pet them and feed them handfuls of small pellets.

What I enjoyed most about the neighboring farms was running through the golden cornfields in late autumn. At the top of the ridge behind our neighbor's barn, long, perfect rows melted into the horizon, farther than the eye could see. The late afternoon sun would dance on the tips of each row, making mysterious shadows that would quiver with the wind. At times I could see a distant man perched on what looked like a toy tractor, silent and disproportionate in size to the endless work that stretched before him. I have clung to these childhood images of effort and sacrifice all my life. Even today when I drive down an old country road my eyes sting with gratitude when I see a farmer in his field.

One of our neighbors, Emil Wallace, had a chicken farm. His house was small, and the yard was fenced in like a giant coop. His front and back doors were left open all summer long, allowing the chickens to wander in and out freely. Emil had one leg shorter than the other, which gave him a distinctive rocking gait. He stood about five-two, rarely shaved, and had a nappy clump of hair that blew to one side. One time when I was passing by, I saw Emil grab a chicken by the head, slap it onto a tree stump, and whack its head off. I watched in horror as the headless chicken darted in every direction, spurting blood all over the place, while its head lay in the dirt. "Dinner," Emil proclaimed with a toothless grin, grabbing the animated corpse by its feet. I was frozen, unable to look away. How did they keep running around like that? Marvelous!

The Devines were part-time farmers. The property was filled with crops, animals, and a few broken down shacks. The scene looked like something you would find in the Smoky Mountains of Tennessee.

Joey's father, Bill Devine, was a stern man with a mean-looking face. His jet black beard matched his dark, formidable eyes. I was always afraid of him. I think he was drunk a lot. Never smiling, he looked like a creepy mountain man, and he always seemed to be sweating over some project in the yard. I can still see the consistent drip that would gather and fall from his angular nose. In the eight years that I lived next door, I don't believe he ever talked to me. For all I know, he thought I was one of his kids. He never talked to them, either.

Joey's mother, Darla, would talk to us, but she was strange. She had bad teeth and thick glasses like Joey's, and never shaved her armpits. You could tell because she wore those thin, white, sleeveless fifties blouses with the Peter Pan collars. She would stand in the doorway counting kids, a cigarette in one hand and leaning on the doorjamb with the other, proudly displaying her luxurious crop. Yuck! It made me sick. Thank God she didn't sweat like her husband did. But I suppose with nine kids you don't have a lot of time to shave your armpits. I often wondered what came first, though, the armpit hair or the nine kids. After all, I would imagine armpit hair is pretty effective birth control-even for people like Mountain-Man Bill.

One thing I could never understand was why Mrs. Devine wouldn't let us come into the house, not even to use the toilet. Sleepovers were out of the question-though we couldn't have messed the place up any worse if we'd tried. I found this out one day when Joey snuck me into the house to show me his bedroom. His sister, Darla, had her own room as did Bill Jr., the oldest son. The rest of the boys were stuffed into a giant loft, which looked like an army barracks but without the discipline. The room had a sickeningly sweet smell from all those hormones and unshowered bodies. I concluded that Joey and I were much better off sleeping at my house.

The Devines had a huge oak tree in their backyard, the climbing of which set the standard for bravery. To gain any respect at all from the older kids, you had to climb solo to the very top, a not-so-casual sixty feet. I had been terrified of that old tree and jealous that my older sister, Lindsey, could climb it with ease. Not to be outdone, and after many attempts, Joey and I finally made it to the top. In tandem, we pushed and pulled the top limbs back and forth, back and forth, making them sway like a giant brush painting clouds in the sky. We did it for hours, recklessly, claiming victory over our fear and rendering that old tree impotent in the face of our bravery. Never would we be afraid of that tree again.

Sometimes we would pretend to be race car drivers. Mr. Devine always had an interesting collection of old junkers strewn across the property. The hot, muggy days of summer would intensify the rank smell of the old car seats, and the corrosive odor of rust would waft over us. Everything was too hot to touch. My favorite vehicle was a black 1935 Ford roadster. The two doors and windshield were missing, and it sat on rusty axles. An old kitchen chair was substituted for the driver's seat, which sat in front of the holes in the floorboards where the clutch and brake pedals once were-probably cannibalized for parts. But the gas pedal was there, which was all we cared about. We would take turns sitting in the silent machinery, imagining ourselves in control of massive horsepower, making every impossible fantasy curve look easy. While I raced, Joey would be working the pit, and I yelled *"Eeeeyyyowww!"* on every turn. It was a perfect race car, often holding our attention for an entire afternoon.

Occasionally we would hike down the hill where Mr. Devine kept his six boxed beehives. Each stood about four feet tall. They looked like swarming filing cabinets. For fun, we would throw rocks at them. (I was always throwing things, mostly rocks and apples, which would serve me well later when I started playing baseball.) We would sneak up slowly, fire a big stone, and run like hell. This would really piss off the bees. We never got stung, though, which was a miracle.

In contrast to our neighbors' property, our yard was always clean and tidy. My mom and dad, Anne and George Kerrison, made sure of that. They were hard workers at their jobs, as well. Dad worked for Municipal Light Company in Cleveland, climbing power poles to repair high-voltage wires-a risky undertaking for an otherwise undaring person. He was tall, with broad shoulders and a kind face loaded with freckles-especially in the summer. Mom was the hostess at the Spanish Tavern restaurant. She was a lovely Greek girl with bushy brown hair, brown eyes, and full lips, always red. Dad was reserved, almost shy; Mom was just the opposite, outgoing and garrulous, which contributed to her being a good hostess.

Dad always looked as though he was deep in thought about something. "George, what are you thinking about?" Mom would often ask.

He would say, "Nothing, why?" But it was always something. We just never knew what. Mom said it had something to do with the war. Dad was a World War II vet-Normandy, Battle of the Bulge, Purple Heart, the whole bit.

For all their hard work, they rarely made ends meet. After paying bills, Mom stuffed the remaining cash, around $200, in a small drinking glass hidden in the top drawer of her dresser. This would have to last the month, usually to buy food and gas. I never felt poor, but I do remember Mom saying no a lot. She was creative in finding ways to get things for us, though, like using cereal box tops and S&H Green Stamps from the grocery store. I can picture her sitting at the kitchen table, proudly displaying her stamp books after her most recent shopping trip. "Look, Mike, almost filled. We can get something soon," she'd say. Once I got a Rin Tin Tin hat that way, plus a bunch of those little green army men.

Dad was gone a lot. Three shifts often had him out all night and sleeping all day-so even when he was home, he was gone. On cold winter nights, after his late shift, he liked having a shot of bourbon and a beer before turning in. Mom would always be up waiting for him. Sometimes she would wake me so that I could visit with him for a while. I remember the bottle of Wild Turkey on the kitchen table next to where he sat and the shot glass that had little flying pheasants etched on the side. Mom had it sitting out waiting for him, with a plate of crackers and a few slices of longhorn cheese.

"Mom, why does Dad drink those things?" I asked. "They smell kinda yucky."

"They're called boilermakers, sweetheart. Your dad had his first one at a little pub in Belgium. I guess he's been drinkin' 'em ever since."

Dad always had the scent of the shop on him-grease and body odor from the long underwear that he wore under his blue work clothes.

The Municipal Light Depot was a massive warehouse filled with linemen's trucks bearing tall ladders, giant spools of cable, tool cribs, a maintenance shop, and a locker room where the linemen could store their belongings. The depot always carried a peculiar odor, much of which was the remnant of stale cigarette smoke.

Before having to go back to bed, I would always get a ten-minute pillow fight or a wrestling match out of him. When he was really tired, we just cuddled. His funny smell never bothered me.

I remember when I decided I was too old to kiss my parents good night. I felt so guilty that on my way to bed, I swapped the kisses for about ten or fifteen good-nights and I-love-yous. It went something like: "Good night, see ya tomorrow, I love you, good night, see ya in the morning, good night Mom, sleep tight, good night Dad, I love you both, see ya."

Dad finally blurted out, crushing his newspaper in his lap, "Jesus Christ! What the hell's wrong with that kid?"

"George, relax, don't you see what's happening? He's not kissing us good night anymore. This is how he's dealing with it," I could hear Mom whisper as I made my way to my room.

"Oh . . . I didn't know. Well, that's fine, but I liked the kisses better."

Then he came and tucked me in.

Mom ran the show. She didn't exactly wear the pants, but it was close. Above all, she was driven and competitive, pushing Dad to do more, to accomplish more. For instance, there was never any question that my sister and I were going to college, no matter what. We were going to be somebody. She argued with my dad a lot.

Her nature came from her father, Alexander Gaitanis, who came to America from Greece at age fifteen with absolutely nothing. Years later, with five daughters and a wife, he really wore the pants. But though Mom's sisters got away with nothing, she had her father wrapped around her little finger. This was her way of sharing the pants, the skillful art of manipulation. For me, she was just Mom-loving and attentive.

Supper was always on the table at six o'clock sharp, and we always said grace before every meal. Dad would start. We would follow.

"Bless us, O Lord, for these thy gifts, which we are about to receive from thy bounty, through Christ our Lord. Amen."

After blitzing through the prayer, we ate. Lindsey and I would finish early and be forced to sit through the unknowable jabbering of Mom and Dad.

Dad was a devout Catholic. Mom had converted. On Sunday mornings we jumped into our 1949 Ford and headed to St. Joseph's Catholic Church. Dad wore the same brown suit and tie every Sunday, and he passed the basket during the offertory. Mom watched him proudly through the fishnet veil that hung from her hat. Lindsey and I, tortured by the drone of a Latin high mass, waited for the first moment that we could break our twenty-four-hour fast, which I found to be wholly unfair since I hadn't received my first communion yet. Mom reasoned, "It's still good penance for you, Michael. You can never have too much penance."

With all the purgatory time I was already facing, she was probably right.

Once home, we would have our traditional Sunday breakfast: oatmeal with brown sugar and raisins, homemade muffins, and fruit salad. Mom would say, "This will hold you over till dinner," which was *always* a late-afternoon pot roast, mashed potatoes, carrots, and Jell-O for dessert. I loved both meals-even the carrots.

Lindsey, five years older than I, got stuck baby-sitting for me a lot.

Mom had to increase her hours at the Spanish Tavern to cover our increasing expenses, leaving Lindsey in charge. Mom didn't like Lindsey handling the gas range, so each night on her way out the door, she would sprinkle a cookie sheet with something frozen. On Fridays it was fish sticks. I grimaced at the smell of them coming out of the oven. It required deliberate gulps of milk to get them down without puking. We knew it was the best Mom had to offer; nonetheless, we did feel sorry for ourselves.

Lindsey was beautiful, with strawberry-blond hair and light-green eyes. Dad said, "She's got a lot of Irish in her." This was confusing to me since I had the same amount as she did, but I was much darker. Dad explained, "You got that from your mom."

As big sisters go, Lindsey was one of the best. With the exception of sticking her fingernail into the bottom of each piece of candy in the Whitman Sampler in search of her favorite (cherry cream), I can't think of anything my sister ever did to annoy me. In her defense this rude behavior seemed logical in that she was simply protecting the rest of us from her inevitable retching upon the misfortune of biting into a coconut piece.

She was always sweet and extremely patient, and provided excellent defense against some of the older Devine brothers, who were bullies. Given our age difference we weren't together much, but on summer nights Lindsey and I and the Devine kids would play hide-and-seek for hours. You can imagine all the great places to hide in the Devines' yard.

Some nights lightning bugs were out, dotting the landscape with their flicker and flash. They hovered aimlessly at eye level, making them easy to catch. Cupping them in our hands, we waited for their tails to light up and then smashed them on our foreheads, illuminating our faces with a kind of phosphorescent war paint. My timing was poor, so I often had smashed bugs on my head and no war paint. But that was an advantage for hide-and-seek. When Dad saw my forehead afterward, he'd say, "Looks like Ash Wednesday came late this year."

Lindsey and a few of the other Devine kids often joined Joey and me as we rode our bikes three miles down Grafton Road to Ohl's country store, where we bought candy cigarettes, slowpokes, and jawbreakers. Ohl's wasn't much of a store, but it had everything you needed between big shopping trips. The ramshackle structure stood alone immediately adjacent to the railroad crossing and was surrounded by brushwood and a white picket fence. The screen door was usually propped open, giving it a kind of homey look. On the porch was a pop machine with a large red lid that you lifted to expose the bottles, which were lined up on rails. You dropped in your dime and slid the bottle of your choice down to the end of the rail, and, *clunk*, it would dislodge from the turnstile. Mom, of course, had encouraged a lemonade stand as a way to finance a trip to Ohl's. With Mom there was no free lunch; if you wanted something you had to earn it. But on occasion I heard an unfamiliar jingling in my pocket, where Dad had slipped me a few dimes without my knowing.

Cargo trains with their steaming locomotives would stop at the crossing in front of Ohl's so the crew could get snacks and pop for their journey. The trains were beautiful, like giant replicas of my Lionel set (another one of my childhood passions).

One day Joey and I rode to Ohl's without permission. A train was parked at the crossing next to the store. This created the greatest temptation of our lives: We *had* to get on that train. After buying our candy (fifteen cents' filled an entire paper sack), we sat perched on our bikes with our kickstands down, both feet on the pedals, leaning to one side for balance. We feasted happily on jawbreakers while staring at the locomotive.

A man suddenly came out of the store, groping through his paper sack. He stopped, rolled his shoulders and head, and stared at us for a while, munching. We munched back. His outfit was classic, right down to his red-and-white neckerchief and pinstriped bib overalls with matching cap.

"God, he looks like Captain Kangaroo," Joey whispered. We both giggled.

He continued to stare at us. His eyes narrowed, and then the impossible happened. "Where you boys from?" he asked, still searching inside his sack.

"Just down the road," I said, pointing down the rails.

"Grafton?" he asked.

"Yep . . . Grafton," I said.

He continued to stare. "You boys want a ride home?"

Joey and I gaped at each other wide-eyed, and in a flash we leaped from our bikes and stood at attention in front of him, waiting for instructions. What followed was the greatest thrill we'd ever had.

"C'mon, follow me," he said, smiling. He turned toward the train. "Oh . . . and put your bikes on the porch. Ohl's will watch 'em for ya."

We climbed into the spartan cabin of the locomotive-though the first step came up to my chest, requiring a hoist from the conductor. Once inside, grinning ear to ear, we sat patiently, arms resting on the open windows. I felt the butterflies beginning to build. And then it happened. The deep, open throat of the whistle, enlarging, building, and finally blasting, filled the silence of the countryside. We held our ears. After the whistle blew, the bell began to ring, the wheels engaged, and the train jerked forward with a screech from the effect of metal on metal. It was as if Joey and I were a modern day Lewis and Clark as we rattled down the rails with the wind in our face. The conductor, whose name I have forgotten, looked as if he was having as much fun as we were.

Unfortunately our adventure didn't end as well as it had begun. Dad was furious when he found out, and, following in his car, he made us walk the three miles back to Ohl's to get our bikes, giving Mike and me a chance to review our mistake-which we both concluded was well worth it. The benefit far outweighed the consequence. "C'mon, Dad, you would have done the same thing," I said. My father-half smiling-didn't say a word.

When I was eight, I stumbled into my second entrepreneurial experience: trading cigarettes. Mom and Dad smoked Winstons and always had two cartons in the refrigerator. I thought I was being very clever when I would steal a couple of packs and then shake the carton forward, sliding the remaining packs to the front, thus creating a void in the back of the carton. It was perfect. Surely my folks would never miss them. With my inventory, I bartered the cigarettes for baseball cards, marbles, candy, kites (kite-flying was huge back then), and other items. I even got to look at Dana Devine's boobs. A ten-second peek would cost me two cigarettes. Dana was thirteen, and her boobs weren't worth the price of admission, so I lowered my offer to one cigarette, and she was only too happy to oblige. After all, this was about supply and demand.

My little business ended abruptly when Mom caught me smoking some of my purloined inventory.

"Oh, my God, the drapes are on fire!" she screamed, not realizing the true source of the smoke.

Moments later she found me under my bed with a fresh pack of Winstons, matches, and an ashtray. I was puffing away madly, and smoke billowed out from under the box spring. I could have sworn I was invisible under there. Mom sentenced me to solitary confinement-a six-hour sojourn in the basement-until Dad got home.

That's when the real punishment was meted out, and it was hardly conventional. Dad decreed that since I loved cigarettes so much, I would smoke a whole pack in front of the entire family. So there at the kitchen table I sat, smoking and crying and crying and smoking. I was humiliated, and my mouth tasted like a plumber's hanky.

Mom wasn't sure it was the right punishment, so she tried to intervene. But Dad lifted his hand, his eyes never leaving mine, and said firmly, *"Annie, leave this alone."* We had little doubt who was wearing the pants that day. Then he handed me another smoke as I sat looking imploringly at Mom, forcing tears and blowing bubbles from my nose for effect. Mom just grimaced, looking helpless and sad. Her baby was at the whipping post-oh, the horror!

Lindsey, holding her hand over her mouth, giggled and snorted through the whole thing. My prosperous bartering business had ended in disgrace. But I did get a peek at Dana Devine's boobs.

Looking back at these snapshots of days gone by, I feel that mine was a fogged-out landscape of a fairly typical childhood. I was a happy kid. We lived a few notches above poverty, and I had a great time. My humble beginnings felt comfortable and secure. But things were about to change.

Chapter 2

Bless Me, Father,
for I Have Sinned

"I don't want to go . . . and I'm not gonna help, either," I said to my father on that August day in 1960.

This feisty remark was the start of a bad day.

Respecting parents was a requirement at our house. Dad promised me that he would tan my hide if I used that tone with him again. I was far too old for such childish behavior, and the sooner I learned that, the better off everybody would be.

"If you don't want me talkin' that way, then why'd ya make us move?" I asked.

Dad closed the doors of the U-Haul, snapped the lock shut, and leaned against the truck. "Look young man, first of all, I didn't *make* us move. Your mother and I *chose* to move. And as much as I like a democracy on family matters, there are certain things that children don't get a vote on. Where we live is one of them," he said. "Besides, the new house is bigger. You'll make new friends. It'll be fine, you'll see. Now, give me a hand with these suitcases."

I lugged the biggest suitcase to the trunk of the car. Dad watched with amusement as I used this opportunity to impress him with my strength. "Can Joey come visit me once in a while, dad?" I asked.

"Anytime he wants. It's only an hour away." Dad began loading the trunk. "He's always welcome to stay with us. You know that."

"Can I go over and say good-bye?" I asked, my eyes filling up.

My dad knelt in front of me. "I'll do you one better, Mike," he said gently. "We'll all go over together and say good-bye. Okay?"

So that was that. We were leaving the tranquility of Valley City and heading for Broadview Heights-my first introduction to suburban living.

When we finally pulled away, Joey Devine was standing in the middle of the road waving to us with tears running down his face. I waved from the back window until he disappeared from view. I was already miserable without him-until it occurred to me that Aunt Jean and Uncle Specks and their five kids had bought a house right behind ours and would be moving in soon. That would ease some of my loneliness.

Mom enrolled me in Assumption (a Catholic grade school), and Lindsey entered as a freshman at Brecksville High. Lindsey was smart, a straight-A student. I, on the other hand, was operating below the red line-the line that set the bar for my potential as a student. Every report card had a red line, established by the annual standard achievement test that was administered by the Catholic diocese. Mine was a whopping C minus.

Having Father Snyder, our parish priest, review your report card was like standing before Saint Peter at life's end-or so I would imagine. It was a terrifying experience. Each semester Father Snyder visited our classroom. The routine was always the same. The entire class stood, and with angelic insincerity we said in unison, "Good morning, Father Snyder."

He responded, with equal disingenuousness, "Good morning, children," while shuffling and blessing his way to the front.

Then the death march would begin. Upon command from our teacher (who was always Sister Mary Something), we rose one row at a time and lined up along the chalkboard. She handed Father Snyder a stack of report cards arranged in order by row, without which he wouldn't know who the hell we were. One at a time he called us up, opened the card as if interested, and made vague utterances like, "Hmm . . . well . . . let's see here . . . this looks quite good, Mary." He looked straight at you with his disturbing eyes. "You got an A in English, and all your grades are above the red line. Very nice . . . very nice. . . . Oh, and look, you got an A in religion. Wonderful!"

I wanted to puke. The girls *always* got As in religion. The next kid went up and got chewed out, followed by the next, who got a mixed report, then another, and another. Then he got to me.

"Well, Michael, let's see how we did *this* time."

Father Snyder always seemed to remember who I was.

He looked gravely at the report card, pursing his lips and rubbing his chin while I stood at attention holding my breath. His eyes shifted from the card to me, then back to the card, then back to me.

Oh, God, here it comes.

"Michael!" he fired. "Your red line has slipped. What happened? And these grades, they're all below the red line. What do you have to say for yourself?"

He always asked questions that he didn't really want an answer to. I mean, what was I supposed to say, "Well, Father, I guess I'm just a dumb ass"? To be sure, I did not say this, but the words dangled so palpably from my tongue that it was if I had spoken. As always, I said nothing, just stood and took the heat, and shamefacedly returned to my desk, where I suffered the scowl of Sister Mary Something.

Father Snyder was no bargain in the confessional, either. Every day after school we had forty-five minutes to go to confession before getting on the bus. Catholics must never take Holy Communion with mortal sin on their soul. Mortal sins were the biggies (we're talking hell-fire). Venial sins were the little guys (maximum sentence: purgatory). They were the ones the girls confessed to-unless, of course, they were French kissing. That was considered a biggie. Looking at Dana Devine's boobs would be right up there, too.

The pressure to confess was so intense that I would often make things up, just so I'd have something to be forgiven for. I kept the grievances fairly piddling, though, like kicking the dog or pinching my sister, to keep the penance under control.

We had mass every morning before school, so it was important to tidy up your soul the day before so that you could go to communion. Father Snyder was in one confessional, Father Gabeline, in the other. Father Gabeline was the number-two guy. All the mothers thought he was *gorgeous*. We all scrambled to be in Father Gabeline's confession line. He got you in and out in three minutes, unlike Father Snyder, who kept you in there for a half hour, followed by another half hour on the rosary beads. The girls rarely went to confession, but the boys were there *every* afternoon. This struck me as odd at first, but then it occurred to me: Twelve-year-old boys had discovered sex. But we never called it that; we always called it "impure thoughts and actions." So if you went to Father Snyder, it would go something like this:

"Bless me, Father, for I have sinned. It has been one day since my last confession. I committed impure thoughts and actions."

I'd say it really fast hoping he'd miss it.

"What did you say? Speak up, son," he demanded.

Now snapped to attention, I'd repeat myself, only this time with a more righteous tone. "I committed impure thoughts and actions."

"Impure actions! What *kind* of impure actions?" he erupted. Once again, a question he didn't want answered-or did he?

Well let's see, Father, I was staring at my Jayne Mansfield poster-you know, the one I keep on my ceiling because I can't afford mirrors. Anyway, one thing led to another, and before you know it, I was . . . doing the same damn thing you were doing when you were twelve years old, nitwit. Once again: thought but never said.

"The Lord doesn't like it when you do those things, you know. Say ten Our Fathers and ten Hail Marys, and light a candle," he'd say sternly. At least he didn't tell me I'd go blind.

The nuns eventually dragged us over to Father Gabeline; otherwise, half of us would've missed the bus. "Don't worry, my son, it's all part of growing up," was Father Gabeline's boilerplate response. He'd move us through like cattle in a meat market.

Spotting the boys who couldn't make it through the night was a cinch. We were the ones sitting in the pew during communion.

The girls would snicker, with no effort to conceal their curiosity. "What were *you* doing last night?"

More humiliation. All this cruel and unusual punishment could have been so easily avoided if they simply switched it around: confession in the morning and mass in the afternoon. But I guess that was the whole point.

Nonetheless, I loved the Catholic Church with all of its tradition and solemnity. As an altar boy, I learned just enough Latin to pass the test, only to have it lapse into a kind of hilarious linguistic soup. None of us knew what we were saying, particularly when choking on clouds of smoldering incense. Father Snyder liked to pour it on thick, too, particularly during Stations of the Cross. *Clink, clink, clink* . . . right in the face. I used to imagine the curlicue angels on the ceiling, dropping oxygen masks onto the congregation like an airplane in distress.

I also loved the flicker of the votive candles, each representing the longings of someone's heart. I loved the *Marian Missal* and the way the pages would crinkle when you turned them. I loved the slutty Catholic girls wearing their mohair sweaters and teased hair doused with Aqua Net, flaunting their "holy water" names like Veronica and Ruth. They were the ones doing the French kissing. I loved the holy cards and the patron saints, and knowing that St. Michael was an archangel. I loved the church structure and how it held us together-and how we got to be so conceited because we were *Catholics*. In all of this I felt the comfort of humanity surrounding me-all ages, all striving, all trying to be better people, all on their stairway to heaven.

The little parish called Assumption, despite its imperfections and foolishness, is where I discovered a love for God, respect for adults, a disciplined spirit, and a burning desire to prove them all wrong about me. Maybe my grades weren't above the red line, but my life would be.

Don't Aim, Just Throw Hard

Dad had been promoted to foreman, with his own truck and crew, and was making more money than before. Our new house was a modest L-shaped rambler with a family room, bigger kitchen, and a huge unfinished basement with room for my trains, punching bag, Ping-Pong table, and dartboard. One side of the basement was long and narrow, perfect for practicing my pitching-baseball had become my new passion. I drew a batter's box at the far end of the wall with chalk. After dinner in the winter months, I threw against the wall for hours, catching the returning ground balls. The goal was to hit the corners of the strike zone. I slipped into a trance, picturing myself on the mound, striking out big leaguers like Rocky Colavito, Mickey Mantle, and Willie Mays. Well, maybe not Willie.

My concentration was interrupted a few times by the sound of breaking glass. "No meat pitches allowed," Dad would say, but sometimes one would get away from me. After I broke the window the third time, Dad surrendered and covered it with a board. I was the best pitcher that ever played the game. I wasn't going to let a little broken glass get in my way. Competing is what it was all about. I didn't just want strike-outs; I wanted no-hitters. I didn't just want hits; I wanted home runs.

Dad loved baseball, too, and coached most of my teams. He believed that loving the game *always* led to the skills to play it well, not the other way around. On summer nights when he wasn't working we headed to the backyard to work on my pitching. I had the catcher's mitt and home plate ready to go, and we threw until dark. I was amazed at his patience when I chucked one in the dirt or sailed one over his head. Without objection, he would turn and fetch the ball out of the weeds.

"That's all right," he'd say. "To hit corners, you're gonna have to throw some bad ones. Don't aim, just throw hard. Good things will happen." Dad thought baseball was my ticket. He believed I had something extra, something special. He'd say, "Ya gotta practice every day, Mike. Don't slack off on this. God gave you a gift, but it's up to you to do something with it."

For me, I could find few things more enjoyable than to make the ball *hiss*, and listen for the pop of the glove at the other end as it passed over the low inside corner. *Don't aim, just throw hard.* This simple principle stuck with me and later transformed into a guiding theme that would help me start my business. It is not a principle of aimlessness but of effort and belief-a great combination for any business: *Good things will happen.*

Finding Strength in Weakness

At age thirteen I entered Padua Franciscan High School. Dad wanted me to go to Brecksville, where Lindsey had left her legacy. She had been a 4.0 student, head cheerleader, and homecoming queen her senior year. Furthermore, Dad had been working on Joe Vadini, the varsity baseball coach. "Ya gotta take a look at this kid, Joe. He can really smoke it," Dad would say. All my friends from Assumption were going to Padua, so that's where I wanted to go. But Dad thought I had a better chance of getting a baseball scholarship at Brecksville than at a large all-boy's Catholic school like Padua. This created another doozy of a fight between Mom and Dad, but in the end, I headed for Padua.

In August 1966 I was introduced to double sessions. Over one hundred boys, most of them older and bigger than I was, showed up to play football. Baseball was still my game, but in those days if you were an athlete you played everything. In Ohio, football, basketball, and baseball were the three biggies. I arrived at the high school with a couple friends on Monday morning around quarter to eight. I was overwhelmed by the size of the crowd that had already formed on the field. It was eighty degrees on its way to ninety, and the humidity hung in the air like death. *How in the world am I going to play with all these guys trying out?* I thought.

The coaches were all business. They looked more like drill instructors than football coaches, and it was obvious that they themselves had played college ball only a couple of years earlier. They all sported a Johnny Unitas haircut and looked like they had been chiseled out of stone. Being newcomers, they apparently had something to prove. I was hoping for some fat, middle-aged English teacher who had to pull double duty as coach-like the guy we'd had in eighth grade. No such luck.

There we were, huddled around our coaches, waiting to be inspired. Coach Bush looked us over and said loudly, "I have fifty uniforms. The last fifty guys standing at the end of two weeks will get one. If you're out of shape, you might just as well quit right now. You won't make it. Last year, thirty guys quit the first day." That was all he said.

I was scared to death, and we hadn't even done anything yet. I grabbed my thermos and chugged down the nausea along with some water. Then the torture began.

After fifteen minutes of stretching, we ran, followed by puking for those who had eaten a big breakfast. We started with four miles (sixteen times around the track) just to warm up. The sun rose higher, bending the air with heat. The stampede of runners converted the track into what looked like a cattle drive-clouds of dust stirred up by a bunch of two-legged beasts. On the last lap we heard the coaches yelling, "Don't be last . . . don't be last. If you're last, you'll do it again." We spurted forward, all jockeying for position, praying that someone was behind us. I finished in the last three, beating only the two really fat guys.

Three guys quit during the warm-up. We stood bent over, sucking air, sweat mixing with the dust from the track. We looked like coal miners. After a two-minute break (no water), we did wind sprints. This lasted for about an hour, followed by dry heaves. For our cool-down we ran through tires for twenty minutes, then topped that off with a hundred push-ups and sit-ups. The first session finally ended, and ten guys had quit. This worried me concerning the afternoon session. *How could this get any worse?*

I opened my lunch bag. Mom had packed me a ham sandwich and an apple. The smell of warm ham made me gag. I ate the apple and stood over the drinking fountain for half an hour.

Some of the guys ate like pigs-another fatal mistake. The afternoon session was twice as hard, and guys were tossing their cookies everywhere. By the end of the first day, twenty-two had quit. It was pure hell, and for the first time football was no longer fun, as it had been when I played in grade school.

That night Dad said, "That's not football, that's conditioning. Wait till you get the pads on. You'll have fun."

I didn't know if I could last that long. We had nine days to go.

Turned out, Dad was right. We finally put on the pads and started playing football. Thanks to speed and a broken-field running style, I managed to jitterbug my way through the line for noticeable gains. The coaching staff was impressed but not sold on my approach of advancing the ball. They preferred to see their running backs squaring up and blasting dead ahead. "Good runners make their own hole," they'd shout. They were from the old school (three yards and a cloud of dust), which always mystified me since three carries of three yards never produced a first down. *No math majors in this group*, I thought. *Besides, haven't they heard of Gayle Sayers?*

At 142 pounds, I viewed their approach as a losing proposition, demonstrated by the violent hammering I received. I ended up on my back, staring into a snorting facemask filled with bad breath. "God, nice breath, pal," I told the facemask.

"Yeah, well, bad breath is better than no breath-*pal*," the facemask replied.

This I found to be true enough on the very next play.

I went back to skittering, allowing nobody to get a big piece of me like that ever again. This decision, in direct opposition with Coach Bush's philosophy, won me a starting position in the freshman back-field-a spot that I would keep on the JV and varsity teams, as well. Above all, it kept me in shape for baseball.

Dad acted unsurprised, almost nonchalant, at this news. But I knew that he was surprised. I learned an important lesson from that experience: *"There is always strength in weakness; you just have to find it."*

I had found a way to get through that line. Whether it was a line of scrimmage or a red line on a report card, lines had taught me well. Lines were obstacles, that's all. Things to overcome.

Chapter 3

A Rough Start

High school started, football season began, and Dad got sick. Dr. Teitlbaum, our family physician, thought it was pneumonia. Dad got chest colds easily, probably from the pleurisy he had contracted during the war while sitting in a water-filled foxhole for two days during the Battle of the Bulge. Of course, smoking two packs of Winstons every day didn't help.

A chest X ray had revealed a shadow on the lower lobe of his left lung. In a state of shock and denial, our family continued to function while we waited for Dad's exploratory surgery. Obtaining a biopsy in 1967 was a perilous undertaking compared to the simple, noninvasive methods used today. For the doctors to get full access to Dad's lungs, they had to open him from top to bottom and side to side by sawing his ribs in half. They rushed a biopsy to the lab, analyzed it immediately, and made a decision while Dad was still on the table. The doctors had hoped that the cancer hadn't spread to both lungs-which would spell the end. (Although having one lung removed was a fairly new procedure, Dad could still live a normal life.) If it had spread, they would simply close him up, wait till he had recovered from the exploratory surgery, and send him home.

The cancer was in both lungs.

We brought Dad home to a small gathering of family and friends. Astonished by his weight loss and ashen complexion, they gathered up a smile, which did nothing to hide their sadness. Dad had been given twelve to eighteen months. No one talked about it. Mom served coffee and desserts and carried on with a phony breeziness as if nothing had happened. That pissed me off.

People are unpredictable during a crisis. Denial sets in quickly, providing a protective shield. But the grief is real-unlike our lives, which become unreal. I believe we are better off letting grief strike quickly, hitting us like a tidal wave, banging us against the rocks. Pummeled but aware, we can acknowledge our humanity, our mortality. We live in truth again, no longer in denial, and when it's over, we can begin to heal. But that's not what we did then.

As promised by his doctor, Dad felt good enough to return to work. His boss had him do simple jobs in the shop, like painting stoplights and building cable. But his illness didn't keep him away from the football field. He made it to four games before it became too hard to breathe the cold air. Those would be the last games he would see.

Lookin' Good

Lindsey, now in college, had fallen in love with Alex Strazzanti. Alex was Italian (as is no doubt obvious from his surname), very handsome, with endless charisma. Our family also fell in love with him. His engaging personality, combined with his ingrained Italian ethos, swept us off our feet.

My sister was emotional when it came to the boys in her life. Sometimes we had found her alone in the living room, listening to Barbara Streisand sing "People," with streams of tears running down her face after one of those bastards had dumped her and broken her heart.

Lindsey had had lots of boyfriends, but she'd never once asked us to meet one of them, at least not in a formal way. So when she officially introduced him to us, we knew right away that Alex was special. Dad was skeptical at first because Lindsey was so young, but he eventually came to deeply respect Alex and welcomed him into our family. They were to be married that summer of 1967, a year earlier than they would have preferred, for fear that Dad might not make it much longer. I believe the desire to walk his only daughter down the aisle is what kept him alive. Dad would not allow himself, or Lindsey, to be robbed of such an important and sacred occasion. The cancer had slowed, and he made a remarkable recovery that summer. We were even playing catch in the backyard again.

On Lindsey's wedding day, Dad finally wore something to church besides that old brown suit of his. He had a great suntan and looked remarkably healthy and handsome in his tuxedo. It was hard to believe he was dying.

Alex had selected me to be one of his ushers, which made me very proud. I was at the front of the church with the other groomsmen, in my tux and pleated white shirt, waiting for the bride. Their names were Jimmy and Tommy Ambresia (brothers), Johnny Bando, Lenny Serio, Petey Olah, and Franky Arminio. I wondered if we looked like a bunch of gangsters standing up there.

I felt as though I'd better change my name to "Mikey" just to fit in. That way when I was introduced at the reception, I'd receive an open *abrazzo* (big hug), and they'd say with their big fleshy faces: "Hey, Mikey, how ya doin'? Lookin' good, baby. Yo, Mikey, lookin' good," while pulling on my bow tie. The old Italian ladies would reach up, grab my head, muss my hair, and give me sloppy kisses on both cheeks.

Lindsey-looking like the cover of a bridal magazine-floated down the aisle on her father's arm with a grace and sureness resembling royalty. It was a spectacular July afternoon, and Assumption Church was the ideal sanctuary for this beautiful celebration.

And was it ever a celebration! I love the Italians; they're all a little wacky and hot-blooded, but, boy, they know how to have a good time. Over two hundred fifty people were invited to the reception, which was more than my parents could afford. They had to take a loan on the house to help pay for it. Still, the wedding was a wonderful union of our two families, the Kerrisons and the Strazzantis, and Mom and Dad had a tremendous time.

My role in the event was easy. I was to be the escort for Dianne DiTori, one of Lindsey's bridesmaids. She was stunning, and at age fifteen, I fell in love. It happened about ten minutes after drinking my first glass of wine. That had been a mistake, of course, but the waiter was pouring for the entire bridal table and when he got to me he just kept pouring. The first glass made me feel all warm inside. The second glass nearly put me in a coma. I couldn't feel my lips, and the room began to spin.

The first course of the meal was, naturally, a bowl of spaghetti. But the bowl was moving. *Why is the bowl moving?* I stabbed a meatball and tried unsuccessfully to get it into my mouth. *Oh God, I hope nobody saw that,* I thought as it fell off my fork, landed on my perfect white pleats, ricocheted off my chair, rolled across the floor, and landed against a guy's shoe. I watched in horror. A dark Italian face with huge watery eyes slowly turned and stared directly at me. *He knows.* I stared back, my mouth wide open, unable to move.

Dianne, who was sitting next to me, put her hand on my shoulder and said, "Oh, shit-I mean shoot. . . . Mike, look at you, you poor baby. You're a mess!" She dipped her napkin into her water glass and proceeded to smear spaghetti sauce all over my shirt. I sat in a stupor, slowly falling in love with her blond hair, black eyes (what a combination), full lips, and cute, turned-up nose. She was a goddess.

I danced with her no less than twenty times that night, never missing a slow one. After each dance I would strut to the bar to hang out with the boys. "Mikey . . . Lookin' good . . . lookin' good. You want a cigar? Have a cigar." I stood puffing proudly (after all, I had some experience with this) and leaned back to watch my girl glide across the dance floor.

Next thing I know, someone whacked the cigar out of my lips. The ashes flew all over me, which looked really great with my spaghetti sauce stain. *Dad.* If looks could kill, I would have been dead.

"Uh-oh!" Jimmy Ambresia turned away, grimacing.

"Sorry, Dad," I said sheepishly.

He raised an eyebrow at me, winked at Jimmy, and walked away. At least he didn't make me smoke the whole box.

Dianne was a good sport to play along with my little fantasy. When it was time for her to go home, she suggested, "C'mon, walk me to my car."

My heart was pounding through my spaghetti-sauce-and cigar-stained shirt. When we reached the car, she turned to me and gave me the most passionate kiss of my life. I was in heaven. I opened the door for her. She got into her car, blew me a kiss, and drove away. I never saw her again.

Unrest

Dad suffered at the end. He kept an empty coffee can next to him at all times to spit in after coughing spells, which got so bad that we finally took him back to the hospital. He told Mom to go warm up the car and he'd be out in a minute. We waited and waited, but Dad did not come out.

Lindsey said, "I'm getting scared. Somebody better go in there." She reached for the door.

Mom caught her hand. "It's okay, Lindsey. Give him some time. He's saying good-bye."

Lindsey covered her face with her hands and cried.

Dad finally came out of the house and got into the car. No one spoke. Mom touched Dad's hand and smiled at him warmly. Dad, trying to smile back, turned his head to the window, his eyes tracking the house as we pulled away. You could sense the memories brushing past him in that moment. He knew he would never be back.

The cancer was eating him alive. I'd arrive at the hospital each day after practice or a game, with Dad still looking for a full report on the team. Like a Hail Mary into the end zone, my stories hurled him downfield, far from his illness, to a world of goalposts and marching bands and crisp clean air, all linked to the lost days of his active fathering and coaching.

A competent father and coach he had been, but that competence had now lapsed into the need to be fed, bathed, dressed, and turned. Each day brought morphine, catheters, lemon swabs, and an oxygen tent-all providing little or no relief. My dad's handsome face and sturdy form had been reduced to a transparent, bony shadow.

Father Gabeline was summoned to the hospital to administer the last rites to my father. Last rites, or extreme unction, is a Catholic sacrament of anointing that, when administered by a priest, absolves a person's sin and prepares his or her soul for heaven. My father was a spiritual man, and he insisted with a lift of his hand that I pay close attention to what was happening. Father Gabeline's Latin prayers of anointing, given in solemn yet warm tones-almost chantlike-were soothing to everyone in the little hospital room, now being used as a chapel. Friends and family had been coming in all day, most of them shocked by what they saw, having seen my father looking so wonderful at the wedding. They'd had no idea.

My father died a few hours later.

Members of the family had been taking turns standing vigil at his bedside. My mother, sister, Alex, and I had gone home to try to get some sleep, having been at the hospital for two straight days. Uncle Specks and Uncle Russ were with Dad and promised to call immediately if anything changed. A knock sounded on my bedroom door in the middle of the night.

"Mike . . . Michael . . . It's time to go," Mom said softly. Her silhouette stood in the doorway.

I sat up quickly. "Is he still alive?"

"Yes, but he's very close."

Alex drove us back to the hospital. The car was cold, providing no comfort. No one spoke.

We didn't make it in time. Mom went into Dad's room first and quietly closed the door. We each waited for our turn-none of us in a hurry.

My heart pounded with fear as I stood in the dark hallway, listening to the muffled sounds of Mom's grief. I had never seen death before.

Mom eventually returned to the hallway, "It's all right, Mike. C'mon in. He's nice and warm, and his spirit is still here."

Some Catholics believe that the soul stays with the body for three hours after death. He looked pretty gone to me. That was not my dad lying there. I couldn't look at him, so I headed out of the room. Lindsey signaled to Alex to follow me out.

"Mike, wait. Are you all right?" he asked.

"I don't know, Alex. I just can't stay in there. It gives me the creeps."

He put his arm around my shoulder, and we strolled down the dimly lit hallway. The patients were all asleep, and everything was dead quiet. After a while we returned.

My dad's room was dark except for a soft wall light over his head. The nurses had put fresh linens on the bed, which were folded neatly across his chest. His hair had been brushed, and his eyes were closed. His jaw, no longer supported by life, sagged to the right. He was so lifeless, so motionless. It made me queasy. The room was filled with a few of our extended family.

Feeling numb and exhausted, I stayed close to the door, trying not to be noticed. Underneath my numbness was rage. I was seething inside, though trying to push the anger down. *How could he do this to us? He left . . . just like that . . . gone! Now look at him, getting more attention dead than when he was alive.*

The funeral arrangements kept Mom busy, and the house was full of people for three straight days. Everyone brought terrific food, and the atmosphere around the house had a kind of lightheartedness. The funeral home had long lines of people waiting to see Dad. The room would occasionally ring with the irony of laughter from people who needed to laugh. This would be followed by tears, usually from the ones who'd been laughing, as they finally gave in to their grief. I had never realized how many people had known my dad and loved him. The man with the smelly work clothes and the old brown suit was the real thing.

At the gravesite the color guard presented my mom with the American flag that had been perfectly folded into a tight triangle while three shots were fired in honor of Dad's Purple Heart. As my mother clutched the flag to her chest, at that moment, having been jolted by the thunderclap of each shot and the bolt action release of shells, I felt the finality of it.

All that remained of Dad's presence was the smell of his old brown suit. I can remember sitting in the back of his closet, a boy the size of a man, with my face buried in that old brown suit, trying desperately to hold on to his scent. It wouldn't be long before it faded away. I feared I was fading away with it.

Kids don't like to grieve. They would rather just get on with things. I read somewhere that grief is like a lazy Susan. It starts out heavy and laden, then it rotates, stopping at pissed-off and crazy; from there it stops at self-pity, then numbness, then silence. You can shake it off for a while, but grief always returns if it hasn't been dealt with. Sometimes that takes years, but it always returns.

Grief is not the enemy, though. Fear is. It's a predictable result of our grief. To escape it, we skitter along life's surfaces, working too much, drinking too much, exercising until we drop, shopping until we're broke-anything to crowd out our fear and medicate our pain. Friends with good intentions would say to me, "But he's *finally* at rest, Mike, surely you can see the blessing in that." Blessing, yes; comfort, no. Because the rest granted to those who go before us is no comfort for the *unrest* of those left behind.

Finding Alex

Time passed slowly that winter. Alex and Lindsey visited frequently, determined to stay close. Alex took a special interest in me, which took up some of the slack for my dad. We had long talks, and he provided lots of encouragement. I depended on him and grew to love him. We were comfortable together.

After college he was hired as a salesman for International Harvester. He told me about his job and the new things he was learning. But he was frustrated. Instead of training him how to sell, they had him washing trucks and providing delivery from one dealer to another. He said to Lindsey, "This isn't why I went to college-so I can wash a bunch of stupid trucks." What's more, he was now facing the draft. The Vietnam War was escalating, so if he didn't enlist, he would surely be drafted.

Alex caught two breaks. First, he was introduced to Uncle Specks's brother, George Janik, a successful branch manager for International Business Machines. Then Uncle Sam (speaking of uncles) took a pass on Alex when they discovered a small curvature in his spine.

It was 1968, and IBM was known for having the finest sales force in the world. Only the best and brightest got in. George arranged an interview for Alex. He passed the logic test, nailed the interviews, and was offered a job as a sales trainee in the Data Processing Division of IBM's Cleveland office.

Alex kept me posted on his progress. Watching him somehow filled me with hope for my own future. I admired him, and I wanted to be just like him. He became a dad, big brother, and best friend all wrapped up in one. I remember him showing up at the house dressed in a blue suit, a white broadcloth shirt, striped tie, and forty-pound wingtips, polished to perfection. He was IBM from head to toe. You could sense that a transformation had occurred as he began to carry himself as a professional. This guy was going places, and I wanted to go, too.

At age fifteen, I would become a salesman for IBM. I just hadn't received the offer yet. But make no mistake, it was going to happen.

Chapter 4

Adversity Taught Me Well

Things went downhill quickly after Dad died. Mom started drinking, and her behavior became dark and erratic. She was losing it. She took a job as a bank teller, working only occasionally at the Spanish Tavern. She was good at her new job, and within a few weeks she was able to balance her station and, later, the entire bank. She received her first promotion: head teller. For Mom, days were short, and nights were long. Dad left behind a small life insurance policy, which had provided some help with the funeral expenses. But it was becoming increasingly clear that despite Mom's improved wages, we were running out of money. S&H Green Stamps weren't going to provide a solution for us this time. We were going to lose our house.

Technically Orphaned

Mom's loneliness grew steadily. We spoke little. She began dating a man named Bill Keane, a retired policeman from New York City who had walked the beat of Manhattan. They had known each other during the war. Somehow Bill found out about Dad's death and after a respectful-though brief-period of time he called my mother. Having never been married, he had been able to save some money, and he no doubt represented financial security for Mom, besides relief for her loneliness.

She began taking frequent trips to New York to visit him, which I found disturbing since Dad had been dead for only a few months. Mom talked him up a lot, determined to win my approval. The truth is, he didn't have a chance with me, but I'm not sure he really gave a rat's ass. He wanted Mom, but unfortunately for him, I was part of the package.

We met on a Saturday. Mom picked Bill up at Cleveland Hopkins Airport and brought him home. He seemed like an okay guy, but the thick New York accent, when blended with a touch of the Olde Sod, was hard on a Midwestern ear.

Mom had a few other goons hanging around the house at that point-after all, she was attractive-so I guess Bill had some competition. The goons never knew what to make of me, though. You'd think they had never seen a teenager before. To break the ice, they'd bring me these pathetic sympathy gifts. One time I got a baseball glove that was plastic, like something you'd give a toddler. *What are you thinking?* I wanted to shout. On another occasion I received a Hardy Boys book and a Beach Boys album-a much better effort but still pretty lame.

When the goons actually met me, confronted with my sturdy six-foot frame, they transformed. Now intensely determined to impress me with their knowledge of teenagers, they would suggest tickets to an Indians game or feign interest in the new bellbottom trousers, the ones with paisley pleats. "Those are really cool," one of them said. When given the chance to break the ice *my* way, I'd suggest a game of catch in the backyard, toss them Dad's old catcher's mitt, and proceed to rifle fast balls at their heads. It was fun watching them crawl through the weeds.

Bill Keane was no exception to the gift-giving game. He gave me walkie-talkies. "Hello there, young lad," he said enthusiastically on his arrival for one visit, extending his large fleshy hand.

Young lad? . . . Did somebody fart? I mean, do I look like a leprechaun or what? I thought. "Hi" is what I said.

We both stood there studying each other. Bill was huge, standing about six three, portly, with a broken, ruddy complexion, cloudy eyes, and skimpy lips. The only thing missing was his blue uniform and a billy club. He was the quintessential Irish cop. One of his eyebrows twisted cockeyed in the air, giving him a pained look. I couldn't tell if he had gas or if he was really, really drunk. But the eyebrow never moved. I stood there, not saying a word, purposely making him feel uncomfortable. In other words, I was being an ass, and I was too young and too cynical to see the possibility of anything good coming out of the situation.

A few weeks later, Mom dropped a bomb on the family: She had married Bill. That's right-she had eloped on one of their weekend rendezvous. At fifteen I wasn't familiar with terms like abandonment or betrayal. I just felt shitty. Above all I felt seething anger and enough rebellion for ten teenagers. My newly discovered independence (okay, rebellion) began by refusing to move to New York with my mother and new stepfather. Technically orphaned, I would now be responsible for my own life. While this seemed altogether appropriate, at least to me, it did not come without some serious consequences.

The only remaining stable elements in my life were Lindsey and Alex, Padua, sports, and my girlfriend, Barb-whom I have forgotten to mention. Barb was a doll. I loved her, at least in a high-school kind of way. She was a soul mate and loved me too, despite my bizarre family circumstances.

To my surprise and relief, I found an unexpected source of backing: my grandmother, Mildred Gaitanis. After hearing the news of Mom's marriage, Grandma offered to stay with me until our house sold. After that, I could move in with her.

A Few Potholes

My grandmother lived in a trailer park about an hour north of Padua. To my disappointment our house sold quickly, and it was time to move out. Everything had happened so suddenly. Lindsey had married, Dad had gone, Mom had gone, and now the house had been sold. My entire world had been turned upside down in a matter of months. The moving van and Mom went in one direction, and I went in the other. Our paths would remain separate for a long, long time. I didn't look at the house as we pulled away, trying to fight off the image of my dad's departure. My grandmother drove the two of us to her trailer park.

As we pulled into the park, my heart sank. I had forgotten what it looked like. Grandma slowed the car to absorb the first deep pothole, then proceeded through the mud as if on an obstacle course. Old cars were carelessly parked along the dirt road in front of each trailer. The trailers, eight feet apart, sat diagonally one after another, with a small carport between each one. Grandma's trailer had two bedrooms, one bathroom, a living room, and an efficiency kitchen. During the summer the temperature inside sometimes reached ninety-five degrees. After double-session football, I slept in front of a fan with a wet towel over my face. The sweating usually stopped around three o'clock in the morning.

"Well, Mike, honey"-she called me "Mike, honey" a lot-"this is the best I can do, sweetheart." She called me "sweetheart," too.

"This is nice Grandma . . . really . . . it's nice," I replied.

She knew I was lying.

I did receive some good news, though. I was within days of taking delivery on a two year old Chevy Camaro-a peace offering from New York but necessary if I was going to get back and forth from school every day. The thought of having a car, and the freedom it provided, soothed me for a while. Being a bit of a gearhead, I jacked up the back end, placed a racing stripe down the middle, and installed dual-exhaust glass packs. This provided zero additional horsepower but gave the car a kick-ass sound and intimidating looks. The Camaro became my second home-and in some ways my actual home.

My grandmother was one of the most loving and unselfish people I had ever known. At first I wondered if she was overcompensating. But she wasn't. She made breakfast each morning before school, and when she wasn't home, I'd find my dinner wrapped in tin foil warming in the oven, along with instructions on how to heat the rolls or mix the salad. And she always provided a can of Hershey's syrup and whipped cream. She knew I loved chocolate milk and ice cream sundaes. I have often reflected on how something as simple as an affectionate note or a warm plate of food can demonstrate a person's love and devotion.

The Camaro came in March, just in time for baseball season my junior year. And, of course, within one month I had my first driving accident. (C'mon, now, it's a right of passage! You didn't have one when you were sixteen?)

As expected, Grandma had no concern for the car, only for me. "Michael, are you all right? Are you hurt?" she exclaimed, running to the car.

"I'm sorry, Grandma. I just didn't see it coming," I said.

"Oh, the hell with the car. Cars can be fixed, grandsons can't," she said.

But she *had* fixed me. She fixed me in ways that I would only understand many years later. She held me accountable to truth and fair-minded thinking. She taught me to solve problems. She killed my rebellion with her kindness. And she gave me hope. I can remember her saying to me one evening when I sat silently at dinner, "Mike, it's not over for you. Do you realize that in the whole history of this world, there has never been and will never again be another you? Get excited about that. If you do, the rest of your life will be exciting, too. You can do anything you want, Mike. Yes, you've had a setback. But it's time to get moving again. The future is all that matters now."

Her message stuck.

Lindsey and Alex pulled up to the Mobil station where I was working one Sunday afternoon that spring. I was always thrilled to see them-especially at that moment, when I was filled with anxiety about my current living situation. Out of the blue, my grandmother had met a wonderful man and was planning on remarrying and moving in with him.

Alex leaned out the window, grinning from ear to ear. Lindsey, peering at me from the other side of the car, wore a similar Cheshire-cat smile.

"Hey, pump jockey, fill it up with high test, and catch the windows, will ya? Oh, and by the way, we bought a house, and we want you to move in with us," Alex added nonchalantly.

It took a second for the words to register. "*What*?! You're kidding! You do? . . . You did? . . . I mean, it's okay?"

"Yeah, it's okay," he assured me. "We talked it over, and that's what we're gonna do."

It was as though Lindsey had reached back in time and popped another cookie sheet of fish sticks in the oven. She had found a family of her own and would now share it with me. This was also instinctual for Alex, having grown up in an Italian home where family was exalted. And, of course, I still had my prize grandmother, who for one year had devoted herself to meeting my needs. We all had found family.

Everything Came Together

After the football season in my senior year, I had been exhausted. I went both ways-offense and defense-and played all the special teams. I would fake a mild injury just so I could get off the field for five minutes. Basketball was to start on the Monday following our final football game. However, I had been anything but excited. *Who needs a six-foot forward in the Crown Conference?* I thought. So I quit. Making money had been a bigger priority.

I had worked two jobs that winter, one at the Mobil station pumping gas, and on weekends I was a waiter at Piper's III restaurant. In my spare time I lifted weights with the Burly Bruin Barbell Club (Padua's competition weight lifters) and took batting practice in the indoor cage. My coach had believed I could earn a baseball scholarship, and I applied to several Ohio colleges, figuring a state school offered the highest probability of acceptance. Not having been a stellar student (roughly C-plus), I figured that if baseball didn't get me in, I didn't know what would. I had no money.

Spring baseball practice began. We were a state contender with a great team, and I loved our head coach, Chuck Prieffer. He was so talented that he would later coach football at North Carolina, and eventually he became special teams coach for the Detroit Lions. Recently he had been inducted into Padua's Hall of Fame. He had an interesting way of keeping us calm under pressure by saying, "Don't worry about what the other guy is doing. Pay attention to what *you're* doing. Let him worry about you-*that's* when you're in charge." I never forgot that advice.

Everything came together that spring of 1970. I batted .397, broke the school RBI record, and led the conference in home runs. Padua won the Crown Conference and two weeks later, the state championship. I played in the annual East-West All-Star Game at Waterfront Park, which allowed us to showcase our skills for the college scouts. Later I was named to the *Cleveland Plain Dealer* "Dream Team."

In the all-star game, I went three for four with three RBIs, no errors, and a put-out at third base. Coach Prieffer stood behind home plate when I was up at bat. I was facing the top pitcher in the state, a guy by the name of Bob Amicarelli. I was anxious, and apparently it showed.

Coach Prieffer called me to the fence. "What are you so uptight about? You can hit this guy," he said.

We had a runner on third and two outs. The game was tied. I had two strikes on me and had just stood there looking at both of them. "God, Coach, this guy scares me. I can't see the ball let alone hit it," I said. The stands were crawling with scouts and sports writers.

"Remember what I told you, Mike," Coach Prieffer said. "Don't worry about him. Let him worry about you. Believe me, he's been warned. Now, relax and do your job."

I hit three straight foul balls. The last one ripped down the third-base line. It was one foot from being a double. I heard the groans when the umpire yelled, "Foul ball!"

I glanced at Coach Prieffer on my way back to home plate. "Relax," he mouthed the word. He discreetly signaled for a curve ball with a twitch of his hand. "Wait on it," he instructed me.

The curve developed slowly, and I hit the ball sharply to deep right field for a triple. I heard Coach Prieffer burst with praise from behind the fence. It was one of those silly moments that you never forget-and it was a moment that would pay off.

A week later, following my graduation ceremony, I was standing with my mother-who had flown in from New York-and sister in the high school lobby (Alex had gone to get the car) when Coach Prieffer fought his way through the crowd over to me.

"Mike, where the heck have you been?" he asked. "I've been trying to get a hold of you for days. Oh, by the way, congratulations." Then he apologized and introduced himself to Lindsey and my mother.

"You've been trying to find me?" I asked.

"Yes, all week. Your grandmother's phone's been disconnected, and no one seemed to know where you were. I've been worried."

"Gosh, Coach, I'm sorry. I moved in with my sister and brother-in-law. I guess I forgot to tell you. My grandmother remarried and moved out of her trailer a few months ago," I explained.

"Mike, you gotta tell me these things. Anyway, I got twenty letters from interested colleges. But this is the one I'm excited about." He handed me a letter from Ohio University. "They were at the all-star game. They want you. This team wants to win a national championship, Mike. And I know Bob Wren"-Ohio's head coach-"real well. They have a phenomenal program. When can we get together?" he asked.

"How about right now?" I replied. I was so excited, I could hardly breathe.

Coach Prieffer laughed. "Come by my office tomorrow about ten. We'll go over the whole thing. You go have a good time with your family."

I was to play ball for Ohio University! Bob Wren had pieced together an Ohio state grant, a National Defense Scholarship (thanks to my dad), and a twenty-year loan at three percent interest to cover the shortfall. It was nearly a full ride. I was on my way, and I suddenly felt I had choices ahead. Would it be IBM, or could I actually play pro ball? I didn't know, but I began to dream big dreams again. I was filling up with the emotional fuel that would get my life moving. Baseball had been my salvation.

Finding Family

Living with Lindsey and Alex was not only fun, it also provided a great education on how to raise a young family. Alex was up every morning at six o'clock. After suiting up in his pinstripes-the gray-flannel variety-he would streak through the kitchen, grab coffee and toast, and be out the door by six forty-five, leaving a cloud of Jade East behind him. "Well, Michael . . . shit, showered, and shaved." He had a weird habit of saying this as he ran out the door. Lindsey and I both hated the smell of Jade East, but she said it was better than the English Leather crap that he used to wear.

And Lindsey, my God . . . she had graduated from high school only six years earlier-at sixteen no less (she was a whiz kid). Now she had a husband, a house, and a little boy named Marc, not to mention a full-grown teenager, to look after. Furthermore, Lindsey was pregnant with her second child, a girl, whom they would name Lisa. I learned quite a bit about diapering, bottle feeding, and burping that year.

I enjoyed listening to my sister and brother-in-law talk at night. Perhaps what I liked most was the feeling of being snug in a safe home. Alex would grumble about his day in the territory while Lindsey, always patient and busy shoving loads of wash in the dryer, would calm him down, redirecting his attention to something new Marc had learned. It was like watching a training film for new families. A new awareness was developing within me-lessons and insight and illumination were now being added.

Sundays after church we went to Alex's mom and dad's house for spaghetti. The Strazzantis *always* had pasta on Sunday-a family tradition for decades and the highlight of the week for me. Mrs. Strazzanti was an Old World Italian mother, always serving, always feeding, always loving. She was crazy about her son, Alex, and said so. She afforded me the same loving attention. I was now family and received all the consideration and privilege that went with that designation.

Mrs. Strazzanti's spaghetti sauce, a recipe for the generations, was to die for. I can remember walking in the front door after church, when the pasta sauce had already been on the stove for an hour and was a deep red mixture of fried tomato paste, crushed tomatoes, sautéed garlic, red wine, and wonderful seasonings of oregano and rosemary. After another hour of simmering, she added veal, homemade meatballs, and Italian sausages. Each meatball had been packed with spices and fried in olive oil before going into the pot, where all the ingredients simmered for six hours, blending the flavors to perfection. Every time Alex's mom lifted the lid to stir the sauce, it smelled like heaven. Alex and I would sneak into the kitchen when she wasn't looking, split a piece of fresh Italian bread, and dunk it into the sauce for a quick snack. Mrs. Strazzanti would catch us in the act, then snap us with her dish towel, pretending to be angry. But after kicking us out of the kitchen, she would present us with a small bowl of sauce, one meatball, and a hunk of bread. *I mucho bella!*

Sunday afternoons were devoted to napping in the family room with one eye on the Cleveland Browns game while Mr. Strazzanti read his newspaper. After the morning pastries and an undisturbed nap, Mrs. Strazzanti would put out a platter of cold cuts, fresh cheese, and a couple of loaves of bakery-fresh bread. "This will hold you over until dinner," she would say.

Eating was an all-day affair at Mrs. Strazzanti's, and she was happiest when we were complaining.

"Mom, you're gonna kill us!" Alex would groan.

"What?" she'd protest, raising her hands. "It's a little sandwich. Everybody needs a little sandwich."

The dinner table was a special place at the Strazzantis', and someone was always invited over: a neighbor, a relative, somebody from work. The table was packed. The only silence was during grace, followed by a flurry of arms reaching, bowls passing, pitchers pouring, salads tossing, stories telling, and lots of love and laughter. And the food. Oh, the food!

Mrs. Strazzanti never sat down. She ran back and forth from the kitchen continually refilling platters and bowls, occasionally returning to her seat for a bite, only to survey the table for the next requirement. She was the real thing, receiving her nourishment not from the table, but from the joy it brought those who sat at it.

In the old-style Italian heritage, the men eat and the women cook. That's just the way it is. Roles are willingly accepted and responsibilities freely taken on. These two people respected each other. Between them there was honor and loyalty. (That same loyalty extended to work. Mr. Strazzanti had worn a two-inch recess in the cement floor of the welding station where his feet had stood for forty years.)

One Sunday, Alex and Lindsey were arguing about something. It wasn't anything too serious, but it was enough to get Mr. Strazzanti-a soft-spoken man-out of his chair. He didn't like the way his son was talking to his wife. He rarely got out of that chair, so I knew something was up.

"Alex . . . Alex!" Mr. Strazzanti bellowed, throwing his newspaper down and charging into the kitchen. "Don't you *ever* let me catch you talking to your wife like that again! That is the mother of your children. You will *honor* her and *respect* her. Do you understand me?" He stood glaring at Alex through his thick glasses. Lindsey, now speechless, turned away, a wry smile beginning to form.

"All right, Dad . . . all right . . . I'm sorry," Alex said contritely.

"Don't apologize to me; apologize to your wife."

Mrs. Strazzanti, paring a cucumber in the sink, looked at Lindsey and gave her a nudge with her elbow as if to say: *Touché!*

Mr. Strazzanti returned to his recliner, grabbed his newspaper, pointed his finger at me, and said, "That goes for you, too, Michael. Someday you'll be a husband. That's not the way you talk to a lady."

I nodded my head in full submission. *Wow! At age twenty-seven Alex just had his butt chewed out. I guess a father never stops being a father,*

I thought.

At a time when I needed it most, I found family. Or maybe they found me. It didn't matter. I heard it said once that losing family obliges us to find our family. Not always the family that is our blood but the family that can become our blood. Should we have the wisdom and courage to open our heart to this new family, we will soon find that the wishes we had for the father who once guided us or the mother who once nurtured us can now be fulfilled. I never left the Strazzanti table hungry. Had I eaten nothing at all, I would always be filled, completely nourished.

High school was finally over. It had been a bumpy road-mostly lonely, always challenging-leaving me with more questions than answers. The one important question I did get answered, though, was whether I could survive. I found that I could. I discovered that adversity had challenged the depth of my stability. What *did* I have in times of trouble? I now believe that it's through adversity that we discover just how strong (or weak) we really are.

But what about when prosperity comes? What do we have then? Prosperity is the true test of our integrity. Like nothing else prosperity reveals the honest-to-goodness truth regarding our most basic values. I believe integrity is hammered out on the anvil of prosperity-otherwise it fails the test completely. Our values don't hold up.

For me, prosperity finally seemed within my grasp, and adversity-at least for the moment-had disappeared. At seventeen I didn't realize that it wasn't the path of adversity I should have been concerned about but the path of prosperity. Adversity had taught me well, but prosperity's path is strewn with the litter of its victims-the ones who fail the test completely.

Would I be one of them? Was I ready for the test?

Chapter 5

Rowing My Own Boat

After high-school graduation I spent the summer in Queens, New York, with Mom and Bill before heading to Ohio University. Alex had been promoted to sales instructor, and he and Lindsey were on their way to Endicott, New York, so I no longer had a reason to stay in Ohio, although I tried to find one.

Queens was like landing on another planet. Even my grandmother's trailer was looking pretty good compared to that nightmare. Bill lived in a shabby brownstone row house built in the twenties, located at Elliot Avenue and Seventy-Ninth Street. The neighborhood offered miles of concrete, no trees, and barely a hint of grass. Sidewalks were dense with people-all sizes, all shapes, all ages, and all colors. Every block had a bar, a delicatessen, a barbershop, a laundromat, and a church.

This is going to be an experience, I thought.

The brick on Bill's house was soiled with a greasy film from fifty years of buses belching smoke into the air. The house was dark, with small windows, and the rooms were filled with antique furniture put there years before by Bill's mother, who was also still there and at age eighty-nine looked rather an antique herself. She sat in a rocking chair, her lap draped with newspapers and yarn. Her spectacles were tiny, her housedress was tattered, and her flesh-colored nylons drooped over the tops of her black laced shoes. When she wasn't sleeping, she was knitting, and when she felt feisty, she gave orders-especially to me. Pitching in was the least I could do, being a free boarder and all, she would say. I had never felt more unwelcome and out of place. I couldn't believe that Bill had been born in that house-literally-and lived there with his mother for *forty-six years.* The place smelled like old age.

The windows were kept open at night, making it difficult to sleep-particularly on the oppressive third floor. If it wasn't the smoggy heat keeping me awake, it was the chatter of the trolley or the strident wail of an occasional police siren. Often while skittering on the surface of sleep I'd hear a hot rod screech around the corner with its high-compression engine roaring to a crescendo, then slowly fading away gear by gear, block by block, followed by yet another roar, only this time, softer, until finally it was gone. Eventually the city would sleep while I lay awake wondering what the hell I was doing there.

At the corner was a Jewish deli, a hangout for the neighborhood gang. It was like a scene from *West Side Story*. The gang members were not happy to see me on the few occasions that I strolled over to pick up some things for dinner. I kept my eyes pointed straight ahead, trying to look confident as I walked between them to enter the deli. Nothing ever happened, but there was one close-enough call that I was scared shitless. This was a tough town, and these were tough people.

My summer job was working as a camp counselor, with responsibility for twelve boys. The pay was lousy, but the boys loved baseball, and it kept me outdoors. My nights were my own, so I began searching for other ways to make money. I started my first small business a week later.

I noticed a city worker stenciling addresses on the side of the curb. I asked him what he was doing. He said it was a project to help the police and fire departments. Apparently at night they couldn't see the addresses.

I called the city to see where the cut-off was and asked if I could stencil beyond that point. It turned out that funding only covered streets up to Queens Highway. Beyond that point it was fair game. I was given the go-ahead. So I ran a test market. I invested in three cans of white paint and a stencil kit and started knocking on doors. I stenciled over nine hundred houses that summer. My camp job was over at four o'clock, and after a bite to eat I was on the street till dusk.

At three bucks a pop and a few tips, I cleared about $2,500. It was a neat little operation with the perfect reference sell. Women stood at their front door waving their cash at me. "Do mine next! Do mine next!" This was a hot market, and I had no competition. After one hundred houses, I hired two twelve-year-old boys to work the other side of the street. I never missed a payroll.

The Home of Thirty-Six Bars

My summer in Queens ended, and in the fall of 1970 I headed for

Ohio University. My girlfriend Barb also attended Ohio. While we remained friends all four years, our courtship ended soon after our arrival on campus. The bus dropped me off at the corner of Court and Union in the small college town of Athens, Ohio. Court and Union Streets are famous for their thirty-six bars, where it was customary for students to arrive early to kill a few brain cells before starting their classes. The two streets were bustling. Anyway, there I was, standing on this famous corner, with a large trunk, my suitcase, and a duffle bag, when I realized that I hadn't thought this through very well. How was I going to carry this stuff? And where the hell was Sargent Hall? A moment later a beautiful girl walked by who was kind enough to escort me to my new home.

"That's it, huh?" I said, staring at a three-story brick structure with a New England look. The walls were covered with ivy, and the windows were large double-hung sashes with white trim. The front porch had four white pillars and several Adirondack chairs with kids flopped all over them. All the windows were open. You could hear the Doors, Santana, and Three Dog Night pulsating into the courtyard, providing entertainment for students and parents, who were scurrying about emptying U-Hauls. It was a zoo. I loved it.

Play Ball

Classes were easier than I had thought they'd be-unlike fall baseball practice. I had never seen an eighty-mile-an-hour curve ball before. Every player was outstanding. I performed reasonably well in the fall workouts (thank God), giving myself a chance in the spring.

I joined the Sigma Chi fraternity. I felt a need to belong somewhere-finding family again, I guess-and Sigma Chi seemed to offer that. After burning out on three-to-a room dorm life, I chose to live in the frat house the following year. The fraternity did not mix well with baseball, however. My burgeoning social life and occasional pot party started to get in the way of playing good ball.

I lost focus and ended up breaking my hand in a game with Kent State. The batter hit a short Texas leaguer over second base. I was in center field. I charged the ball, calling off the shortstop, who was also charging. Realizing I was late to the ball, I dove straight ahead, attempting a scoop catch. I crash landed with a skid, trapping my hand under my chest, and broke all four bones in the palm of my hand. It was a serious compound fracture.

The doctor had to cut off my glove before he could stop the bleeding and set the bones; I threw up from the pain and nearly fainted. Rightly, I blamed myself for the accident. I had been reckless, and now I was at risk of losing everything I had worked for.

Six weeks later I returned to the field. I took batting practice and was in shock over the pain I felt. I couldn't grip the bat securely, and the vibration felt as though I had broken the bones all over again. My hand throbbed for the rest of the season, and I never regained my ability to hit the ball hard.

What had gotten me into Ohio University-baseball-had broken into a bunch of pieces along with my hand. I washed out of the game for good. This was a devastating setback and left me terribly depressed. What was I supposed to learn from this? Why did it have to happen? I had been jacking around the night before the game, and now I was paying the price. Sure enough, prosperity's path had been strewn with one of its victims. Thankfully, though, I was able to keep the scholarship.

Life in a Cathouse

The summer after my junior year, I bought a 1961 Ford Falcon for $300 from a fraternity brother-the Camaro had been short lived, and I had been without wheels from the time I had graduated from high school-and drove it up to Cleveland to search for a job and a place to live. No way was I going back to Queens.

My uncle Specks tried to hook me up at Republic Steel, shoveling coal into a furnace, but the economy was weak and most companies weren't hiring. Uncle Specks and Aunt Jean allowed me to stay with them while I continued my job search. After a week I found nothing, and I was worried that I'd have to return to Queens after all. That thought alone provided all the motivation I needed.

I received a tip that Gaydos Welding might be hiring grinders. I drove over immediately, parked the Falcon in one of the visitor's spaces, and walked into the office to introduce myself. A woman handed me an application without looking up. I filled it out, handed it back, and asked her if they had any openings. "Nope, but we'll call you if something changes," she said. She still hadn't looked up.

I went back three straight days in a row. The woman behind the desk was getting angry, but I didn't care. I returned to my car and sat in the parking lot for two hours, until closing time. Then a man came out of the building. He locked the front door and headed for the Lincoln parked beside me. Having your own personalized parking space was typical for the three-martini executive of the seventies, which gave me a head's up that this was the owner of the company.

I popped out of my car. "Mr. Gaydos?"

He glanced at me over the Lincoln's roof. At five five-and roughly two hundred pounds-he could barely see over it. He was sucking madly on a freshly lit cigar that dominated most of his face. He wore dress slacks and a white short-sleeve cabana shirt and sported a large tattoo on his forearm. He looked like Edward G. Robinson.

"Yes," he said.

"Excuse me, sir. I've been sitting in this car waiting for you for two hours. My name is Mike Kerrison. I've been here every day this week, looking for a job. I'm a college student, I'm on my own, and I've run out of time and money. I'm an excellent worker, I have references, I'm strong, and I learn fast. Can you help me?" *Oh, my God, I'm talking way too fast. This is not the way I rehearsed this.*

The cigar stopped wiggling in his mouth, and he stared blankly, not sure what to say.

"How old are you?" he asked.

I lied and told him I was twenty.

"Have you ever worked in a factory before?" he asked. He was leaning on the Lincoln's roof, staring straight at me as if waiting for me to lie again.

"No, sir, I haven't," I admitted. *This doesn't look good.*

"Do you think you can operate a grinding machine?"

"Absolutely," I said. I approached his car.

He rubbed his eyes as if soothing a headache. "When can you start?" he asked, still rubbing his eyes.

"Immediately." At that point I was praying silently.

He continued staring at me, studying me.

"All right, then, start tomorrow morning. Be here at seven-thirty. Ask for Mary. She'll sign you up. You'll start at five bucks an hour. Okay?"

We shook on it.

"Don't be late." He began to get into his car.

"Mr. Gaydos . . . one more thing," I said. He popped back up, looking agitated.

I winced. "I'm only nineteen."

He shook his head, snickered, and said, "Four-fifty an hour, and don't lie to me again."

He pulled out of the parking lot, nodding as he passed.

I was ecstatic-and relieved. I learned tremendously valuable things that day. Always call at the top. I also learned that little white lies have consequences-in this case twenty dollars a week. And, finally, I learned that you must accomplish a goal in your mind first, as though it's already done. Then you just play it out. Don't get hung up on the perfect approach; just take action. If your motives are pure, good things will follow.

I had a job. Now I needed a place to live.

I found an interesting newspaper ad, describing a house that rented rooms in the basement. I cut the ad from the paper and headed there. The house was a small, simple rambler, nicely maintained-or so it looked on the outside -and situated in a respectable but isolated section of Middleburg Heights. Feeling encouraged, I rang the doorbell. A woman answered.

"Hi, can I help you?" she asked.

"Yes, I hope so. I'm responding to the ad in the paper regarding rooms for rent," I said. She smiled and invited me in. She had a toying look on her face, as if she wanted to adopt me or something.

"My name is Dottie, what's yours?"

She had bushy jet-black hair, enormous breasts, heavy makeup, and wore skin-tight Capri pants. I didn't see what was on her feet because I was having trouble getting past her boobs.

"I'm Mike . . . Mike Kerrison."

The eight-hundred-square-foot basement had been divided into five tiny subterranean chambers made out of paper-thin knotty pine panels. Under the stairwell were two makeshift aluminum showers-which seemed to only offer cold water-and a curtain hanging from a wire, behind which you were expected to dry off. The walls provided no privacy for any voice above a whisper. From the exterior, most people would find the house inviting-neighborly, in fact. And Middleburg Heights was well regarded. But the place, which was out of the mainstream of the neighborhood, was only one cut above a rat-infested flophouse, differing from the shelters only in that it had privacy in the form of a locked door.

Dottie had one room left, the smallest of the five. It had no windows, an exposed light bulb pulsing dimly overhead, and a small nightstand next to the bed-perfect for my hot plate, salt and pepper shakers (that I had stolen from Manner's Big Boy), and a few eating utensils. The place smelled of mildew, stale cigarettes, and cheap wine. It was unrelievedly oppressive, which explained why it was only a hundred bucks a month. But the hard reality of my financial condition made the decision simple. I moved in.

"The other tenants are at work, so you'll have to get acquainted with them later," Dottie said as I watched my hundred-dollar deposit disappear into her cleavage. *Oh to be that hundred bucks*, I thought. I pulled up the moving van-the Falcon-and unloaded my one suitcase, a duffel bag filled with dirty clothes, and one change of bed sheets that after three years of college had been laundered to transparency. I settled in.

Floyd Peterson, a scruffy-looking man in his sixties, occupied the largest corner bedroom. Dottie called him the anchor tenant. He had been there five years. His look was that of a felon after a month in solitary, giving him a translucent hue like a creature deprived of sunlight. He invited me into his room for a drink. Hesitant at first, I decided to be neighborly and went in.

The room was overflowing with pornography-magazines, posters, books, and movies were stacked everywhere in unstable configurations. Even the most committed pervert hadn't seen anything like this before. He searched recklessly through the smut and found a glass smeared with sticky fingerprints. *Oh, my Lord, he's not gonna use that, is he?* He poured straight Canadian whiskey out of a pint bottle that he had no doubt been swigging from all day. I reached for the grimy glass and gagged at the thought of drinking from it.

"There you go, and take a look at that, Mike," he said, flinging a filthy photograph in front of me. He lit his cigarette, spit tobacco from his lips, and giggled.

"My, this is quite a little collection you got here Floyd," I said in what I hoped was the proper admiring tone. "You must be very proud of it."

He just sat there hunched over, grinning at me with his stubbly face, sucking on the pint bottle. His eyes were rimmed in red, and his fingers were long and frail with knuckles twice the normal size. He looked ill.

I swirled the drink in my glass, figuring it might kill some of the bacteria. "Well, Floyd, thanks for the drink. I'd best be going. Got some unpacking to do." I closed my eyes, tossed the amber dregs down the hatch, and bolted for the door. I couldn't get out of there fast enough. What a creep. How could people live like this? And than I realized: *God . . . I'm living like this.*

Later that evening I heard someone walk down the hall. It sounded like a woman's footfalls. I could hear her fiddling with her keys and struggling to open the door to her room. After Floyd, I wasn't real fired up about meeting anybody else, but I erased my doubts and poked my head out my door. To my surprise I saw a petite, sweet-looking girl about my age, looking very frustrated.

"Fucking door," she said, kicking it. "Why do I lock this stupid thing? There's nothing in here, anyway." She twisted and yanked. "*Damn* this thing!"

"There's nothing in my room, either," I said. She looked back at me, startled. I raised my hands in surrender. "Sorry, didn't mean to scare ya. I'm your new neighbor. My name's Mike."

Looking both embarrassed and suspicious, she studied me. "Donna . . . nice to meet ya. Sorry about the language," she said.

"I've heard worse," I said. "Can I help you with that door?"

She was poorly dressed, her hair was dirty, and she had dark circles under her eyes. She obviously had been crying. On closer inspection I could see that she was beautiful and feminine. *What are you doing here? Someone so pretty. When did you give up on yourself?* I thought.

Her door popped open. She thanked me and disappeared into the room, glancing over her shoulder as she walked in. I shrugged and returned to my room.

I was finishing a disgusting bowl of hot-plate Hormel chili-which, to my embarrassment, had stunk up the entire basement-when someone knocked on the door. It was Donna. She looked lovely. She had showered, donned cutoffs and a Hiram College sweatshirt, and smelled like a bouquet of spring flowers-a timely remedy to offset the stench of my chili. It was quite a transformation from the person I had met an hour ago. I was immediately attracted to her.

"I had to find out who was polluting our perfect air," she said, holding her nose.

"Oh! . . . Sorry . . . I guess that would be me." I could feel my face redden.

"Let's start over. I'm Donna Bayus. Pleased to meet you," she said, extending her hand.

I reached for her hand and introduced myself.

"Welcome to the neighborhood," she said. "Have you met all the weirdos yet?"

"Only Floyd." I stood aside, allowing her to enter my cubicle.

She started laughing. "Oh, Mike, what a pervert! Did he invite you into his room?"

"Oh, yeah, I got the full treatment." I offered her the plastic chair while I sat on the foot of the bed. "Aren't you afraid to be down here with a guy like that?" I asked.

Flipping the chair around, she straddled it and lit a cigarette. "Oh, he's harmless, I think." She offered me a smoke. I declined.

"Yeah . . . well . . . don't be too sure." I said.

She shrugged. "Besides, he's not the guy who scares me. Bill is."

"Bill?"

"His room is in the other corner. He's huge, like six-five. There's something wrong with him, though. He can hardly talk, and he won't look at you-ever," she said. She took a deep drag on her cigarette.

"How does he take care of himself?" I asked.

Donna shrugged again. "Who knows? I think he works for Dottie. Kinda like a maintenance man. I don't think he pays rent." She surveyed my room. "He's a bodyguard for Dottie, too," she added.

"A bodyguard! What the hell does she need a bodyguard for?" I asked.

"Dottie's a prostitute. Didn't you know that? Haven't you seen the creeps coming in and out of here all night?"

"No, this is my first night," I said.

"Oh, brother. Keep your eyes open. You'll see all kinds of strange things around here. She rents that room by the week," she said, pointing at the wall next to me. "She says she gets a better rate that way. Last week we had this big biker guy down here. Scared the hell out of me. He was always slipping in and out of here all secretlike, and he kept peeking out his door . . . like he was expecting something. He had a gun, too."

"Jeez! It sounds like *we* need the bodyguard," I said.

"Yeah, there're some spooky people coming in and out of here. Just mind your own business. You'll be okay."

"So, Donna, what do you do that allows you such fine accommodations?" I quipped.

She smiled and stared at the floor. I waited for her answer. It turns out that she was a hooker, too. Dottie had brought her in, providing her a place to live and a steady flow of business-all for a cut of the action, of course. Donna was only eighteen and still in training. In fact, a few days later, Dottie had suggested to Donna that she try out a few of her new tricks on me-you know, for practice.

"It wouldn't mean anything, Mike. You'd be helping me out. And, it would be free," Donna explained.

"Don't tempt me, but I think I better pass. Maybe Bill can help you out. For sure Floyd," I said, chuckling.

She didn't think that was very funny. And I have to admit that resisting her advances was not easy.

Donna and I became good friends that summer. We ate a lot of bologna sandwich dinners together. She was terrific company and surprisingly smart. I was troubled by the sound of her door opening and closing throughout the night, and I would lie in my bed, listening for foul play, prepared to get up and beat somebody's head in-which on one occasion was nearly the case. If it hadn't been for Bill (the semi-retarded guy who ended up being our pal), I would never have been able to rescue Donna from the big bastard who decided to get rough with her.

In the middle of the night, I was woken up by the sounds of her struggling and yelling, "No! Don't! Stop it!"

I ran down the hall and pounded on Bill's door. He was asleep. "Bill, get up! Right now! I need your help! Donna's in trouble!"

Suddenly the door was flung open and Bill flew out. He shoved me aside, charged down the hallway, slammed through Donna's door-tearing it off its hinges-and jumped on top of the son of a bitch and Donna. Bill bear hugged the guy, trapping his arms to his side, dragged him up the stairs buck naked, his unit flapping between his legs and hurled him out of the house. The guy lay sprawled on the grass. I had picked up the john's clothes and now threw them at him.

"Hey, you got my shoes in there," he protested.

Bill ran downstairs, grabbed the shoes, raced back up in three strides, and came barreling after him. The guy started running across the front lawn with Bill chasing him and throwing the shoes at him, hitting him in the back of the head.

"Ow! Shit! You're crazy man, you know that? Fucking crazy!" The guy jumped into his car and desperately locked the doors. He finally got his car started, and as he peeled off, Bill began running alongside, kicking the fenders. I stood staring in disbelief.

Bill finally gave up the chase and came back, panting.

"God, Bill. You were gonna *kill* that guy! Settle down. It's okay. Donna's okay." I put my hands on his shoulders to calm him. He was soaking wet. "It's okay. Let's go in the house now."

Dottie had been standing at the front door, watching. I signaled for her to wait. Bill had calmed down and went back into the house.

I walked to the front door to address Dottie. "God, Dottie, I think it's time for you to find a real job, for crissakes. This is getting crazy. You're gonna get us all killed!" I said. Donna's only eighteen. This has got to stop."

She stood there staring at me, nearly in tears.

"Plus I'm sick and tired of having to take cold showers." Frankly, though, with Donna next door those came in pretty handy. I stepped onto the porch, grabbed Dottie by the arms and said, "Please, stop doing this. Please."

Donna and I talked until six in the morning. It took me the entire night to convince her to go home. She shouldn't have been selling herself. We went down to Bill's room to thank him. He was already asleep.

"And you thought you were afraid of this guy. What would have happened to you if he hadn't been around?" I asked.

She left at the end of the week. I came home from work that Friday and knocked on her door like I always did. When there was no response, I pushed the door open. The room was empty. I then found a loving note shoved under my door. She had decided to go home. I never saw or heard from her again. I often wonder how her life turned out. She was the first woman that I had been intimate with without ever touching. I can't say she was an important person in my life-we knew each other for only a short time-but she represented something for me. She was a forgotten kid, caught in the jaws of adversity. Would she get out? Would she repair herself? Would I?

That was a strange summer. Although I had been living with reprobates in mutual poverty, I felt a certain kind of felicity to it all. I had now seen the other side of life, up close. I now knew personally people in this world who had nothing-no future, no dreams, and no hope. I saw their choices and the regrettable consequences they held. When I think of my own four kids, I am grateful that they haven't had to see these things up close as I did-or had to live the way I did. Yet I sensed a mysterious benefit. I learned to be brave-a quality that doesn't exist for a person whose life is always wonderful.

Another year had flown by. From the age of fifteen, I had been on my own. I had already covered a lot of ground for one so young, doing a lot and seeing a lot-but I never would have guessed that my journey of discovery would take me to a place as bizarre as a cathouse in Middleburg Heights, Ohio. I packed up my things and headed back to OU for my senior year, celebrating my deliverance from Floyd and Dottie and the multiple creeps who had been my weekly neighbors.

One more year. I could see light at the end of the tunnel.

Meeting Lynn Lynch

I was on my third consecutive hour of playing poker-a clear sign of the "senior slump"-when I was rescued by a phone call. One advantage to being a senior is that your life is about to take on more meaningful pursuits than just mindlessly scraping poker chips from a table, ducking classes, and growing facial hair. Counting my reds, whites, and blues, I reckoned my entire net worth was somewhere around forty dollars. I hurried to the phone.

"Hello?"

"Hey, it's show time." It was Alex. I was always excited to hear from him. "Lynn's ready to see ya"-Lynn Lynch was Alex's boss-"and he was hoping you could come up during spring break."

"Really? God, Alex, that's fabulous news! What do I need to do?"

"Just sit tight for right now. Keep the grades up. When we get a little closer, we'll have to buy you a suit and get you to Chicago somehow. What does your hair look like?"

I looked at my reflection in the soda machine. "Fine," I lied.

"Good. Oh, and get rid of those lamb chops, too. Bottom of the ear, no farther. Okay?"

"Okay. No sweat. God, Alex, I can't believe it! It's really happening isn't it?"

I could practically hear him smile. "It's here."

Alex picked me up at O'Hare Airport on a Friday night in late March 1974. He had just moved the family again-after another speedy promotion-and was now a marketing manager for a new group called the General Systems Division (GSD), which had been established to sell smaller computers to emerging-growth companies.

The mission for GSD was to create a new breed of salesman, combining the sophisticated team-selling approach of the Data Processing Division with the street-fighter style of the Office Products Division. What emerged was a new sales model designed to close business in three calls: an introductory call, a survey call, and a closing call. This model would be copied by everyone in the industry. In fact, it's still used today.

Alex drove me to his new home, where I was greeted by Lindsey and the kids. It was an exciting time for them, as well. After dinner, he and I talked about the interview.

"Just be yourself, be natural," he advised. "After some small talk, Lynn's gonna ask you why you want to be a salesman. What are you gonna tell him?"

I shrugged. "I don't know, Alex. It seems like I've been selling since I was fifteen years old. Maybe not products, per se-although I did sell cookware for a month during my final quarter at school. Yipes, that bombed. But, I won't go into that. I thought for a moment. "I'm always selling myself, Alex. I have to. There's always employers, coaches, teachers, parents. . . . I'm selling all the time. Talking to people comes naturally to me. That's why I think I'd be good at this-not to mention that I'm tired of being broke."

"That's perfect!" Alex said. He relaxed his feet on the coffee table. "And tell him about the cookware stuff. Most people wouldn't have even tried. He'll like that."

"Really?"

"Yeah, really. And don't worry about the test. You'll do fine."

My heart jumped a beat. A test! I was never a good test taker.

Mary, Lynn Lynch's secretary, delivered the good news about that part. "You did nicely, Mike. I understand Alex had you scared to death about this test," she said.

"He did, as a matter of fact."

She chuckled. "Mr. Lynch will see you after lunch. In the meantime, I'll set you up with the other managers."

I went back into the test room and let out a yell-the open mouth kind with no sound where your eyes pop out and your face turns red. I was bursting, ready to nail those interviews.

After lunch Alex picked me up in the hallway and escorted me to Lynn Lynch's office. He stopped before entering and studied me. "You know, you clean up pretty good," he said, straightening my tie. I had on a gray pinstriped suit, white shirt, and a red-and-yellow striped tie. "Ya ready?"

I took a deep breath. "God, I hope so."

Alex smiled. "You're ready."

Lynn Lynch was a huge man standing six foot five, with hands twice the size of mine. He had a large face partially borrowed from his receding hairline, his voice was husky from smoking cigars, and he wore a five-and-a-half-millimeter smile and a warm expression. I was immediately comfortable with him. We talked about college and baseball and IBM. I told him that I had wanted to be a salesman for IBM since I was a teenager. He seemed amazed by that.

"Mike, tell me: Why do you think you'd be a good salesman?"

I repeated what I had said to Alex. Lynn loved it, and we talked for about an hour. He sat forward from time to time, puffing on his cigar as though in disbelief at some of my stories. I hoped that he was as impressed with me as I was with him. The interview ended with a warm handshake.

Lynn walked me to Alex's office. "Hold on to this kid. I need to talk to the other managers," he said. He turned and winked at Alex as we watched his big frame disappear into the hallway.

"He likes you," Alex said.

That afternoon Lynn offered me a job-at $950 a month. I was rich. I could hardly breathe I was so excited. My eyes filled up. This was a moment that I had dreamed about-one I had feared would never come. I would not let Alex down. I would be the best salesman this branch had ever hired.

PART TWO

The Business Years

Chapter 6

Everything Happens for a Reason

In June 1974 I received my degree-a BBA in management. Before graduating I snuck back to Chicago one weekend to find a place to live. Lindsey had been scouting around for me and found a place called International Village. The apartments were terrific looking, so I grabbed one. As it turns out, the place was a swinging singles compound-a habitat for lonely hearts.

On weekends these lonely hearts would cluster at the swimming pool bar like school kids jamming around a lunch table. At the center of the circle were a few older guys with great suntans, big bellies, and thick gold chains displayed proudly on their greasy chest hair. They were surrounded by a flock of women in their twenties and thirties who were sporting full makeup and skimpy swimsuits, busily painting their toenails, smoking cigarettes, and flirting. The whole scene looked pathetic to me, but I figured it was a place to hang my hat-at least for a while.

The table was now set. I left campus for good on June seventh, drove straight through to Chicago, moved into my apartment over the weekend, and reported to IBM the following Monday. My world was accelerating-a world far different from the one I had just left.

Alex was the branch training manager responsible for getting us ready for "*A mod*," the first of a series of six-week mini-schools. IBM started us out selling a dictating unit (a relatively simple device) before tackling something as complex as a computer. They wanted us to master the sell cycle first, which by itself was plenty.

My first role-play attempt was a disaster. Alex poured me into a bottle, leaving me speechless and unable to recover. A couple of managers and a few seasoned trainees were entertained by my slaughter as they watched Alex administer the IBM tradition of stripping me down to nothing, then slowly building me back up again. It was like Navy Seals training for sales reps. After one year, if you made it through, you could sell anything.

Alex demonstrated how to make the call. It looked so natural when he did it, even though he was following a structure. He told me the selling structure can be compared to the frame of a house. The frame of a house supports the unique characteristics of the house-colors, moldings, wall treatments, lighting, vaulted ceilings, etc. This gives the house beauty and distinction. It's what we see. The frame (structure) is indiscernible, but it's always there, holding the house together.

Selling is no different. Your personality, individual traits, and natural style-the characteristics that give *you* distinction-are supported by the selling structure, just like the frame of a house. This gives you the freedom to be natural in a sales call (rather than trying to be someone you're not), knowing full well that the structure, also indiscernible, is there holding the call together. The comparison made perfect sense to me.

Sales training generally took one year at IBM, after which time you were expected to assume a territory, take a forty percent pay cut, and go on commission. If you didn't sell something quickly, you'd starve. Although I didn't like it at the time, I became and still remain a proponent of a highly leveraged compensation plan with no caps. For me, a salesman who needs a big salary sends up a red flag.

I was sent to Endicott, New York, for *A* mod, which provided the equivalent of an advanced degree in accounting. A mod also introduced the structured sales call for the first time, which was pounded into our heads for one year. Following *A* mod were *B* and *C* mods. *B* mod taught us how a business operates, and in *C* mod we learned systems design and computer programming. Then came sales school-two weeks of grueling role-play, all on videotape for later review. This was the biggie. If you flunked sales school, you were out. You never went on quota; you were given two chances in case you bombed the first one. The pressure was enormous.

I ended up fourth in my class out of twenty, and rather than feeling good about my performance, I felt like a failure. Was this sour grapes or just plain arrogance at the thought of being in *fourth* place? Unthinkable! This kind of behavior held the clues as to why I sometimes could blow myself out of the saddle.

Starter Patch

I finished my training in ten months, when a territory became available. Lynn Lynch, with his morning cigar in one hand and a giant mug of coffee in the other, flagged me down in the hallway.

"Mike, good job in sales school, by the way. We're proud of you." He smiled and took a sip of his coffee. "Well, are you ready to start making some money?" he asked.

"Absolutely!"

"It's what you've been working toward, and we think you're ready," he said. "You start Monday morning. Report to Dick Daniels. He'll assign a quota and fill you in on the details. We expect a fast start out of you, Mike." He shoved his cigar between his teeth, swatted me on the shoulder, and walked out of the office.

I took a deep breath, exhaled hard, and went to find Alex.

"Well, have you sold anything yet?" Alex asked.

"Hell, yes, I got a whole drawer full of orders," I said, playing along. "By the way, Alex, you're smoking a lot. What's up with that?" Alex had always been a heavy smoker. That he was now on his second pack was evidenced by the crumpled pack in the garbage can-and it was only noon. That was not a good trend.

"Yeah, I know . . . I gotta quit." He quickly changed the subject. "Look, you're gonna get teased by the guys about getting stuck with the starter patch."

"What do you mean?" I asked.

"Your patch has a reputation in the branch as having the worst potential. But don't listen to them. In thirty days that will be the best patch in the office," he promised. "Trust me."

A patch was your territory. A starter patch was a territory no one wanted-a patch given up for dead.

"What's gonna happen in thirty days?"

"Just trust me," Alex repeated.

I met with Dick Daniels the next morning. By reputation, Dick was a "dick," but despite that, he always made his numbers, and he had a conventional style that accommodated itself to IBM's conservative, sanitized mold. By contrast, my style had not been far removed from fraternity parties, poker games, and an occasional toke. This was certainly a new reality for me, and I was determined to fit in, produce admirably, and win his favor.

Dick's insistence on being a dick was at least understandable. His eye had been knocked out by a golf ball that he accidentally whacked into a tree. The accident had occurred during an IBM outing, and rumor had it that he got a settlement big enough to retire on, which he would no doubt exchange in a heartbeat to get his eye back. Anyway, I don't think he ever really recovered from the accident, leaving him depressed and cranky.

He had a weird way of soothing himself with humor. He loved telling jokes, but he had this habit of cracking himself up just before he delivered the punch line. "What?" or "What he say?" or "I didn't hear that?" were the usual responses from the peanut gallery. On his second attempt to deliver, he'd crack up again, only this time wheezing and snorting and turning red, as if someone had punched him in the stomach. Trying to recover, he would signal for patience. "Wait a minute . . . wait a minute . . . wait a minute." Then he would lean back and squirt drops into his glass eye.

The peanut gallery, now shocked and repulsed, would thin out, leaving a couple of obligated listeners-me being one of them. He'd finally deliver the punch line (which was never funny except to Dick, of course). Then he'd crack up a third time, his face now flowing with tears, both real and artificial, that I sensed were somehow linked to that stupid golf ball.

The fact is I liked the guy, quirks and all. The old soldier, despite his unusual sense of humor and melancholy disposition, taught me many things.

I got my patch, my quota, and I was ready to roll. Selling in 1975 was still door-to-door. You parked the car at the end of the block and worked your way down the street. I had a manufacturing territory consisting mostly of tool-and-die shops. Franklin Park had dozens of them, which made the town look more like a business graveyard than a host to the American Dream. Most of the buildings were falling apart, their walls were covered with graffiti, and the el-Chicago's primary commuter train-would rattle and roar overhead every ten minutes. The air smelled of smoke and chemicals, and police sirens wailed continually.

This was my patch. No wonder no one wanted it. You could get killed there.

Something to Prove

Thirty days passed-and then IBM announced the new System/32, one of the most exciting developments since the System/360. It would revolutionize small-business computing. Now, for less than $1,000 per month, you could automate your entire operation.

"Well, how does your patch look now, big boy?" Alex asked.

"This is unbelievable! I gotta get out there!" I grabbed my fair share of marketing materials and headed to Franklin Park. Getting in the door was easy-people respected IBM. But I found out early that exchanging pleasantries in the vestibule did not make money. Just because I had this great new system to sell didn't mean the streets were now paved with gold. I'd have to work the patch creatively. Furthermore, the System/32 was half the price of its predecessor, the System/3, so to make the IBM Hundred Percent Club, I'd have to sell twice as many systems.

The pressure to make the Hundred Percent Club was enormous. If you blew your numbers, your career was toast. The club was a four-day annual recognition event-always held in a warm climate-where the members were treated like royalty. If you weren't there, you were nobody. As usual, I couldn't settle for a realistic goal like making the club-I had to go for Rookie of the Year. Once again, I didn't want strike-outs, I wanted no-hitters. I didn't want home runs, I wanted grand slams.

Telemarketing was considered inelegant and ineffectual in those days. But to me it was the only way to make big numbers. I prepared my approach and got busy on the phone, inviting company presidents to attend a half-day workshop that would demonstrate how the System/32 could provide them a competitive advantage. My branch office hosted a fancy lunch and offered a special drawing for a golf trip and a set of Ram Golf irons (Ram was a customer). The approach was highly criticized by insiders, but after fighting to get my way, I proceeded with my experiment.

It worked. Eleven companies attended the first seminar. I sold three systems in thirty days. My first new account, Ansan Tool & Manufacturing, gave me an order that same day. This seminar strategy became my marquee. In 1975 I was Rookie of the Year at 232 percent of quota. During the first four years, I sold over seventy systems, made four consecutive Hundred Percent Clubs, was New Account Leader twice, and finished in the top three of the region all four years.

I love selling, and fortunately I've always been good at it. When I first started at IBM, I stayed close to the good sales reps and watched their every move. Following them around, asking them questions, watching them do their jobs, and making calls with them was the best training available. I wanted to know their secrets, what made them stars.

Some people believe that great salespeople are born, not made. I don't believe this for two reasons. First, any bright, hard-working, and motivated person can learn and eventually master the mechanics of selling. Second, I believe people are formed by the sum total of their experiences. We aren't fully formed at birth. The doctor doesn't deliver a baby, give it a slap, and say, "Well, this one looks like a salesman"-although he might argue that it sounds like one. The point is, selling can be learned.

The part of selling that can't be learned, however, is *drive*. Nor is this trait something that you're born with. You develop it. And once you have it, it is nurtured and fed by your successes, and strangely enough also by your failures, all resulting in a cumulative effect-thus creating even more drive. This voracious drive is relieved only through total focus, commitment, and the pursuit of big dreams-the biggest, in fact. And, of course, drive doesn't lead only to a sales profession. You don't have to look far to find driven doctors, lawyers, athletes, ministers, teachers, and so on. Drive develops a special capacity in people, one that pushes them beyond their own capabilities in whatever their chosen profession. They are never happy with second best.

Unfortunately drive is a double-edged sword. It cuts both ways. At least it did for me. After my Dad died, I began to feel inadequate, abnormal. The world seemed like a party to which I hadn't been invited. I developed a desperate feeling of detachment. At times it was debilitating, depressing. But this is where the drive came from: a burning desire to get back to normal, to feel adequate, to be respected. I felt it was something I had to earn, something I had to prove. This drive brought tremendous success to my life. (It also brought devastating failure.) But I had support on the way.

The Beer Garden

That support was Dawn, whom I married in 1975. I met her at Butch McGuire's, one of Chicago's famous watering holes. I know, I know: "You're kidding, right? You actually met her in a bar? How glamorous."

It was a Saturday night, May 10, 1975, to be exact. Glen Arnold, one of IBM's sales superstars and notorious party animal, called me. He had a gift of gab that would charm the devil himself. We had become good pals.

"Hey, asshole, what're ya doin'?" came the voice on the other end of the line.

"Oh, hi, Glen." I knew it was him right away. No one else used such charming greetings, such as asshole, dickhead, or butt face. "I'm working on a presentation for Monday," I replied. "How're *you* doin'?"

"I don't know, let me ask her." He cackled, thinking he was hilarious.

"God, Arnold, you are sick," I said.

"Yeah, I know. So let's go to Butch's and have a few beers. Maybe we'll get lucky," he said.

I rolled my eyes. "No way. My head still hurts from last night." Friday nights were devoted to softball under the lights followed by more than a few beers. The evenings would end at Denny's for a 3 A.M. breakfast with me, Alex, Glen, and a few others from the team all stuffed into a booth, behaving like high-school kids-flirting with the waitresses, blowing straws, and generally acting like idiots.

"C'mon, one beer. You can do that shit tomorrow," he said.

"One beer, that's it. I'm going to bed early tonight. And no women," I demanded.

"You're the boss. I'll pick you up in an hour."

We decided to sit at the bar. The beer garden was chilly that night. The smell of stale smoke was making me queasy, and the place was filled with daters having burgers and milkshakes. I wished I had stayed home. Then two women walked through the door. It looked like the parting of the Red Sea as the floor rats stepped aside, allowing them to pass.

"Oh, my God, look at this!" Glen said, sticking his elbow in my side.

She looked like Natalie Wood. The other girl, also very beautiful, was less noticeable, but only because she had walked in second. They headed for the beer garden. Glen was off his stool in a flash.

"For chrissake, Arnold. Get a grip." Disgusted, I watched him wiggle through the crowd, and in no time he returned and gave an order to the bartender. Jeez. He was already buying them drinks.

"Get your ass over there and meet the other one," Glen insisted. "She's *beautiful*." He gathered their drinks in his hand. "You want another beer?" he asked.

"No. I'm fine. I'll be over in a minute."

"Okay. But hurry up. We got some action goin' here," he said, with a cackle. Glen was a horned toad, always chasing somebody. In those days an insecure type, he drove a Corvette, which Dawn later nicknamed the "rolling penis." In her view it was an automotive symbol for impotence. A little harsh, I thought, but she wasn't far off. Not about Glen but about the car.

I went to the men's room to collect some energy and some courage. "You look like shit, Kerrison," I told myself, taking inspection in front of the mirror. I had on my old college bell-bottoms that were at least two inches too short, dirty tennis shoes with holes, a plain white T-shirt, and my Sigma Chi jacket, which was too small and had a torn zipper. I wasn't feeling very sexy as I headed for the beer garden.

"Hey, man, where'd you go?" Glen asked as I sat down at their table. He handed me a beer that I didn't ask for. "Ladies, this is my friend Mike Kerrison. Mike, this is Colleen Zenk and her friend Dawn-uhhh, what was your last name?"

"Duhaime," she said.

"That's right, Duhaime."

Of course it's right, blockhead; it's her name, I thought.

"Hi." I clicked bottles with Colleen and attempted to make eye contact with Dawn. Nothing. "Whoa! No chemistry here," I said under my breath. Meanwhile, Glen and Colleen were chirping like lovebirds.

"You look like you don't want to be here," I said to Dawn.

"That obvious, huh?" she responded.

She *was* beautiful. She exuded a certain confidence and was cool, elegant, and remote under her ketchup-and-gravy suntan. Her hair was dark and shiny and fell softly on her shoulders. She was stunning. I stared at the ground, searching for words. A glimpse of my tennis shoes reminded me that I just might be the biggest geek in the entire joint. I didn't have a chance with this girl.

But somehow I became brilliant. I was funny, intelligent, experienced, and determined to win her heart that night. We talked until 1 A.M. Then I walked her to her car and kissed her goodnight. I was hooked. The next day we took a long drive in the country.

We were married four months and ten days later. We were crazy to do it, but for reasons we couldn't understand at the time, we rushed into marriage. Anyway, Dawn was running away from something, and I was trying to get back to normal-whatever that was. We were both loaded with personal issues, and since we didn't really know each other, we spent the first couple of years with a marriage counselor (with whom we still exchange Christmas cards). We worked hard on the marriage, but eventually we failed. We stayed together a long time.

The Eagle

Before introducing you to Dawn, I was telling you about drive, and while it is a critical component to success, if left unchecked it can turn on you, cloud your judgment, and place you on life's jagged edge.

In 1977 IBM announced a new award called the Eagle that would go only to the top one percent of the sales force. IBM was the master of motivation, positioning and marketing its top awards as effectively as it did its products. To be an Eagle you had to install twenty systems in one fiscal year. Not sell twenty, *install* twenty. It looked impossible since the most I had ever installed was thirteen.

I had a new boss. Rick Halperin was a young hard charger on a fast track-tall, good-looking, athletic, and loaded with charm. Alex liked him but thought he was a showboat. I really liked him, and Rick made no bones about it: I was going to be his meal ticket. When being promoted, it was customary for new marketing managers to be assigned a "horse." Rick told me that before he would accept the job, he insisted on having me on his team, which didn't make Dick Daniels very happy. Rick was determined to make me an Eagle, which wouldn't hurt him much, either.

Most of the sales reps looked at the Eagle as lunacy, a laughable pursuit. I wasn't laughing. Someone was going to do it. Someone always does. I set out to make sure it was me. I already had five systems in the backlog, which meant I needed fifteen sell/installs and no cancellations or deferrals. It was daunting but doable.

Making Eagle became an uncomfortable obsession, leading to seventy-hour work weeks, sometimes no sleep, and skipped meals. I was exhausted and edgy, especially with Dawn, who rarely complained when I went back to the office after dinner or on weekends. She provided encouragement. But she knew it was going to be a bumpy ride.

I knew I had the ability to make Eagle, but confidence was still hard to muster. My insecurity would come exploding out of me as though past failures and recent successes were somehow colliding. I was a potent mixture of drive and determination, turning and twisting with feelings of inadequacy and low self-esteem. The effort to keep going was excruciating. I cut myself off from everything except the pursuit of this goal.

From the look of things, out of two thousand reps there would be only four or five Eagles in the whole country. IBM had a leader board for this, too. Rick was constantly checking in with me at this point. "Everything all right? Do you need anything?" he constantly asked. We were both obsessed.

By October I had everything I needed, with five systems installing in December. Then I received a cancellation and a deferral, from two different clients, leaving me two systems short, and it appeared that there was no chance for delivery in December without immediate replacement orders. Rick and I were able to save the deferral, but the cancellation was real. I was still one install short. It looked hopeless.

Panicky, I went back to an old prospect that despite my best effort I had been unable to move and made what is known within IBM as the "knee-pad" call: I begged.

After hearing my pitch, my client, named John, told me, "Mike, I talked to my dad, and he said he would be willing to help you out, but were gonna need some favors from IBM, too."

I assured him that we would reciprocate, but I had to have the order immediately.

"No problem. My dad will be back in the country on Wednesday," John said. I felt some relief.

I reported back to the branch, only to find out that the absolute cutoff for orders was Monday to get a December delivery date. Here I thought I had it worked out, and instead I got snake-bit again. I had to have a contract, and I had to have it now. I called John back.

"Sorry, Mike, Wednesday is the best I can do," he said.

Over the weekend I agonized about the situation. How could an entire year of work come down to this-two lousy days?

On Monday morning I did the unthinkable and forged the contract, then turned it in at the end of the day and left the office. I got my delivery date: December 29th. Now I *had* to have the real contract signed on Wednesday so that I could make the switch, and no one would know.

I called John Tuesday morning. "Are we all set for Wednesday?" I asked, trying to sound casual.

"Barring any problems with Dad's flight, we should be set to go," he said.

"Thanks, John. I'll see you tomorrow at one o'clock sharp."

I slept poorly that night. Dawn asked me what was wrong. "You got your delivery date didn't you? What's the problem?"

"No problem. I'm fine."

But I wasn't fine. I was ashamed of what I had done, and I felt an impending sense of doom. I stared at the ceiling all night, unable to sleep, searching for justification as if I had earned the right to be a little dishonest. It was a colossal case of denial. I was an imposter, and I had put everybody at risk.

Now my dishonesty was about to bite me in the ass.

Rick took me to breakfast on Tuesday morning to celebrate and go over all of my installations.

"We're almost there, Mike. We just gotta get these babies shipped, and we're home free. You'll be the second Eagle in the country on December twenty-ninth," he said.

I could barely eat.

Arriving at the office, I found an *urgent* message from John in my phone slot. As I charged to my desk, our receptionist-just finishing up a call-yelled to me, "Mike . . . wait. . . . He said something about a forgery."

I felt a lightning strike in my soul. I broke into a blaze of sweat. Perspiration was running down my back. My face was blood red. *My, God, how did he find out? Who else knows? Is there time to cover my tracks?* Thoughts raced through my mind like a tornado. I had finally done myself in.

Unbeknownst to me, earlier that month the region had changed its procedure for handling contracts. Instead of giving them back to the sales rep for personal delivery, they now mailed them from the branch directly to the customer. My worst nightmare had happened.

I turned around and headed out of the building to my car.

John was watching for me from his office window as I pulled up. I was startled to find him standing in the vestibule as I walked through the door. *God, he's not even going to allow me in the office.* Right there in the vestibule I confessed everything. He decided not to tell his father-though he did cancel the order. He asked that I send a letter from the branch manager, acknowledging that the order had indeed been canceled. On the drive home, I actually considered forging the letter, too, but I couldn't bring myself to do it. I returned to the branch and looked for my brother-in-law.

I walked into his office and closed the door.

"What happened to you? You look like shit," Alex said.

"I *feel* like shit." I told Alex the whole story. His face never changed expression.

"Good God, Mike. You gotta be kidding me. Tell me you didn't. What the hell were you thinking?!" He got up from his desk and went to the window. He turned toward me and folded his arms. "It's just a stupid award, Mike. Nobody gives a shit. You're one of the best reps in the country. Isn't that good enough for you?" Then he groaned in disgust, dropped into his chair, and stared at the ceiling. His eyes began to fill up.

I felt sick to my stomach.

He sighed and looked at me again. "All right, let's not panic. Have you told Rick about this?"

"No, I came to you first."

"Well, we've got to tell him right away."

"I know, I know. But that's *my* job, Alex. I'll tell him . . . alone."

He sat staring at me, shaking his head, clearly still in disbelief. I left his office and went to find Rick.

That Big Blue Door

The offices were quiet, which was often the case late in the year. Rick was out with another rep, scrambling for year-end numbers. I sat at my desk, trying to look busy while I waited for him to return. My stomach was sour, and I had a terrible headache.

Finally I heard commotion at the end of the bullpen, which was a sea of steel desks, uncomfortable chairs, and one phone for every two reps. IBM didn't believe in the comforts of the office; they wanted you on the street, selling. Rick's voice sounded from the back entrance, amid laughter and joking.

I stood up and signaled him from the end of the hall, "Rick, I need to talk to you."

He smiled and pointed at his office while yanking off his galoshes.

I entered his office and sat down. Moments later he followed me in.

He was filled with energy. "Michael, me boy, we got the Midway account." He tossed the file in my lap and hung up his coat. He had been working on Midway for almost six months. It was a huge account. "This puts me in the club." He plopped into his chair, held up his arms, and yelled, "Score, baby!"

I managed a weak smile.

"Man, Mike, what a great week this has been. You make Eagle. Now Midway. Unbelievable!"

My stomach was now doing flip-flops. "That's great news, Rick. Congratulations." I didn't know what to say. I was about to ruin his great week.

"So what's happening? Everything all right?" he asked, blowing the cold from his hands. He squinted at me. "You got a funny look on your face. Something's wrong."

"I'm afraid so, Rick. It's not good. In fact, it couldn't be worse," I said. "You're not going to believe what I did."

His face darkened. "Tell me."

I proceeded to explain why I had done what I did. When I had finished, Rick sat in silence. Then he got up and said that the branch manager would need to know what was going on.

Still in shock, Rick returned from his meeting with Kevin O'Brien, our new branch manager, and asked me to join him for a cup of coffee. We walked down the hall to the cafeteria. Rick filled two mugs and led us to the table by the windows.

"Kevin wants to send you home for now, Mike. It's going to take awhile to sort this out. You're on leave of absence with full pay. Keep your chin up."

Rick's voice was cool, distant. He was now operating right out of the IBM procedure manual. I tried again to explain what had happened, but he cut me off.

"Just go home, Mike. I'll call you tonight," he said.

The drive home was suffocating. What was I going to tell Dawn, an innocent victim, about to get clobbered by this terrible news?

Dawn was supportive and kind. She did not judge me, nor did she seek an explanation. She just wanted to know if I was all right and if there was anything she could do to make me feel better. She knew what to do in a crisis.

I still didn't sleep.

IBM formed a special panel made up of corporate people, including two industrial psychologists. IBM was deeply concerned about any employee caught cheating, but as I understand it, the formation of this panel was an unprecedented move on IBM's part. One of the psychologists had a long conversation with Norma Nissenson, our marriage counselor. Norma loved Dawn and me, referring to us as her miracle couple, gratified that we hung in there. Norma described for the panel my loyalty to IBM and my desire to be the best. The psychologist was softened by her passionate plea to protect me, and he was surprised by her thorough understanding of IBM and the Eagle award.

"You mean he discussed the Eagle award with you?" he asked.

"Many times. Mike loves IBM."

I wasn't at the meeting, but Norma filled me in later. I met with the panel after Norma's meeting at IBM's regional offices. I got there early, wearing a dark suit and a conservative tie, determined to be understated. Four men and two women were waiting in the conference room. They stood as I walked in. The oldest gentleman spoke first, explaining that while my situation was serious, he hoped that things could be worked out and I could return to my job. But he made it clear: no guarantees. His smile was compassionate and sincere.

My sense was that while their primary function was to examine me, the panel seemed to be examining IBM, as well. They were searching for the company's role in all of this. Were the reward systems forcing their best people to crack? Did IBM apply too much pressure to perform? I assured them that I was responsible for being in this jam, not IBM. They appreciated my humility, but they didn't seem convinced. I sensed that I was not the only one this had happened to.

A few days later the phone rang. It was Alex. He sounded upbeat.

"I don't know what you did with that panel, but it sure worked. The report that we got from Norma Nissenson didn't hurt you, either. She insisted that IBM would be making a terrible mistake if we threw you away. Everyone here agrees with her. So . . . you keep your job. Now, Mike, you gotta understand that this incident will probably set you back a year, maybe two. But it will eventually be forgotten. So starting right now, I want you to put this behind you and get back to work."

When I returned to the office, I thanked Kevin and Rick for standing by me. We shook hands, and I returned to my desk, where I was greeted warmly by the guys in the bullpen.

"Hey, man, shake it off, it's a slap on the wrist," Glen Arnold said.

Alex put his hands on my shoulders. "This thing is over, Mike. Don't ever think about it again," he said.

But I knew it wasn't over. My career would be haunted by this mistake forever. If a promotion didn't come, I'd always wonder. Sure, I had my job, and I was grateful for the second chance, but my fire was gone.

Three weeks later, in November 1978, I resigned from IBM. This was a chilling experience. Everything had to be done by the book. Rick had prepared my resignation papers, insurance forms, a final commission statement, and a check. It was like being paroled from a maximum security prison-or so I imagined. Rick pointed to a box containing my personal items, which had been removed from my desk. In an instant I was reduced to a statistic. No longer rookie of the year, two-hundred-percenter, new account leader. Just a number, a casualty. The big blue door that had once welcomed me so warmly was coldly slammed in my face. I walked to my car carrying my box of belongings. One of my friends walked down a different row of cars, his head down, purposely avoiding me.

My car windows were iced over from the freezing rain that had been falling. I got in and sat staring straight ahead, unable to move, iced up on the inside, as well, feeling empty, and filling up with fear. When would I stop this self-abuse? When would I stop relying on image and performance to feel good about myself? Straining to see out the icy window, I realized that this was about as clear as I could see anything. My life was like the window, cold and out of focus. My integrity was lost, my identity shaken. Who was I if not a salesman for IBM?

God has a purpose for our lives. Everything happens for a reason. The IBM episode had proven once again that *my integrity was being hammered out on the anvil of prosperity*-otherwise I would fail the test completely. All of us have done something that we are ashamed of. What's important is that we are not maimed by our shame. Shame lies behind the self-esteem issue that hampers so many of us. Instead of disliking what we did, we dislike ourselves. One isolated mistake leads to a piling-on effect. Let's not just beat ourselves up about that one mistake; let's pile on all the mistakes we've ever made so that we can *really* feel bad.

I also discovered that shame can be a false driver. It goads us to over-achieve, trapping us in the role of people-pleaser, pushing us to the brink to prove to ourselves and the world that we have value, that we're okay. But this is not the way it has to be. We can recover from our shame, forgive ourselves, and move on. How do I know this? Because I had to do it. Recovery took a long time, but God kept me on the anvil, hammering out the dents. And when most of the dents were smoothed out, he put me back in the race, where eventually my passion returned, and I could once again see and appreciate my "giftedness."

I believe that giftedness goes beyond a mere inventory of our talents. I believe it is our lifeblood, our grace. It's the song that our heart wants to sing, the race that our legs want to run. It's where the fire in our belly comes from. I urge you to tap into your giftedness, which runs central to who you are. This is the core from which your achievements will abound, from which your joy will flow. It's where your worth as a person is tied not to performance but to God's grace. Your giftedness is the catalyst that will give you courage to start your business if that's where your gifts take you. These gifts are from God and are to be used for his purpose. How else can we show him our gratitude?

And that's what had happened to me at IBM.

Chapter 7

Drifting

My next job came quickly. Itel Corporation was sucking up IBM reps like a Hoover vacuum cleaner. Jim Wells, a past superstar from the IBM Data Processing Division, was now one of Itel's top executives. He had left to join Itel a couple of years earlier and now invited me over for a talk.

Itel was the largest computer-leasing firm in the country. Theirs was a Cinderella story, a firm aspiring for the first time ever to hit $1 billion in sales in the first ten years. Digital Equipment Corporation had done it in eleven, and it was the singular focus of Itel's founder, Pete Redfield, to beat them. Itel's lease portfolio was the envy of the industry, allowing them to wield significant control over most of IBM's biggest accounts. IBM had never answered to anyone in the industry, but with Itel controlling the leases they were now forced to play ball. Itel's strategically strong position captured the hearts and minds of Wall Street and sent the stock rocketing skyward-placing them at the top of IBM's hit list.

I arrived at Itel's Chicago regional office for my interview and was immediately impressed. The offices were elegant and the sales team had work centers that were shockingly more desirable than the austere IBM sales bullpen. People were hard at it, hustling about looking very focused and intentional. Conversations were vigorous, as if each deal was critical. The environment had a buzz, an electricity. *What do you know? There is life after IBM*, I thought.

Jim Wells was a handsome man, confident, almost arrogant, and very young for an executive. In fact, everybody at Itel was young. Jim took time to explain the leasing business and the concept of the time value of money. Itel had discovered how to package the investment tax credit (ITC), bank debt, and equity partners, creating low-cost leases for large

IBM mainframes. Everybody won-the equity partner, the bank, the client, and Itel, which routinely pocketed $250,000 on a single deal. Their profitability was staggering.

"We're going to send you to San Francisco to meet Pete Redfield and Bill Adair," Jim told me. "They pretty much have final say on new sales reps." Bill was number two at Itel and executive vice president.

I was astonished that the top two guys in the company would have final say on salespeople. These guys were flashy.

Jim was my sponsor and accompanied me to San Francisco. We arrived on a Sunday afternoon in May. A young woman picked us up at the airport and took us to the St. Francis Hotel. Jim treated me to an elegant dinner, and later a few of the local salespeople joined us for dessert to answer any questions I might have. We drank cognac and smoked cigars. It was all very glamorous and extravagant. At age twenty-six I was taking the bait, hook, line, and sinker. They knew how to sell greed.

The dinner ended, and I returned to my fifteen-hundred-square-foot club room. I called Dawn.

"Hi, Dawn," I said cheerfully.

"Hi. How's everything going?" she asked.

"Boy, Dawn, talk about getting wined and dined. I'm a little uncomfortable with all this," I admitted. "And you wouldn't believe the room I'm in. Correction, *rooms*. I wish you were here to see this."

"Hmm. Let's see if I've got this straight. I'm at the bottom of a diaper pail, and you're at the top of the St. Francis Hotel. What's wrong with this picture?"

"My lucky day," I said, chuckling. I could hear the baby in the background. I felt far from home.

"What do you think you're going to do?" Dawn asked.

"I don't know. I think I'm going to take it. It'll be an adjustment. But these guys are having fun and making some big money. I could use a little of both right now."

"Boy, you could, couldn't you? You know, if you're uncomfortable, maybe you should wait and talk to Alex first," she suggested.

"I think they expect an answer tomorrow, Dawn. Besides, I'm afraid to tell Alex. He'll just talk me out of it." I stood staring out the huge picture window at the radiant Bay Bridge, bathed in soft light from the streaking cars. Loneliness had set in again.

"Listen to what they have to say in the morning, and then decide. Trust your instincts on this one, Mike. You'll know what to do," Dawn advised.

I met Jim for breakfast the next morning. By eight o'clock we were in a cab on the way to the interview. The elevator doors opened at the top floor of the Wells Fargo Building. It took us nearly ten minutes to walk to the executive suites, a path that meandered beneath oak and maple architecture. To the left were floor-to-ceiling windows overlooking the bustling Bay Bridge and the shimmering San Francisco Bay beneath. I could see the richer blue of the channel, way out. A tanker, deeply laden, rode the channel north, and closer, this side of the bridge, a pair of container ships worked south. The rest of the bay was speckled with small boats that danced in the glare and dazzle of the morning sun. They were the shiny toys of yachtsmen-chrome and brass, canvas and teak. The view was magnificent.

Jim stopped and pointed to the container ships. "See those, Mike? They're ours. We now lease ships, containers, railcars, and aircraft. Neat stuff, huh?"

We stood shoulder to shoulder, appreciating the spectacle of it all, then leisurely continued toward Redfield's office, admiring the walls adorned with expensive art and trimmed with thick crown moldings. As we approached the executive suites, I couldn't refrain from rubbernecking at the offices. They were decorated with Oriental rugs and dark cherry furniture, each one graced with a silver coffee service. The place was oozing with wealth. I was overwhelmed.

The interview wasn't really an interview but rather a sales presentation that allowed Redfield and Adair to brag about their company, themselves, and their top ten salespeople who had collectively made over $2 million the prior year. That got my attention. I asked them how much number one made. I think that question alone landed me the job.

"That would be Harvey Kinzelberg," Redfield answered. "He made three hundred thousand."

Over lunch, Jim Wells and Bill Adair offered me a job as a "finance lease specialist," one of Itel's flamboyant euphemisms for salesman. I could either stay in Chicago or move to Minneapolis. The offer was generous, with full benefits and a lavish expense account. Itel spent a lot of money entertaining clients. That was part of their culture. For instance, it was not unusual to slip a client tickets to the Masters or the Super Bowl. Perks were all part of the game. These guys worked hard and played hard. I took the job.

After a day spent sightseeing, I was sitting in first class, heading back to Chicago, when a man stopped by my seat.

"Excuse me, are you Mike Kerrison?"

I looked up. "Yes, I am."

"Hi. I'm Harvey Kinzelberg. Jim Wells told me to look for you," he said.

I smiled. "Nice to meet you, Harvey. I understand I'm going to be working for you."

The seat beside me was empty, and Harvey asked, "Mind if I join you?"

"Please do," I said. Harvey was legendary at Itel. He had written nearly $60 million in leases the prior year, generating $5 million in profit.

After some chitchat, he opened his briefcase and pulled out his latest deal. "We made a million bucks on this," he said.

"A million dollars! How in the world did you do that?"

"Hair, my man, lots of hair," he replied, displaying a broad, sneaky grin.

I shook my head. "Sorry, that's a term I'm not familiar with."

Harvey leaned toward me. "Every deal has an angle, Mike. A loophole. Something special that the client needs. Your job is to find it. Take this deal, for example." He pulled out a yellow pad covered with calculations. "This customer already agreed to a five percent fee. But you don't stop there, you keep searching. I discovered the angle when IBM couldn't make delivery on the second System/370. It would be six months late. The two System/370s were replacing the 360s, but the client couldn't replace the 360s with only one 370 because there wasn't enough power. And they couldn't afford to pay rent on three machines either, not to mention the lack of space. They were screwed." His face was filled with excitement.

"So what did you do?"

"I started thinking about it. What did we know for sure? And then it became obvious. Itel could buy the two System/360s using the client's purchase accruals and lease them back, cutting their rent in half while they waited for IBM to ship the second 370. The first 370, now affordable thanks to the leaseback, could ship immediately, but that lease would not commence for six months, until the second 370 would finally arrive. They were so happy and confused that I just told them they had to do it."

I was lost. He continued. "We'll charge interim rent for six months on the first 370, extending the lease to when the second system arrives. The two 360s will end up staying in an additional three months as backup for the client's conversion, which of course I saw coming. The three months will be enough to reduce the System/360s book value to zero. So the six months of interim rent on the first 370, plus the market value of the two 360s-which will be in inventory at zero-plus the original five percent fee adds up to a million dollars." He sipped his wine, threw the yellow pad on my tray, and said, "And that is how you put hair on a deal."

I understood about half of what he had said. I had a lot to learn about this new business. I hoped I was up to it.

I worked day and night learning how to run the numbers, read a balance sheet, understand complex accounting treatments, negotiate with bankers, sell equity partners, prepare extensive contracts, remarket used equipment, and handle high-ranking executives. IBM's training and time in the field combined with Itel's pizzazz gave me everything I needed.

A Fresh Start

We decided on Minneapolis instead of Chicago. Dawn's parents, Bonnie and Al Duhaime, had moved there from Chicago right after we were married. Her dad, also a salesman, was tired of commuting to cover his biggest accounts. Dawn was excited to tell them we were coming. She missed her folks, and Chad would have his grandparents nearby. The whole idea seemed perfect, and I could escape the mistakes of my past.

Dawn and I were given one weekend to find a house. Itel would pay for the move. We found a quaint two-story Tudor in the old country-club area of Edina. The homes were beautiful brick structures, mostly Tudors, country French, and colonials. The boulevards were lined with magnificent elm trees that formed lush canopies over the streets. Every square inch was perfectly manicured, the human touch added by kids riding their bikes and mothers pushing strollers. People from Edina were called "cake eaters," a label scoffing at their affluence and snobby demeanor-though some Edina people loved the label. While they considered themselves the beautiful people, they were actually the *Ordinary People*-Edina being the home of Judith Guest, the famous author whose book became a best-seller and later an award-winning motion picture. If you saw the movie, you'll understand Edina.

I sat at my father-in-law's dining room table, trying to figure out how I was going to pay for this new house. The price was double what we had paid for our little rambler in Chicago.

Dawn's father said, "Michael, you need to stretch for this place. The house will double in value in five years. I guarantee it."

I didn't take much comfort in this, however. I walked into the kitchen and sat down, rubbing my forehead. "Well, if I don't get a commission check, we'll be broke in nine months," I said.

"Mike, you have *never* not gotten a commission check," Dawn pointed out.

We bought the house in Edina.

About a month later we moved. Dawn and I, Lindsey and Alex, and their kids stood together in the driveway, watching the moving van pull away. I was feeling sick inside. My sister and brother-in-law had been my lifelines for a long time.

"Ya know . . . in a way I wish we were going with you," Alex said.

"Alex, you don't mean that," I said.

But in a way I think he did. He was starting to burn out-an occupational hazard for most IBMers. We exchanged hugs, and then my family and I were off to Minneapolis to start our new adventure.

After a month on the job, I closed my first deal with Target Stores, a seven-year tax leveraged lease on a $7 million dollar System/370. Then I closed Northern States Power as well as Onan Corporation. The three deals made my quota for the year. Harvey helped me structure every one of them. The guy was truly amazing with the numbers, always thinking outside the box. I was on a roll and loving it.

Just when I felt as though I was back on track, Harvey called to tell me that he was leaving Itel.

"You got to be kidding me! I just got here!" I said.

"You'll be fine. Besides, you need to be self-sufficient. You can handle this without me. Anyway, this has been in the works for a while," he said.

"Where are you going?" I asked.

"I'm gonna start my own firm. I don't need Itel to do these deals. I can do them on my own," he said. "Plus there's some decisions at corporate I just don't agree with."

"Like what?" I asked, sitting forward in my chair.

"I can't really say, Mike. Don't sweat it. It doesn't affect you anyway."

I was stunned. If Itel was such a good deal, why was he leaving?

IBM continued watching Itel like a thief in the night. Only we were the thief-and a predator, taking IBM's best people. Not only did we have control over IBM's install base, we now had a competitive mainframe going head-to-head with them.

Hitachi, determined to enter the U.S. market, had decided to use Itel as a private label distributor. The Hitachi mainframe was faster, cheaper, and about half the size of IBM's. They were killing IBM in the Japanese market, and they were beginning to penetrate Europe.

The Guns of Navarone

During the summer of 1979, IBM announced the 4300 series, a low-cost mainframe with extraordinary price performance. It was small, simple to operate, totally compatible with prior products, and aimed like the guns of Navarone at any company trying to penetrate that market. IBM had exhibited brilliant timing, catching Itel with their pants down.

Itel had $300 million in residual values sitting on the balance sheet (unrealized revenue that could only be earned by remarketing the equipment at the end of the lease). The price performance curve of the 4300 series wiped out their residuals, rendering Itel insolvent overnight. Some of the residuals were insured by Lloyd's of London-but not enough to cover the shortfall and gobs of bank debt that had accumulated. Creditors spent months in bankruptcy court, crawling through the mess. The Cinderella company overlooking the bay now sat buried in its own destruction like the day after a nuclear holocaust. Pete Redfield was horrified. The once unconquerable genius on his way to a billion dollars in sales had been reduced to ashes with a twitch of IBM's nose.

I called Harvey Kinzelberg immediately. He was already set up in his new business and capitalizing on Itel's misfortune. "Did you see this coming?" I asked.

"I did. But I didn't know it would be this soon, or this bad," Harvey replied.

"How did you know?" I asked.

"It was obvious, Mike. I'd been telling Adair for a year that we needed to get out of that Hitachi crap and start focusing on the portfolio. IBM has been leaking this announcement for months. Everybody saw it coming. I knew Itel was screwed the minute IBM announced it."

"Harvey, you saw this coming, and you didn't say a word to me. I moved my family up here. I bought a house. I'm out of a job, for God's sake!"

"First of all, you're not out of a job. Second of all, the two smartest things you ever did were the day you walked into IBM and the day you walked out. And if you want, you can work for me."

Harvey was right. IBM was a wonderful company, but I could now see that they wanted their reps with blinders on, like old pack mules, looking straight ahead, never side to side.

"Would I have to move back to Chicago?" I asked.

"Yeah, at least for a while."

"Okay, I guess we can talk later on that. When the dust settles. I appreciate the vote of confidence." I hung up the phone, once again uncertain about my future and drifting in uncharted waters. Somehow, though, I wasn't afraid this time. Instead I felt a sense of adventure, of destiny taking shape like a photograph emerging in a darkroom.

No More Drifting

When I walked through the door that night, I held up my business card. "You see this, Dawn? This is the only thing Itel has to offer me. The only thing that needs to change is the name of the company on this stupid card, and my world is exactly the same. I'm going to do this myself. If Harvey can do it, I can do it. I'm sick and tired of being controlled."

"Are you serious?" she asked. She was setting the table for dinner.

"Dead serious," I replied.

"I'm ready when you're ready," she said, shrugging. "Hey, go up and get Chad. Dinner is going on the table in five minutes."

I couldn't believe her reaction. She was so nonchalant.

Over dinner I questioned her again, and she said, "Mike, I have no doubt you can do this. Besides, I don't think you will ever be happy working for someone else. At least not since you left IBM. I say go for it. What have we got to lose?"

The year I had spent with Itel was not wasted. I had learned many valuable lessons. Itel revealed the danger of not sticking to the knitting. They had entered markets that they didn't understand. The executives had lost their company because they got greedy. They had made so much money for so long that they thought they were invincible. While trying to beat IBM at their own game with a plug-compatible mainframe, they neglected their core business-the lease portfolio. They were vulnerable and didn't know it. The innovation, moxie, and salesmanship that had made them great went up in smoke with their big cigars. No one had planned a defense, sought new leasing structures, or taken the time to get really close to the client. They had no second idea, no safe haven.

I began to picture my own company. I didn't know how to run a business, but I knew something about people and how to treat them. I knew how to help them find their gifts and reach for something more. I wanted to make a difference. I had seen two companies up close, and I had been mentored by superstars such as Alex and Harvey, each one teaching me what to do-or what not to do. Now it was my turn. No more drifting.

Chapter 8

Flying Solo

I did my best thinking at the kitchen table. I got up early on Saturday, snatched Chad from his crib, made coffee, and the two of us sat eating Cheerios while I ran some numbers. Dawn took her turn sleeping in. The night before we'd had a huge snowstorm, and we had been up until well past midnight digging ourselves out and talking about how to start this crazy business. The work and excitement had worn us out. We slept like dead people.

Now I sat staring at the snowdrifts, letting the coffee do its job, trying to imagine what this business would look like. *I have no money, no office, no secretary, and no experience running a business. I don't even have a name for my business. What makes me think I can do this? How does anybody do this?*

I soothed my anxiety with a quick game of Nerf ball with my two-year-old son, which consisted of me lobbing the ball off his forehead. He sat in his high chair blinking strangely, not sure whether to laugh or cry. Dawn had been stirring around and soon bounced down the stairs to join us.

As she turned the corner, she yelped, "Hey, don't hit him in the head!"

"What do you mean? He likes it. Watch." I fired a perfect strike at his forehead. It bounced across the table straight into my lap. Luckily, Chad laughed hysterically. "See? I told ya."

"God, Mike, you're still throwing things," she said with a grin.

Dawn scooped Chad out of his highchair, cuddled him on her lap, and asked in her baby-talk voice, "How's my handsome little boy doing?" She looked at me and smiled. I smiled back. I was overcome by the awesome responsibility that I now faced. I didn't want to let my family down.

"So how's it lookin'? Ya gonna do it?" she asked.

"I want to, Dawn. But we don't have the money. I just don't know how to swing this. Christ, we'll starve." I shook my head in utter frustration.

"You know what, I'm gonna call Sue Larson. Do you remember her? She's a friend of my mom's."

"Yeah, I think so. Why would you call her?"

"She mentioned this guy once. Apparently he's loaded. One of these eccentric-millionaire types. You know-houses, yachts. He owns a bunch of businesses, I guess." Dawn was feeling Chad's gums in search of new teeth. "I think he helped Sue's husband with his business."

"Oh, I see. Sue Larson's going to find money for us. Now *there's* a pipe dream." I folded my arms and stared out the window.

"Well, Mike . . . who knows? This might be a good day for pipe dreams. I'll make the call."

Entering the Stone Age

A day later Dawn delivered the name and phone number of Andrew Stone. "Here's your man. Sue said just pick up the phone and call him."

"You gotta be kidding me. Are you sure? What am I supposed to say to this guy?" I asked.

"Can't help you there, big fella; that's your department. Just pick up the phone."

Dawn had a clever way of issuing a challenge along with her encouragement. These challenges occasionally smacked of "get off your dead ass and do this." She didn't think I was lazy-far from it in fact. But she knew I had spent too many years not fully believing in myself.

I called Andrew that afternoon, and to my astonishment he agreed to meet me for breakfast at the Decathlon Club, where he worked out mornings. I arrived early, wearing my favorite blue suit, a blue oxford-cloth shirt (button-down, of course) and a red tie. I looked great, and I felt prepared. It was a cold morning, so I had arranged for a table by the fireplace, which I thought was a nice touch.

He had described himself perfectly, for I had no problem spotting his stocky build and his wildly curly hair, which was still wet. He looked disheveled, juggling his briefcase, duffle bag, newspaper, and sports jacket.

I stood up. "Andrew, Mike Kerrison . . . how do you do." We shook hands. "Can I help you carry something?"

"Hi, Mike. No, no, I'm fine. Sorry I'm late. In fact, I don't have a lot of time, so let's order breakfast and keep moving."

Oh, brother, I could see it coming: the big brush-off. I had already been rejected once at First Bank Edina, trying to borrow money for this deal. Some stupid little banker, not much older than I, sat and listened to my impassioned story on how I was going to build an empire. If I'd had a dollar for every time he yawned, I wouldn't have needed the loan.

Andrew was the controlling, fidgety type. You didn't have to worry too much about breaking the ice with him. He broke it for you. In other words, you'd better enjoy being the passenger because he's driving the bus.

He got right to the point. "So what's on your mind?" he asked. "Sue said you're trying to start a business."

"Yes, that's right, Andrew. I want to start a computer brokerage firm. The industry is brand new, and it's growing very fast. I've spent my entire career in computers, and I know if given the opportunity, I could do very well at this," I said.

"Computer broker, huh? You mean like Comdisco? Boy, how do you compete with them?" he asked. Comdisco was the largest computer dealer and leasing firm in the industry, now that Itel was out of the way.

"You're familiar with Comdisco?" I asked.

"Very-I was one of the original investors before they went public. Did okay on it."

Our breakfast arrived. Andrew immediately shoved a huge wedge of pancakes into his mouth and within two bites chugged half a cup of coffee.

I hope he makes decisions as fast as he eats his breakfast, I thought. "Actually, Andrew, I have no interest in trying to compete with Comdisco. I'm going down-market, offering leases and used IBM equipment to small and midsized companies. This market has been ignored," I said.

"Yeah . . . keep talking."

"I know the low-end customers and how they think. I spent almost five years at IBM in that market and over a year with Itel, where I learned the leasing business. There are sixty thousand IBM machines out there, and no one is filling the need except for a few little companies," I explained. I finally took my first bite.

"How would you start?" he asked, sucking his teeth.

I swallowed quickly. "With my old IBM clients, of course. I installed over seventy systems in Chicago. In fact, I've spoken with a few of them already, and they're eager to see me do this."

"Why is that?" he asked, waving to someone across the room. I was afraid I was losing him.

"I can save them money on equipment and reduce their lease payments up to thirty percent and still make thirty percent on the deal." At that point I threw my Hewlett Packard calculator in front of him to recapture his attention. "I can work miracles with this, Andrew. No matter how complicated the numbers get, I can figure them out."

He chuckled. "Yeah, I bet you can. So what do you need from me?"

"Well, the only thing standing in my way is having enough money to pay my bills at home while I start this up. And I'll need to buy equipment to fill my orders. Here, take a look at this." I presented a five-page kickoff plan. "At IBM we use to call this a two-hundred-percent plan. I think I can generate two hundred fifty thousand dollars in gross margin the first year."

Suddenly Andrew had all the time in the world. He looked over the plan carefully and continued to ask questions.

"How much do you need?" he asked.

Here I thought I was just going to get to know this guy, and *wham*, he wants to know how much money I need. The fact is, I didn't have a clue. I didn't know what a business plan was, let alone a cash flow forecast. I was a salesman.

"Thirty thousand." I pulled the number right out of the air.

"Thirty thousand . . . you're sure?" he asked. "I think you're going to need more."

Damn, I low-balled myself, I thought. "What do you think it should be, Andrew?"

"Fifty, but we'll start with thirty," he said.

Did I hear that right? "So that's it, Andrew? You're ready to go forward with this?" I asked to be sure.

"I'm ready. Let's start. But before we do anything, you must understand that I will be the majority shareholder of this new business. I've gotten screwed too many times as a minority holder. So if we're going forward, you need to agree to this."

Wow. This must be the way the big boys do it. I got the impression he was closing me. I felt uncomfortable, but I accepted his terms.

He reached into his pocket, and handed me two five hundred dollar bills. "Here, go over to Hank Carney's and buy yourself some office furniture and anything else you might need. And then call this number and ask for my controller, Phil Pocket. He'll set you up with an office in our suite. In the meantime Phil will pull the paperwork together for our deal.

Okay?"

"Okay!" I said, jubilantly.

We shook hands, and he dashed out the door. I sat in disbelief. Had this really happened? One hour ago I merely had an idea, and-*presto!*-it was now a reality. I ran to my car and drove straight home as fast as I could.

I burst through the front door. "Dawn! Dawn! We got the money!" I shouted.

"What?" Dawn's voice trailed from somewhere upstairs.

"We got the money! Andrew Stone . . . We got the money! We're in business!"

"Oh, my God, you're kidding! How much did we get?"

"Thirty thousand."

"Holy shit, that's unbelievable! How'd you do it?" she asked, rushing down the stairs, grinning from ear to ear.

I gave her a quick briefing on what had taken place and what Andrew was like. She listened intently to every word I said as I recreated the entire scene. Her face was filled with excitement. Then she hesitated.

"Are you sure you're okay with only forty-nine percent? I mean, that doesn't seem right to me."

"Well . . . yeah . . . I'm okay with it. It's not like I had a choice, Dawn. I already told you that."

"I know, I know. But you're going to be doing all the work. I just want you to be happy with this whole thing," she said.

"I am. I'm thrilled. It'll be fine," I assured her.

Her question bothered me, though. I had no clue about the consequences a minority shareholder faced. If I had known then what I know now, I would never have done that deal. Forty-nine percent is useless. You control nothing. You can even get fired. But on the other hand, I might never have started my business otherwise.

Enough of that, I thought. *Think positive.* "I'll tell you the rest over dinner. Call a baby-sitter. We're going out," I said.

Dawn and I went to the fancy Fifth Season restaurant in Minneapolis, where we dined and dreamed. It was a perfect ending to a perfect day.

Phil Pocket and I had connected before Dawn and I left for dinner. Andrew had already informed him about our deal, and Phil was making the necessary preparations for my arrival. The next morning I went to Hank Carney's to spend my thousand bucks.

"Oh, yes, Mike, Andrew told me to expect you," Hank said. "I have a few things already picked out."

I was impressed. Andrew Stone was in command of things.

I felt like a kid in a candy store. Picking out furniture at Hank's was just as exciting as filling a sack at Ohl's with bubblegum, jaw-breakers, and rock candy. In forty-five minutes I bought enough stuff to fill up a small truck.

"Mike, I think you did well. This will certainly get you started," Hank said.

I thanked him for his encouragement and headed home.

My furniture showed up on a Friday. Andrew was down in Florida, apparently entertaining customers on his yacht. Phil was at the office to greet me. He was an interesting guy but not impressive like Andrew. He had a skinny mustache and a pasty, almost transparent, complexion. His suit was wrinkled in the back and hung heavily on his skinny shoulders. He had the look of an immigrant just off the boat, and I thought I detected a slight hint of alcohol on his breath. I quickly dismissed my suspicion.

My office-one of several in Andrew's suite of offices-was long and narrow. The walls were yellow with wavy brown pinstripes, and the floor had a green shag carpet. It smelled musty from lack of use.

"It'll look better when you get your furniture in here," Phil said. "As you can see, it's a bit dated. We haven't used this room in years."

"No, no . . . this is fine, Phil. This is just fine," I said as I strolled through the ugliest office I had ever seen. My used desk was ugly as hell, too, but I loved it because it was huge. I called it my aircraft carrier. None of the furniture matched, giving the office a kind of "early attic" look. Dawn later surprised me with a couple of decorative plants, which helped somewhat. The office was sickly, but it was comfortable, it was mine, and I was proud of it. I still had much on my to-do list, but all I could think about was selling something.

Everything was happening so fast that I was still struggling with a name for this new enterprise. Dawn and I got up early Saturday morning. After feeding the kids-Cammy had just been born-we drank coffee and brainstormed for a business name.

"The name should provide clues about what we actually do," I said. "I don't want some trendy nonsense name as though we're trying to be impressive. I want it to be clean, simple."

After a two-hour debate, we settled on *Computer Options, Inc.* And we created a tag line for the company: "The best option." It was perfect.

I got to my new office early Monday morning-my maiden voyage. As I pulled into the parking garage, the reality finally hit me: *I pulled this off. . . . I can't believe it, I really pulled this off. . . . How did I pull this off? . . . How am I going to do this? . . . I'll just get on the phone. . . . I mean, what else is there to do? . . . I need to make a sale-immediately!*

Andrew's secretary, Nora, was already in the office and had the coffee going. She was to be my receptionist, and secretary as well, until I could afford my own. After a pleasant conversation and some mutual orientation, we were both off and running.

Without hesitating, I picked up the phone and called everybody I could think of to let them know what I was doing. Most of them wanted me to send a business card. *Good Lord, I don't have one yet-or stationery or even my own phone number.* I made a list and engaged in a blizzard of setup work.

The following day Andrew returned from Miami and took me downtown to meet his banker. "Mike, this is Paul Broughton. He'll handle all your banking needs," Andrew said.

We shook hands.

"Mike, we have opened up a checking account for Computer Options, Inc. Andrew has started the account with seven thousand dollars. We will need your corporate tax ID number and your social security number. Also, are you planning to be an S or a C corporation?" Paul asked.

I began to feel panicky, fearing that he might discover that none of this stuff had been done yet. I got through the preliminary meeting without blowing it, but I could see that I needed a lawyer-fast.

Once the legal stuff was completed, by Bob Buttertsrodt, my first lawyer, I had nothing left to do but sell.

Most people build a business plan first, then work the plan. My plan was in my head. It was intuitive. It had to be since I had never written a business plan before. Though one thing I knew for sure: *Nothing happens until something is sold.* So that's where I put my time. All of it. I would find plenty of time later for the other chores.

After three weeks of phone prospecting, I finally landed my first deal with Fargo Paint and Glass Company. I made $2,600. It was a sweet little deal, but at this rate I wouldn't have much of a business. I needed to get my name on the map through an inbound marketing plan to supplement my outbound telemarketing. I needed to make the phone ring.

Jackpot

I persuaded Andrew to let me spend seven thousand dollars for a mass mailing. I bought a list of names from one of the trade journals, then sat down with Dailey Printing to design a marketing brochure. The brochure outlined our mission, equipment for sale, prices, and a couple examples of savings. We went all out on this mailing. The brochure looked professional, and it made a statement, creating an illusion of experience and stability.

We whipped it together in about three weeks and got it out the door. In the meantime I continued dialing for dollars. I closed a couple of more little deals, but I wouldn't survive for long boiling a bunch of chicken bones.

Andrew was in my office every day with the same question: "Any checks today?"

Two weeks passed without one response from the mailer. I was both discouraged and surprised, having expected a faster start than this. Doubts began to enter my mind. I became a worrier.

"Let's go to a movie. It's time for a break," Dawn suggested.

With two little kids at home, a movie theater was one of the few places where we could finish a conversation. So going to a movie was also a mini business-therapy session since we could brainstorm about this and that.

We arrived early so that we could sit and munch popcorn with no interruptions. In the quiet of the dimly lit theater, I rambled about my business insecurities while Dawn listened patiently.

"God, Dawn, I spent all that money on that stupid mailer, and I haven't gotten one call. Not one," I groused.

"Will you relax? It's too early. I bet you'll hear something on Monday," she said. "Now, sit back and relax. The movie is about to start."

Dawn had to fill me in on what was happening in the movie. I was in another world most of the time, ruminating on mailers and problems and deals and life in general. As I have said, I became a worrier.

Monday morning came and went. Nothing. Another week went by.

Then it happened. After my morning appointment with Paul Broughton, who was getting nervous, I returned to the office. As I walked in the door, Nora yelled, "Jackpot! This phone is ringing off the hook. I've had three lines going all morning. If you can't read these messages . . . Well, I did the best I could. Take a look at this." She handed me a stack of response cards that was at least two inches thick. I could feel the adrenalin building. This *was* a jackpot. Between mailers and messages we had over two hundred responses by the end of the day.

I called Dawn and gave her the news. "Stay in the office. It's okay. This is what you've been waiting for. Everything is fine here," she assured me.

That night I worked until midnight. The leads were everywhere. I arranged the messages and cards into two piles: buyers and sellers. Then I broke the piles down by equipment type. The matches were perfect. I had matches for System/3s, System/32s, keypunches, sorters, CRTs, and printers. I even had a match for an old Burroughs bookkeeping machine. I was so excited, I could barely function.

I went home and slept for four hours, then headed back to the office. That day would be the test. I would work coast to coast for eleven hours. First I called the sellers, to determine price and availability. I didn't do a lot of negotiating at that point except to warn them that their prices were too high. When I finished the sellers, I called the buyers. It was like running a table in a pool hall. The pockets were filling up. The rest of the week was no different. By the end of the week, I had closed nineteen deals. That meant nineteen sale contracts and nineteen purchase contracts.

I had created a monster. Checks had to be cut to buy equipment. Freight had to be arranged. IBM had to de-install the equipment and certify it for maintenance. I needed insurance on the freight. The equipment needed to be refurbished and some needed to be repaired. Colors had to match. Dates had to match. Installs had to be arranged. And now the phone just kept ringing off the hook. The faster I went, the slower I got. I was a wreck, completely overwhelmed. Most of this stuff I had never done before. And to think: People were willing to commit thousands of dollars over the phone, without meeting me first. That just blew me away.

I found a company on the East Coast to do all my freight, insurance, and refurb. Then I found another on the West Coast. Phil chipped in with contracts, and he designed a crude open-order system that he put up on a white board in my office. We had no accounting system yet, but things began to fall into place little by little.

Suddenly the challenge was to write new business while servicing the old. Two out of three calls was now from a client with a problem. You don't ignore problems if you expect to stay in business. You drop everything-immediately!-and take care of your customer. Everybody chipped in-Phil, Nora, Dawn, even Andrew. But the business was already getting away from me. After only six weeks I was ready for my first employee.

It Was a Miracle

A month had passed since the initial bonanza. But the mail kept coming. I was living in a world of postcard blizzards. An improving world, I might add. I once heard it said that success is an accident well placed.

Let me explain.

At the end of a long day I leaned back in my chair, slipped off my shoes, and whipped my feet onto the desk. A stack of postcards spilled off the edge. *Shit. These things are a pain in the ass. But a good pain in the ass.* I rested my bloodshot eyes for a moment and gave my back a rest, as well. I had been working like a one-armed paper hanger.

After a wonderful fifteen-minute nap, I knelt down and picked up the splash of cards. I kept staring at one card with a System/3 Model 15 for sale. IBM's list price was over $500,000. If I could flip this one quickly, I could make some real money. Moments later a call came in from Bell & Howell Mamiya Company. The camera division had been spun off from Bell & Howell corporate as a stand-alone company and had been given three weeks to get their accounting system off the corporate System/3. They were desperate. They had to have a System/3 Model 15 now. The call came while I was down the hall

"C'mon, Nora, this is a System/3!" I bellowed.

"Well, what was I supposed to do, drag you out of the john?" she protested.

I dialed the phone as fast as I could, staring at the message. *Need immediate delivery on a System/3 Model 15D . . . In Chicago . . . Must be IBM certified. Call ASAP.*

Miraculously, their new data-processing manager was Gary Sheath, a loyal customer from my IBM days. The deal was quiet. I was the only broker talking to him. Gary assured me that as long as I could deliver in two weeks, I could have the business. Price was not the issue-delivery was. I bought the machine off the card for $150,000 and sold it to Mamiya Camera Company for $375,000. The configurations were identical. I was in shock. So was Dawn. It took me a half hour to convince her that this was on the level. Not only did this deal launch my company, but I learned the entire business cycle, all the critical steps associated with buying, refurbishing, shipping, and installing a large, sophisticated computer system. I handled every single detail myself on this one. So much was at stake. The system went in smoothly, and Gary became my best reference. It was a miracle. I was on my way.

Take Action

Only five other companies were doing what I was doing. I had gotten to the market early, which is both good and bad. The good news was that I could create the market-or at least heavily influence it. The bad news was that the market had no rules, no infrastructure, making it hard to get things done. I was crossing a bridge and building it underneath my feet at the same time. But if I could cross this chasm, the potential was limitless.

Getting started with a new business means taking action. If you spend too much time trying to pin everything down, you will never start. It's like trying to nail Jell-O to the wall. I've often been asked, "Is one time better than another to start a business?" Simple answer: *No.* When I started mine I was twenty-six years old, married, with two children. I had no experience running a business and no money. Jimmy Carter's SALT II treaty had just failed, the country faced double-digit inflation, interest rates had reached a record twenty percent, Ted Koppel was covering the hostage crisis every night, and gasoline prices finally hit one dollar.

Gee . . . I think I'll start a business.

My point is that you won't find a perfect time. If you have a skill or a product or an idea that you really believe in, act on it. If you are good at what you do, and people truly need what you have, you face no real risk. You agree? So-go sell your idea to someone, get the money, and start. The money is out there for good ideas and hard workers. Many resources exist. Bankers, venture capitalists, angels, private investors, SBA government loans, and others are all at your disposal. You just have to get out there with your message. Someone will help.

Don't spend too much time on the launch plan. I've seen hundreds of plans stuffed with perfection but *no action.* They end up wooden and useless because they're neither believable or actionable. That's not to say you shouldn't have a plan or that you shouldn't run the numbers. Of course you should. But keep it simple and heavily focused on the *critical launch activities.* You can figure the rest out later, once you're off the ground. That's the way I started, and within three months I had enough working capital to last a year. That's not something you can plan for. That comes only with action.

Another Miracle

Making the phone ring was a requirement in our industry. For some reason, buying used computer equipment was an inbound sale versus outbound, so you had to let the prospect know where you were. *Computerworld*, a fast-growing industry newspaper with fifty thousand subscribers, was another way to do that. I called the marketing department to find out how to place an ad.

"I don't have anyone to do the graphic arts work. Can I just draw something up freehand and send it to you? Maybe one of your artists could sort of spruce it up for me," I pleaded. They had never done that before, but I was able to talk them into it. I sent the rough copy. The ad was to appear in the next issue.

The following Monday the mail came in, all of which I tossed aside except for the new issue of *Computerworld*. Like a kid on Christmas morning, I began tearing through the classified section in search of my ad. I found it.

"Oh, my God! How could this happen? Shit, those idiots! Those stupid idiots!" I railed. My hand-sketched ad had never been converted. Apparently the classifieds editor had thought it was finished copy, as if it was some kind of attention-getting thing. I was stricken at the sight of this pitiful ad sitting in the midst of all my competitors. I finally got my name in lights-and I looked like a fool.

Turns out, though, that my goofy-looking ad was a hit. Customers commented on how clever they thought it was. "Your ad was the first one I saw. I mean, it just stuck out. How did you come up with the idea?" one caller said.

I spent the week taking orders and accepting praise. "Oh, thank you. We worked really hard on that ad," I'd say, rolling my eyes.

What's even more amazing is that some of my competitors started doing funky things with *their* ads. We were the trendsetters-the new architects of marketing excellence. Unbelievable!

Business is like golf. Sometimes you get a lucky bounce out of the trees.

Bad Checks, Bad Decisions

I had more business than I could handle. I needed another salesman-fast. I wanted to approach Mike Duhaime, Dawn's older brother. He had recently married and was working for Prudential Insurance.

Dawn was dead set against it. "What if something goes wrong and it doesn't work out? Then what? C'mon Mike, this is my *brother*. You've got to find someone else," Dawn pleaded.

I kept working on her, trying to convince her it was okay. "Honey, I need to move fast. Besides, I have a good feeling about this, and your brother won't have to work nights anymore."

She finally gave in, and I hired Mike. Just as I expected, he was bright, quick with the numbers, and began to produce early.

"I'm glad he's off to a good start, but I hope this doesn't come back to bite us," Dawn said.

I told her to relax. Nothing would happen.

Mike and I were both selling up a storm, putting added pressure on my crude accounting system, which sadly consisted of two measly file fold-ers-one marked accounts receivable, the other accounts payable-that were getting thicker by the day. We were out of control.

Mike suggested, "I got a buddy that I play racquetball with who used to be an accountant. Maybe he can do some moonlighting for us."

I was afraid to spend money on anything, but I knew we needed help, so I hired him. His name was Gary Turtle, a super guy and perfect for what we needed. He worked two weekends in a row, putting together a balance sheet and income statement.

After the second weekend, I looked over Gary's records. I was bewil-dered. "If we're making so much money, why don't we ever seem to have any? Where the hell is our cash?" I asked.

Gary gave me my first lecture on the dynamics of cash flow, which he demonstrated to be altogether different from earnings. "They're cousins, Mike, but they can be distant cousins if not managed," he explained. "Didn't you say you had a controller watching these things for you?"

"Oh, that's Phil Pocket, Andrew's controller. I don't know what he does, really, but he keeps the checkbook and pays all the bills," I said.

"Say, I'm going to need that checkbook. I have to reconcile your accounts, track your cash, and I should set up payables," Gary said.

"Okay, I'll get it for you."

Later that evening Gary called me at home. "Mike, you better come down here. I need to show you something."

"Is everything okay?" I asked.

"I don't know for sure, just come on in."

I raced out the door, telling Dawn I'd be back late and not to hold din-ner.

Arriving at the office, I found Gary in the conference room buried in a sea of paper. I removed my jacket and sat across from him.

"Well?" I asked.

"Mike, didn't you tell me that Andrew gave you thirty thousand seed capital and that he put seven thousand in your account to get things started?" Gary responded.

I swallowed hard. "Yeah, why?"

"Look at this. See what's happening here?"

I watched carefully as Gary laid a bunch of checks in a row in front of me one at a time.

"These checks are all marked insufficient funds. Look at the sequence. The first check for seven thousand bounced, followed by eleven thousand, which also bounced. This progression continues all the way to this check for thirty thousand. Andrew bounced eight straight checks," Gary said.

"I don't understand. What are you telling me?"

"I think he's kiting checks. Every deposit that Andrew has ever made for your company has bounced. And the checks are made out from different companies, one company covering for the other. No money has ever been deposited. He's invested *nothing*."

I was dumbfounded. I sat staring at the checks. "Oh no, Gary. He owns all these different companies. You know all those different colored phones on Nora's desk? She answers all of them for Andrew. I've heard all these names before," I said, now shaking my head. "How could this happen? Wouldn't the bank catch this?"

"The bank must be cooperating in some way. Somebody has to approve a bad check," Gary said. "The bottom line is, you're short thirty thousand. That's why you've been feeling squeezed. I thought you should know right away."

"No, it's worse than that. Andrew borrowed ten thousand from the company last week. I didn't even know you could do that"-by the way borrowing money from your company, while perfectly legal, is a dangerous practice; don't do it-"and Phil Pocket has been taking money, too. Last week Dawn was sitting in for Nora when this woman walked in. A bleached blonde in a slinky outfit. She asked for Phil, but he was out. Dawn saw that she was agitated and asked if she could help. The woman was jittery but finally told Dawn that Phil Pocket had given her a company check for five hundred bucks, but her bank wouldn't cash it because it was from a third party. And what really pissed her off is that she gave Phil fifty dollars cash because . . . well . . . her fee was four fifty. That's why he wrote the check for five hundred."

"Really? Then what happened?" Gary asked, his eyebrows rising.

As Dawn had reported the story to me, she had hid her suspicion and asked, "Can I see the check?"

"Well, I guess, but I was told that some guy named Mike Kerrison wasn't supposed to know about this," the blonde had replied.

"Well, I guess we better not tell him then," Dawn had responded, snatching the check from the woman's hand. Her casual walk down the hall to my office turned into a sprint, and she handed me the check, explaining what had happened.

Gary stared at me wide eyed. "You've got to be kidding!" he finally said.

I shook my head. "I wish I was."

"Keep going, keep going."

"I invited the woman into my office and had her sit down and explain to me what was happening. The long and short of it is she's a working girl. Apparently she turned a trick for Pocket and gave him fifty bucks cash to boot-probably weekend drinking money," I said.

"Let me see if I got this straight. Pocket pays a prostitute with a company check. She delivers her services, and then gives him fifty dollars spending money. Andrew offers you thirty thousand to start your business, puts in nothing, borrows ten thousand from you, and gets fifty-one percent of your company." Gary shook his head in disbelief. "Wow! you should have called *me*, Mike. *I* would have taken this deal."

I was mortified.

"Well, that explains why Andrew has Phil handling the checking account. Otherwise I would have found this earlier when I got the bank statements," I said.

Gary nodded. "No question."

"You think this guy's a crook?" I asked.

"Hard to say, Mike. Look at it this way-he takes fifty-one percent of the stock, puts no money in, has a banker in his pocket, kites a few checks, and after a few months of solid operations he hopes the whole thing goes undetected."

"I do know Broughton has been on that yacht," I muttered.

Gary grinned. "Well, duh . . . there ya are."

I called the bank first thing in the morning after a sleepless night. I was livid. I went right to Bob Ford, the president of the bank, and demanded a meeting. Hearing the distress in my voice, he made room in his schedule to see me right away.

We talked the situation through and got it straightened out, but Bob had a face full of egg over this one. "Gosh, I'm embarrassed about this, Mike. This should never have happened. I obviously have some internal control issues. And so do you. I think it's time you had a little talk with Mr. Stone."

I called Andrew at home that night and arranged a morning breakfast meeting. I was scared, but I had to confront him. My offer was simple: He would deposit $30 thousand in certified funds, covering all the bad checks. I would pay him a reasonable return over five years in exchange for his fifty-one percent ownership. Furthermore, I could keep my office, rent free, for up to six months while I looked for a new place. And, finally, I wanted Phil Pocket out of the office immediately. That was the deal-take it, or face prosecution.

Nora told me that Phil Pocket had a fit when he found out. "How the hell can he throw me out? These are your offices. Who the hell does he think he is, anyway? I'm not going anywhere. If he wants me out, he'll have to throw me out himself," Pocket said to Andrew.

That was all I needed to hear. That night after work I pushed his entire office into the hallway and changed the locks. I left a note on top of the pile with a copy of the check that he had written to the hooker. The note read: See to it you pay her the $500 you owe her. I'll be checking up to make sure you do. Don't disappoint me again. Kerrison.

After all that nonsense, I got my company-free and clear. About a year later I found out that Andrew ended up having to serve five years in federal prison somewhere in Texas. I never got the full story. I don't judge Andrew or hold him in contempt. In fact, despite his character issues, I liked him. He was engaging, funny, and smart. I often wondered how successful he would have been had he put all that talent and energy into something worthwhile. The irony of the whole thing was that I had started my company under the illusion of having financial support. I was walking a tightrope without a net, but since I didn't know, I had no fear. Like it or not, the fact remains that without Andrew, I might have never started at all.

When you go through something like this, the back-office staff takes on a whole new level of importance. Now that we had cash in the bank, we needed to get some control. When Gary wrapped up his auditing project, he recommended that I hire an operations manager to begin strengthening the back room. So I hired Sherry, Gary's wife.

"You're going to have to trust me on this one, Mike. She's exactly what you need," Gary told me.

He was right. We nicknamed her "Ma Turtle," which was fitting for her matriarchal style of management. First she automated our proposal process, allowing us to configure, price, and customize a proposal in ten minutes, which cut the order-writing routine by fifty percent. She installed our first accounting system-nothing fancy, but it worked. She set up and staffed our "Orders and Movements Department," arranging and tracking refurb, staging, testing, freight, and installation for our customers, and had all machines inspected for IBM maintenance, a contract requirement. Plus she answered phones, typed contracts, set up files, and made bank deposits. And I don't remember one moment when she didn't have at least three cigarettes burning somewhere. It's a wonder we didn't go up in flames.

Selling creates customers, customers create problems, problems steal time, which eventually steals sales, creating even more problems-the worst kind, in fact. So as soon as possible in your new business, you must establish a set of controls, develop office procedures, and put in a customer-support system that will quickly identify and resolve customer problems. If the president has to solve all the problems, the company will never grow, and eventually you'll go out of business. The president must graduate from top salesman to owner/operator to manager/builder to leader/planner. This progression takes time, and new skills are needed along the way. But the first step is to graduate to owner/operator. This is hard to do when you're a salesman.

Quick Review

To start your business, you need *lift*. I read somewhere that it's like your first solo flight. You're on the ground . . . on the ground . . . on the ground . . . faster . . . faster . . . faster . . . then *poof*, you're soaring on a mystical pillow of air, captain of all you can see.

You need to think your business through, but don't overthink it. Make a plan, but don't overplan. Just take off. Sell something-the wind beneath your wings. Forget about the fancy business plan, with all of its color charts, spreadsheets, and complex action items. You won't follow the plan, anyway, because it's too soon, the action items are too muddled, too contrived. And you're not ready for a "gold-plated" mission statement that's bold and full of virtue or a calligraphic set of profound business values to hang on the wall of your perfectly planned office. That's not to say that you aren't on a mission, that you don't need principles, or that your office environment isn't important. It's all important-but not as important as *lift*.

Besides, your business must evolve and eventually become all of these things first, at which time your mission and principles will have purpose and meaning. Before that, it's just window dressing-you're playing at the business. Later, when you know exactly where you fit, who you are, and the direction your business is going, your planning will be crisp, your mission will be clear, and your values will reflect what you have created. It will have integrity. Now you can hang it on the wall.

Passion and vision are the drivers for all of this. Dreams are born in the mind and heart, not in a three-ring binder stuffed with dry, lifeless numbers where, without passion, the dream dies. You have chosen to do what you love, remember? You are splendid at it, and people need what you have. So do it-whatever it is-until your legs fall off and your eyes roll out of your head. You won't mind, believe me, because you're creating something great, and it makes you happy. Not working becomes the real work. *Poof!* You are now in business.

Vulnerability Is a Condition of Leadership

Okay, you're off the ground. Sales are growing steadily. Now your infrastructure (back room) must expand, providing support for the outside clients, as well as the inside clients (your sales force). Do not overspend on infrastructure, and don't get complicated. You can upgrade systems later, when you need to. Once you have some structure, a sense of flow and process, you can grow . . . for a while. And don't give me this bull that you don't want to grow, that you want a nice little business you can control. The fact is, good companies grow. Why? Because they're good.

An effective CEO leads the growth effort. As such, he will always be judged by hindsight. He has no way to escape it-he must be vulnerable. If he isn't, he is not performing the job he signed up for. Vulnerability is a condition of leadership. It's the heat President Harry Truman referred to in his famous remark "If you can't take the heat, get out of the kitchen". From my point of view, either you grow or you die, which leads to the same two problems for all businesses: growth problems and liquidation problems. Growth problems are better. If you're not interested in growing, open a flower shop, and give this book to someone else because you don't need it.

Three more points:

One, the start-up companies with the best survival rates are the ones that can generate a cash flow in ninety days. These businesses do not consume bundles of start-up capital for research and development. The founder enters a solid market-preferably early in its life cycle-that he knows like the back of his hand. He aggressively grabs a piece of that market and then immediately establishes ways to differentiate the company from its competitors. His pure will, motivation, and talent launch these ninety-day wonders. This is the "bootstrap" approach-requiring a ninety-day plan that shouldn't take more than ninety minutes to do. I'm exaggerating, of course, but you see my point. Go for the quick kill by entering a market you know-and "stick to the knitting." In ninety days you will have a cash flow. I promise.

Two, establish a sales-oriented culture in your company from day one. Everybody sells. When you hire staff personnel, make sure they understand that their primary purpose is to help a salesperson sell. If you are not helping directly, you'd better be helping someone who is. This culture will eliminate contempt between sales and staff. It's not about playing favorites or who is more important, but rather what is more important. Sales are just plain way more important. This is something you *never* apologize for.

Three, don't hire family members or close friends if you can avoid it. Later in the year I had a major falling out with Dawn's brother, Mike. It's not important what happened. What is important is that it put a significant strain on Dawn and other members of the family for quite some time. The situation has been resolved for many years now-but not without some tears and heartbreak. I have found that the greater the emotional involvement you have with an employee, the less likely you are to make a prudent judgment. When managing any organization, one duty is inescapable: managing people. So to keep things right, to remain objective, you need to manage your people as nature would. Show neither malice nor pity. If you do, you will jeopardize the authority that your people have granted you. But nature doesn't work well with family members. So you'd best not hire them.

Making the *Inc. 500*

Two weeks after Sherry started working for me, I hired my next salesman, who lived two doors down from me. Jack Collins had heard about the used computer industry and how it was growing. His situation at Watkins Corporation, where he was president, kept him away from his wife and three kids, and he was primed for a career change. We met for lunch, and after hearing his background, I felt he would be perfect for the job. His concern was whether he could learn the computer business. I promised to teach him everything.

Jack picked me up every morning at six for our morning run around Lake Harriett. That is where I conducted his training. After a brief stretch we started our jog, during which I taught him about computers, software, applications, leasing, war stories, customers, techniques, selling, objection handling, contracts, structuring deals, competitors, refurbishing equipment, operations, IBM, and on and on. These mini-lectures quenched his thirst better than his water bottle did.

"You know, Mike, you should document all of this, or dictate it or something. This is the basis for your training materials," he said.

And so I did. That's how I got started training my sales force. I was good at it, and it brought me tremendous joy and satisfaction. Jack hit the ground running and, as I had hoped, became a marvelous producer.

We were now in our new offices. Dawn had found a beautiful new office park called Parkdale Plaza in neighboring St. Louis Park. It was expensive, and given my roots I was afraid to spend money.

"Dawn, we can't afford this. We don't need anything this fancy," I protested.

"You told me that you were going to build the best sales organization in the industry, offering the best service and the best products," she countered. "If you really meant that, then you have to have the best offices, too. Don't scrimp on this, Mike. This is way too important. This place will be a reflection on you and your company."

I turned to Sherry for support. "Sherry we can't afford this. Can we?"

"You can't afford *not* to do this. Dawn is right. I say we go for it." Sherry folded her arms.

It was two against one. I lost. I also knew they were right. Sometimes you need to look and act bigger than what your balance sheet might bear out.

We now looked like a real business, and we had only been at it for nine months. Sherry, thinking ahead, negotiated some flexibility in the lease, allowing us to easily expand or move to another location in the building. We knew we were going to grow. We just didn't know how fast.

Next I began working on Pete Jackson, an acquaintance from the IBM Omaha office and one of the best salesmen who ever came out of Big Blue. He had been promoted to marketing manager in the Twin Cities and had just moved up with his family. "No, I've got to do this for a while. But I appreciate the offer," Pete told me.

One afternoon I invited Pete to lunch. With Jack's permission, I took a copy of his year-to-date earnings with me. I thought Pete's eyes would fall out of his head when he saw what Jack had earned in his first six months.

"You've got to be kidding me! This is three times what I make," he said.

"That's what I've been trying to tell ya, Pete, and Jack's not even from the industry," I said. "Now are you ready to go?"

"I'll call you tonight. I have to talk to my wife," he said.

Pete started three weeks later. IBM was livid.

Now there was four of us. Jack, Pete, Mike, and I brought in a ton of business, and we were having a great time. Sherry had hired two young women to handle accounting and reports, and we now had a full-time receptionist.

I can't emphasize enough the importance of a great receptionist. I believe it is one of the most influential jobs in the business for protecting morale and promoting good will. How many times have you made a business phone call, only to be treated like crap at the other end? They don't know, they don't care, they can't help, good-bye. The receptionist is the first contact a client or recruit has with your company. It should be an overwhelmingly pleasant experience. For this reason I hired winners for that job and paid them twenty percent more than market. I promised to move them through the organization if they promised to give me two years on the phone. That was the deal, and they had to stick to it. Tami, our first receptionist, remembered your name just by hearing your voice a couple of times. The clients loved her. They became friends. Hire only *great* receptionists, train them to understand your business, and treat them like gold. They will take this ordinary job and transform it into something special.

We hit $1 million in sales in our tenth month of operations. Our little group-spouses included-celebrated with a fancy dinner at Charlie's Café. This ragtag team had a real sense of accomplishment and anticipation. I thanked everyone for their dedication and offered a challenge. I held up a copy of Inc., a brand-new business magazine. *Inc.* has a special issue each year called the *Inc. 500*, which recognizes America's fastest-growing companies-the *Fortune 500* for the little guys.

I told our people that I wanted to be on that list. We wouldn't be eligible for five years, but I knew we could do it. I enlisted their help and commitment to this extraordinary goal.

In 1985, our first year of eligibility, we made the list. We were ranked number 149, with a compounded five-year growth rate of 1,381 percent. We reached $26 million in sales and we were profitable every year. That same year Microsoft made the list for the first time-ranked number 163. I enjoy telling people how we beat the pants off of them back in the eighties.

But as Paul Harvey would say, "And now the rest of the story."

Chapter 9

Riding the Series/1

We rode the IBM Series/1 all the way to the *Inc.500*. It was a magic carpet ride. The system was originally designed for engineering applications, so you might find it installed at Ford or Honeywell doing CAD/CAM design or running a machine tool-it was never intended for commercial business. The Series/1 was powerful, operating at speeds three times faster than the System/34, IBM's most popular midrange computer. The problem was it ran a UNIX operating system, and back then no one wrote business applications on UNIX-at least no one that I knew of.

I was first introduced to the Series/1 at Carlson Companies, headquartered in Minneapolis, where I had gone to sign a contract to buy a System/34. The DP manager took me into the warehouse to show me the machine and get the serial number for the contract. As we walked through the storehouse of goods, I abruptly stopped.

There, wrapped in original IBM packaging, were some two hundred running feet of new Series/1 computers and peripherals. I counted over seventy computers, one hundred printers, five hundred CRTs, and enough cable to wire Chicago.

"What's all this?" I asked.

The DP manager sighed. "You don't want to know."

"These are Series/1s. What are you using these for?" I asked, now strolling along the aisle and touching the computers as if they were jewels.

"That's just it. We *aren't* using them. They were ordered for our Radisson Hotels to run the front offices, but the project got canned. That was a year ago," he said.

"IBM wouldn't take them back?" I asked.

"Nope, and the guy who ordered them is long gone."

"Why haven't you sold them?"

"We've tried. There's no market out there," he said.

"No market? There's always a market. Somebody's buying them." I paused. "I'll get them sold for you," I said.

"Well, have at it, my friend. If you get these boat anchors moved, I'm a hero. We paid two million for these babies and had to write the whole thing off last year. It killed our budget and pissed off a lot of people, including Curt."

I knew he was referring to Curt Carlson, the chairman and CEO. I smiled. I loved a good challenge.

I returned the next day, having talked to three software companies that wrote programs for the Series/1. I had no doubt there was a market-and it was growing. I signed a remarketing agreement with Carlson. We would take the machines on consignment and split the revenue seventy-thirty.

We sold everything in four months, paid Carlson nearly $1 million, and made $300,000. From this one deal we emerged as the nation's market leader for used Series/1s. In three years we sold and installed over two hundred systems, fifty of which went to Doubletree Hotels-to run, of all things, their front-office applications. One man's garbage is another man's gold.

Hiring Mark

The Series/1 also brought us Mark Dover-possibly the finest salesman I have ever known. During my search for Series/1 software companies, I ran into a small firm down in Austin called Texas Data. Mark was my initial contact with the firm and their top salesman. We hit it off immediately. He told me everything I needed to know about the Series/1 and the dealers making a market, and I was impressed with his industry knowledge and charming personality. I shared with him the opportunity we'd had at Carlson Companies and persuaded him to use us as a supplier for his Series/1 clients.

Within one year he became our largest customer. Mark sold a turnkey solution-hardware and software-for the distribution industry. He had a deep understanding of business applications, processes, and complex selling techniques, and he knew how to sell executives. Software sell cycles usually take three months or longer. Mark was closing one a month-phenomenal! He bought fifteen systems a year from us at an average selling price of $75,000. Quick with the numbers and fair with negotiations, he looked for a win-win. He would always ask, "Mike, are you okay with this deal? Can you make money?" And he meant it. If the deal got too skinny, he would ease off on the terms or allow me to raise my price. He knew when to give in and when to hold firm.

Mark and I were having one of our regular end-of-the-week conversations when I detected his discontent with Texas Data. It occurred to me that I maybe should hire the guy. That night I talked the situation over with Dawn.

"Gosh, Dawn, I'm torn. He's my best customer. If I hire him, I'll be losing two million in sales a year."

"Yes, but if he leaves Texas Data, you've lost him anyway. You already told me he's the whole company. Besides, how would you feel if he ended up at one of your competitors?"

I made my move.

The next morning I called Mark and invited him up to Minneapolis for a visit, telling him straight away that I was interested in having him work for us. He arrived on a Friday. We spent most of the day looking over the company, my vision for it, and how he could contribute. He was excited and seemed anxious to get an offer. Later I drove him around so that he could see the city, and that evening Dawn and I would take him out for a special dinner.

Mark and I made a quick stop at my office to wrap up the day. I wanted to find out where he stood. I wasn't at all expecting what came next.

"Mike, I sense that you are going to offer me a job, and quite frankly I hope you do," he started. "But there is something you need to know about me before you go any further. I wasn't going to say anything, but it would be unfair to you to find this out after you extended an offer."

I suddenly felt anxious. What could he possibly need to tell me? My first impulse was that he was an ex-con or something.

"Well, Mark, just spit it out. I mean, we've got nothing to hide here," I said.

"I'm gay."

"Excuse me?"

"I'm gay. I'm a homosexual. I have a lover. His name is Kevin. We live together," he said.

I froze like a deer in headlights. That was the last thing I had expected him to say. There we were, slouched on my conference-room chairs like a couple buddies drinking beer and watching the Super Bowl. I abruptly snapped to attention. I was embarrassed, confused, but most of all curious. Rarely at a loss for words, I somehow recovered and wiggled out from offering him the job. I felt bad, but I needed time to think. He was still the best salesman I had ever known, and it was one of the best business relationships I had ever had.

When I got home, Dawn was in the bathroom, putting on her make-up. *Should I tell her now or wait till after?* I wondered. I wanted her honest assessment.

"Hi, Mike how'd it go?" she asked. "Did you offer him the job?"

I plopped down at the end of the bed, and she studied the long look on my face.

She sighed. "He didn't take the job did he?"

"He's gay."

"*What?*"

"He's gay. Can you believe it? I mean, there is no way I could have known. This guy is manlier than Rocky, for crying out loud. And now we're supposed to take him out to dinner," I said.

"Holy smokes . . . no way . . . I mean, this is way too weird. I can't go out with you guys," Dawn said.

"You want me to go out with him alone?"

"Oooh! That's a little spooky. You want me to pick you out a nice outfit?" She giggled.

"Very funny. Look, you're going with me. Besides, I need your help on this, Dawn. I really don't know what to do. Mark is a terrific person," I said.

"Well, fine, let's just go out and have a good time. It'll be okay." Dawn could see my anguish over this decision and decided to support me. "One question, though. You don't think he has any interest in you do you?" she asked.

"Well, he has a lover and considers himself married. I guess that makes me safe, huh?" I said.

"Wow, this is gonna be different," Dawn said.

After dinner that night the valet brought the car around. I held the door for Dawn and turned to shake Mark's hand, thanked him for coming, and wished him a safe trip home. I got in the car and looked at Dawn.

"Well, see what I mean?" I said.

"I do. He's absolutely charming. I could be friends with him. I can't tell you what to do, Mike, but if it were up to me, I'd hire him. He's tremendous. He reminds me of you," she said.

I gave her a double take.

"Relax, Tarzan, I didn't mean that way," she said. "It was meant to be a compliment."

"God, Dawn, I just don't know what to do."

"You'll know what to do. Sleep on it, and trust your instincts," she advised.

Mark returned to Austin, and on Monday morning we were back on the phone doing business as if nothing had changed. That week he ordered two systems and never once mentioned anything about the visit. He put no pressure on me whatsoever. I was the coward. I didn't offer him the job, and, worse yet, I didn't even offer an explanation. I just let it die. I told Pete, Jack, and Sherry about the whole thing. Their reaction was similar to mine, provincial, but more unbending. So I chickened out.

Mark continued our business relationship. That told me a lot about his character and integrity. Most people would have ended the relationship in the face of my prejudice. But Mark wasn't like most people. He was special. I felt ashamed that I didn't have the courage to stand up to the others in the office. I wanted to hire him, but I just couldn't do it.

Two months later on a Sunday night, the phone rang. It was Mark.

"I've decided to leave Texas Data, and I wanted you to be the first to know. I've been offered a job with another computer broker, and depending on how our conversation goes, I'm going to take it," he said.

"I see."

"Look, Mike, I know why you didn't offer me the job. I completely understand. I want you to know two things, though. I don't hold anything against you, and you made a huge mistake not hiring me. Furthermore, if you *do* hire me, I will never allow my personal life to interfere with my professional life, and I will outperform your best salesman two to one. I'm good at what I do, and I want to work for your company. I want to work for the best," he said.

I was flabbergasted and acted on instinct. "God, Waldrep, how do I resist a sales pitch like that? Consider yourself hired. Call me in the morning, and I'll take you through the details. And, Mark, I'm really glad you called. You're right. I should have done this two months ago." I hung up the phone and smiled.

Mark Waldrep shattered all the company's sales records. In my best year I had done $560,000 in gross margin, Pete was second with $530,000. Mark, in his first year, did $660,000 against a quota of

$280,000. He was a magnificent performer, and, what's more, the staff liked him as did the other reps. Except for one. One of my top reps could not handle that he was gay and decided to leave. I was happy to watch the door hit him in the ass on the way out.

I did not agree with Mark's lifestyle, but I had no right to judge him for it. Nor did anyone else. He deserved the job because he had integrity and extraordinary talent. I learned to separate a person's private life from his or her professional life and to act not on prejudices and old beliefs but on knowledge and understanding. I developed an open mind and the ability to see past such circumstances and see people for who they really were.

I don't claim great virtue in this way of thinking. After all, this is the way it should be. I took a risk hiring Mark. But the payoff was huge. Without him we wouldn't have made the *Inc. 500*.

Chapter 10

Going a Little Crazy

When you grow the way we did, from $0 to $26 million in five years, you go a little crazy. By 1985 we had fifteen salespeople covering the entire country. Our office grew from 8,500 to 30,000 square feet to keep pace with our growing employee base, new refurb center, and expanded parts inventory. With competition ever increasing, we found these improvements necessary to maintain an edge. We kept the phone ringing through a simple marketing campaign, using a database of sixty thousand IBM sites that we had collected over the years. Each month we sent out postcard mailers announcing promotions, pricing trends, and special equipment deals. The cards were horrible colors like lime green, hot pink, and canary yellow. Our prospects waited for these cards like a junkie waiting for a fix. One month we missed a mailing only to have hundreds of companies call and say, "Hey, I didn't get my postcard this month. Am I still on your list?" We received over one hundred prospect calls per week from those postcards. After five years of dumping two million cards on the market, we became the de facto pricing standard for IBM midrange computers. Repetition paid off, and it cost us about ten percent of what the big advertising firms were recommending.

Marketing is meant to be strategic. Let me give you an example. Over time we were able to record in our database the exact locations of different types of disk drives and printers in the market-nearly fifty thousand entries. When IBM made a new announcement (which we learned how to anticipate), we could immediately spot the prospect, swap new for used, inventory the old models at bargain prices, and corner the market. The key to making this work was speed. Since we knew where the bones were buried, we could get there first. Telemarketing would hit the phones on the day of announcement and cover sixty percent of the market in five days. Our prices weren't better, but our timing was. By the time our competitors showed up, we had already been there and gone. Now they had to buy their equipment from us to fill their orders since we had the inventory-so we were able to corner both retail and wholesale. They called us the dealer's dealer. Without the integrated database and telemarketing team, we would never have been able to do this.

Remember: Marketing can establish formidable competitive advantage. It's not just for finding leads.

Our back-office staff doubled, and we automated our business applications-on a Series/1, by the way. Pete became my vice president of sales, Sherry became VP of operations, and we now had a controller. A small but effective organization model had developed, relieving me of the burden of a growing sales force and the increasing pressures of customer service. My duties shifted from top salesman to owner/operator, still very much involved with customers, but now I could devote more time to planning, training reps, and finding ways to grow.

One of the biggest keys to success was our superior sales force. We provided huge earnings opportunity, but they had to perform. Our salespeople were held accountable to a territory and a quota. If they made their numbers, they went to the President's Club-an-all-expense-paid trip to places like Hawaii, Bermuda, Florida, Nassau, and Arizona (which Dawn and a couple of my staff members planned until the trips got too big). Spouses were always included, which was a priority for us since IBM never invited them. We had roses in the room when they arrived and a small gift on their pillow for the last night. I was amazed by the influence a spouse can have on a salesperson's quota. While at the President's Club, we always pre-announced the next year's club. Spouses would turn and ask, "Are we going?"

We had a special award called "In the Club, At the Club." With the annual trips being held during the first week of April, we had at least one rep make the current year's quota in time for the trip. They received a $3,000 bonus, two award plaques (this year and last), and an invitation to next year's club. It was tremendously exciting for them and not bad for retention since headhunters were calling them every day.

Hiring, training, and inspiring a leading-edge sales force are prerequisites for growing your business-they imbue the spirit and drive of the entire organization. Great salespeople must be challenged. Those who continually break sales records might have done far less if they had been challenged with less, and they would have realized less of their potential and their individuality.

I remember from my IBM days when Tom Watson Jr.-one of my heroes-would relay his popular story about why there is a need for "wild ducks." The moral is drawn from the story by the Danish philosopher Søren Kierkegaard. He told of a man on the coast of Zealand who liked to watch the wild ducks fly south in great flocks each fall. Out of charity, he took to putting feed for them in a nearby pond. After a while some of the ducks no longer bothered flying south; they wintered in Denmark on what he fed them.

Over time they flew less and less. When the wild ducks returned, the others would circle up to greet them but then head back to their feeding grounds on the pond. After three or four years they grew so lazy and fat that they found it difficult to fly at all.

Kierkegaard made his point: You can make wild ducks tame, but you can never make tame ducks wild again. Once you spoil them, it's over. You have clipped their wings. Likewise, I am convinced that every sales force needs its wild ducks. And when you find them, don't ever tame them. Instead, manage them. And watch your company grow.

The End of Indiana Jones

One disadvantage of early success is that you then believe that everything you touch will turn to gold. You overestimate yourself. The year we made the *Inc.* 500, the company was on autopilot, booking about $3 million a month by year's end. The opportunities appeared endless. I was now envisioning $100 million in sales, requiring that we grow at a rate of thirty percent per year. I had no concept of the changes the organization would have to make to achieve that level of growth, but I could no longer depend on wits and instinct. What the organization needed was a sound business plan consisting of an honest assessment of our people, a core business-health check, an evaluation of our strengths and weaknesses, a detailed forecast and cash flow, and an adequate line of credit. That's just for starters. It would also require a radical change in our infrastructure, customer service department, procedures, policies, human resources, and management reporting. Finally, the company needed managers because I couldn't do it alone.

The single biggest challenge I faced was whether I could personally develop the necessary skills to take a fast-growing organization to the next level. I could no longer be Indiana Jones with a briefcase. I needed to become a professional manager, a builder, and a visionary. But in 1985 I hadn't gotten that far in my thinking. As far as I was concerned,

I was still Indiana Jones.

I had all the answers. Arrogance replaced humility. I figured the way to continue growing was to throw more salespeople into the mix and open new territory and markets. And here is where I went crazy.

First, I established four new divisions; the General Systems Division (midrange computers and our original core business), the Data Processing Division (mainframes), the Office Products Division (word processors) and the Telcom Division (used telephone systems). The rationale was to unleash the three new divisions into our existing customer base. No one thought through the complications of multiple reps calling on one account or the commission problems that would ensue. As a result, we lost huge amounts of synergy and coordination.

The Data Processing Division was an entirely new segment for us. We did little competitive research, no analysis of expected growth, and had no financial tools to assist us with writing leases, which had been the basis for success in the first place.

Office Products had a different set of problems. The transactions were small, so we had to write a lot of deals to make any money. The amount of staff effort to support a $2,000 word processor sale was the same effort that went into a $70,000 computer sale. The margins were junk, and it was labor intensive and a customer-service nightmare.

The used telephone market was brand new and showed a ton of promise. But refurbishing and installing a phone system was far more complicated than a computer. Our engineers could not cross over. It's amazing how pissed off customers get when their phones don't work. They're far more understanding when their computer is down.

IBM announced the first personal computer in 1982. You remember-that's when Charlie Chaplain started running around everywhere in those ads. So of course we *had* to get into that, too. I bought a tiny PC software company called Datasource Systems (which is still in business today, by the way). This was literally a basement operation, started by two engineers from 3M-pioneer resellers of packaged PC software like Lotus 123 and DBASE II. The tiny ad they ran in *Computerworld* produced $80,000 per month, taken on Visa and Master Card. It was a new world. We performed no due diligence, did zero planning, and knew nothing about PCs. It was a hunch, an impulse buy, and it failed. We sold the company one year later for a loss.

It doesn't take a genius to recognize the folly in the approach I outlined above. Growth is not a pushbutton process. You don't drop a quarter in a machine, and out pops a new business. For new business development to succeed, you need the right players, a separate launch plan, patience, and some extra money because you're going to make mistakes. You also need to take your time. The old joke about how do you eat an elephant rings particularly true in this case. Answer? One bite at a time.

Maintenance Innovators

While throwing new divisions at the wall, I had one that actually stuck. As I mentioned earlier we opened our new refurb center. Bob Erdahl, one of the best customer engineers in the country, helped me set it up and staff it. Bob and I first met through the Carlson deal. He did all our reconfigurations and testing for the Series/1s. Though not formally employed by us, he was in the refurb center every day working on something.

I learned of a small third-party maintenance company in Texas providing service for IBM midrange computers. Bob and I met and broke bread over the possibility of our doing this. It was a natural fit. Bob researched the engineers, and I ran the numbers. We decided to do it. Computer Options would own sixty-five percent and Bob would own thirty-five percent. Within one month we wrote a dozen maintenance contracts, providing our customers with faster response time, experienced engineers, and fully tested IBM parts, all at a twenty-five percent discount. It was a success. Once again, in the first ninety days we generated a respectable cash flow without a big infusion of up front capital.

Bob and I were in complete agreement on the market requirements, the launch activities, and who was responsible for what. Our skills were complementary. Mine was sales and marketing, and I had the client base; his was service, and he knew all the good engineers. We were both excited and propelled by desire, that magic stuff that creates lift: on the ground . . . on the ground . . . on the ground . . . *poof!* Another bootstrap company. Bob and I named it Maintenance Innovators, Inc. (MII).

After a month I hired MII's first salesman, Joe Arel. He was another Mark Waldrep-smart, aggressive, proven. Joe and I developed a seminar strategy much like the one I had used at IBM. Before long we were holding two seminars a month and writing at least five contracts at each seminar. We sweetened our business terms, offering the first month free, an on-site parts kit, and thirty-day cancellation rights for any reason, guaranteeing free and safe return to IBM maintenance. These practices were unheard of in the industry. We learned that a competitive advantage can be gained by *avoiding, not following* industry standards and best practices, which are a sure path to ordinariness. I find a hint of the problem in the verb itself: following. You don't follow to get the edge, you lead. Before you know it, it's your business practices that the others are following.

So the lesson is: Ignore industry standards, and create your own. That was MII's secret.

We told the story through radio advertising, expanded media coverage, and outbound telemarketing, creating enormous demand for our services. In two years we had over four hundred fifty clients within a four-hour radius of the Twin Cities. The company was on its way to $5 million in sales in its second year, and we were forecasting $15 million in three years. Another *Inc. 500* performance was easily under way.

The combination of fully refurbished equipment at half price, a low-cost maintenance contract, and flexible leasing options would provide a formidable offering. The synergy between the two companies would be extraordinary. It was a good thing, too, because the other divisions couldn't get off the runway. On the ground . . . on the ground . . . on the ground . . . *splat!* We looked like the early Wright Brothers.

My people kept warning me, "Mike, you're trying to do too much. We can't handle all of this." But I would hear nothing of it. Skies were blue-or so I thought.

Fifty-Fifty

Life is so unpredictable. Just when everything seems to be falling into place, a bomb gets dropped on you. It was a beautiful spring morning. The sun was streaming gently through the blinds as I sat with my feet up, drinking a fresh cup of coffee while contemplating the day. I had just reviewed the results of our second quarter-another record performance. All was well with the world. Moments later, Sherry appeared at my door, her face tormented.

I sat up in my chair. "What?" I asked.

"Dawn's on line two. She needs to talk to you right away." Sherry pulled my door closed.

"Shit, what's going on?" I asked myself aloud. I reached for the phone. "Dawn, are you okay? Are the kids okay?"

"We're fine . . . but I have some bad news, Mike." It was obvious she had been crying.

"What? . . . Tell me." I felt a warm rush in my face.

"Alex has cancer."

I'll never forget the words. The air flew from my lungs, and my stomach contorted as though I'd been stabbed with a butcher knife. I sobbed. I couldn't control it. It just gushed out. *This can't be happening. This just can't possibly be happening. He's only forty.*

"How did you find out?" I asked, trying to recover.

"Lindsey just called. You better call her right away, Mike."

"Oh, God, Dawn, it's happening all over again."

"I know, Mike. I know. I'm so sorry. But we don't have all the facts yet. Just call her," she said.

I was taken by surprise when Alex answered the phone. You never know what to say when something catastrophic like this happens, particularly to someone you love. What do you say? *I'm sorry. I'll pray. Don't worry, everything will be okay.* What kind of nonsense is that? Our heads always seem to find something to say, but we detach our brains from our hearts. How else do you get the words out?

At the sound of my voice, Alex broke down and cried, unable to speak. We both sat there on the phone and sobbed. Nothing was said, which said it all. It was just a time for two great friends to cry. He eventually handed the phone to Lindsey.

"Hi, Mike," she said softly.

"Lindsey, what happened?" I asked.

"We were out to dinner last week, and Alex complained that he couldn't swallow his food. He said his throat was closing up. I made an appointment with his doctor, and they ran all the tests. We just got the results last night." She paused.

"And . . . ?"

"He has stomach and esophagus cancer. Apparently it's been there a long time. It doesn't look good, Mike," she said.

"Oh, shit. What else do we know?" I asked.

"Surgery . . . immediately."

Lindsey then explained that the only surgery possible for this type of cancer was a new procedure that had recently been developed.

"Who's going to do it?"

"That's just it. Apparently there is only one surgeon in the country who knows how to do it. We don't even know if we can get him. We were told it's very, very dangerous."

"What's the guy's name?" I asked.

"Skinner. Dr. Charles Skinner."

"Let me see what I can do. I'll call you back in one hour. I promise,"

I said.

I was on the foundation board for Methodist Hospital and was able to find Dr. Skinner through my contacts there. Skinner agreed to do the surgery. He had developed the procedure himself, in which he would take a section of Alex's colon and use it to build an esophagus and stomach to replace the portion that would be removed. Apparently he had performed the surgery only a few times-and the survival rate was fifty-fifty.

Alex was scheduled for surgery at the University of Chicago Hospital. Dawn and I flew in to support him and to help Lindsey with the kids. Friends and family came from all over to see him the night before the operation. I shuttled folks back and forth from the airport to the hospital all evening. Several of the guys from Alex's wedding came in from Cleveland and New Jersey. I was so glad to see them again; it had been fifteen years. We partied and prayed in the confines of the sterile hospital room. Alex was joking and putting on a show, as always. Everybody would roar, and then it would become silent. It was a tough night. But the morning would be tougher.

The surgery nearly killed him. I'll never forget what he looked like when he came out of the OR. Lindsey and I followed Dr. Skinner down a dimly lit hallway to a set of double doors. The doors opened, and we found Alex strapped down by his arms and legs to the bars on the recovery bed. He was awake and in agony. A thin sheet was draped over him. Alex had huge shoulders and a barrel chest that now gave way to a gaping void beneath his rib cage. It was grotesque. The anesthesia had worn off, but he was unable to have pain medication until he was considered stabilized. I had never seen human suffering like this. It ripped me apart. We held his hands and prayed.

I returned to the waiting room and found fifteen-year-old Marc and fourteen-year-old Lisa waiting for news about their father. I watched their innocent, open faces as Lindsey told them with courage and poise everything Alex had been through. For me it was like a time warp. Here was Marc, the exact same age I had been when Dad died, facing the exact same thing. And Lisa was at the age when a young woman needed her father. I knew what these kids would go through if they lost him.

Dawn returned home, but I stayed for two weeks and sat next to Alex, who was wired up like a lab animal and breathing with a respirator. He was a fighter and made it through. Once he was out of the woods I headed back home to my family.

It's easy for us to go back to our lives and pick up where we left off, detached from oncology reports, chemo, hair loss, and all the rest. Life goes on for us. We're grateful for our health, our family, our good job. We're full of hope and dreams, striving toward something. But not so far back in our mind we're aware that someone is suffering-someone we love. And as we go forward, part of us suffers, too. I hate cancer. I even hate the word: *cancer . . . cancer.* It has a sickening, slithering sound. It's a hater of people, with an inherent malevolence that drops us in our tracks like a hunter's prey.

Alex was one of the most important people in my life. Losing him would be unimaginable. So I didn't think about it. I just continued to go a little crazy.

Chapter 11

The Meltdown

In 1986 I had the worst business year ever. In fact, it was a nightmare. Looking back on it now, I have to chuckle because it all seems like a big soap opera. But at the time it felt as though the world was ending. I had all the trappings of success. The business had just made the *Inc.* 500, we were profitable as hell, we were growing like mad, we were moving into a dazzling new facility, and I was gaining stature in the community as a real whiz kid, with feature stories in the *Minneapolis Tribune, Minnesota Corporate Report*, and a special TV appearance on *Business Showcase,* a regional program.

I was the young entrepreneur making a ton of money for the first time-which is often when you start making mistakes. Perhaps it has nothing to do with age; maybe it's just the money. You get cocky, you ignore advice, you force the company into unsafe territory, and you work less and play more. Houses, cars, vacations, furs, jewelry become your idols. You get lost in the success.

Dawn and I were caught up in the greedy eighties, going to the Symphony Ball, hobnobbing with the big boys in the community, taking on high-profile civic responsibilities, and playing in every tennis tournament under the sun. And when we got bored, we jumped into our Mercedes 380SL and went to Gabberts to buy furniture. Face time was our credo. We were disgusting-measuring our success by how many party invitations hung on the refrigerator door.

Hey, I'm not knocking a 380SL or a packed social life, and having money is no crime. What will put you into a tailspin is the attitude that you've made it. When you put your faith in these things, you regress, because taken by themselves, these things are empty.

And empty is what I felt. Why wasn't this lining up better? I had worked hard, achieved success, had a great family. What was the problem here? Denial . . . that was the problem. Alex was sick, and I just couldn't make sense of it. I was angry. Really, really angry. And my anger turned into a deep depression. I began to slow down. Each movement felt heavy, as if I were underwater. Now every twenty-four hours gave me about three, then two, and finally one hour of life reserves, concentration, personality, and motion. I was "beat up from the feet up."

One Saturday morning I was sipping coffee at the kitchen table. Dawn finished the breakfast dishes, poured a few Cheerios on the baby's tray, and joined me for a cup. I was in one of those staring-into-space moods.

"Did you have fun last night?" my wife asked.

"Hmm . . . yeah . . . sorta. You?"

"I guess so," she shrugged.

We sat silently for a minute.

"No . . . no . . . actually, I didn't," I finally said. "I absolutely didn't. Dawn, don't you feel as though we've been to the same party a million times? The same people, the same stories, the same stupid jokes? I was lying in bed last night thinking about it. I'm sick and tired of coming home from these stupid parties and asking myself, *How did we do tonight?* Like we're in some kind of competition. The whole scene is disgusting to me. Why do we do it, anyway?"

"I don't know, Mike. Don't go overboard with this. Besides, we wouldn't worry about what people thought of us if we knew how seldom they actually did," she quipped.

"Now, there's a point," I said. "I've overestimated us again."

Nonetheless, she felt the same way I did. Here we were at thirty-something, repeating high school, for crying out loud-playing the same silly games. Ridiculous.

Dawn was reflective that week. And one evening as we were getting ready for bed, she announced that she was quitting drinking alcohol.

"I've been thinking about what you said. You know, Mike, I've seen too many people suffer with this stuff, particularly in our own family. First we take a drink, and then the drink takes us." She walked into my closet, where I was taking off my tie. "I mean, just once I'd like to have a conversation at one of those parties with someone who was sober. I want a relationship with *them*, not their booze. And our kids are getting older, Mike. They're watching. I want them to like what they see when we come home after being out. So I'm quitting," she said firmly.

I admired her decision. At first I wondered, *Do I have to quit, too? Not even a glass of wine with spaghetti! C'mon!* But, you can't go halfway on this kind of decision. So I quit drinking, as well. That was seventeen years ago. Neither of us has missed it one bit. We made a responsible, sensible decision. We felt good about it, and we began to see things differently.

But I was still down for some reason. Something was still wrong; something was missing. I fought off the melancholy by working harder, trying to avoid life's delicate surfaces, holding on instead to life's safe harbors: family, friends, sports, work, chores, money, food, sleep, health. Just keep moving. And when I was on the brink of leaving Earth's atmosphere, I would suddenly and without notice come crashing down, flat on my face.

Something was definitely wrong.

Making Mistakes

This up-and-down pattern continued. When I was up, usually after a good report from Alex, I was invincible-brilliant, in fact. This brilliance led to more mistakes, evidenced by my impulsive decisions to start three new operating divisions, buy a PC company, launch MII, and open the refurb center all at the same time. I was all over the map. I knew where I wanted to go, but I was blind as to how to get there. For instance, who would run all these spin-offs? What skills would they need? How would I pay them? How much cash would we burn through? What controls would be required? Would we need higher inventory levels? Did we have enough space? What would happen to the credit line? How many salespeople would we need? What capital assets would be required? What new competitors would we encounter? Could we beat them? What procedures and policies would we have to implement? What infrastructure would we need to support a growing sales force and increased customer service? And on and on and on . . .

I had few answers to these questions, and the questions themselves barely hit my radar screen in 1986. I was invincible, remember-bullet-proof. We would simply set new quotas for the reps, fortify our staff, reset the clock to zero, and let her rip. Who needs a plan? I'm not minimizing our accomplishments. What we did was great. And I still believe that it is action, not planning that carries the day when you start. But without a planning model, we would now pay the price.

At a time when the used-computer market was already softening, I was kicking the company into high gear-going for $100 million. If I had valued business planning, with full knowledge of the threats we faced and our weaknesses, I would have instead been preparing for a rainy day. But when you're a thirty-one-year-old millionaire, you don't see rainy days. I was heading back to the anvil again, where this time I would take a real pounding.

The biggest mistake I made was hiring an outside executive to run the new DPD division. His name is not important to the story, so we'll just call him Larry Steelman. He had held a big-shot position at Xerox Corporation, and getting someone like Larry was a real coup, given his executive pedigree and status in the community. Larry had ten years on me-a fact to which I assigned far too much importance. He made a similar miscalculation, believing I was this young prodigy with a golden touch-his ticket to lasting fortune and fame. I was still in awe of the corporate brass, something left over from my IBM days, I suppose. During the time I was cutting my entrepreneurial teeth on the street, he was sipping coffee in the boardroom.

Larry got the upper hand early. He was a fierce negotiator-big company politics had taught him well. I gave him an enormous salary (what he called "a salary becoming an executive"), a cushy start-up quota, and free reign to develop the new division, which was another mistake because blue-chip execs usually don't make good entrepreneurs. Worse, I put everything in an employment agreement-which, of course, he also insisted on. I find it interesting that the old "golden handcuffs" end up binding *you*, not *them*. Employers are always at risk under these agreements, and the laws favor the employee. Stay away from these agreements. They are always trouble.

My feeling is that if you offer someone a proven business model, a terrific corporate culture and an exciting incentive compensation plan, that should be enough. If he or she can't see it, you have the wrong person. Go find another. My advice: When hiring executives, if they don't want you badly enough, stay clear. You need to have a shared risk. Make sure something is at stake for both of you. Otherwise you're inviting cancer into your company. (There's that word again.)

I made him a vice president right out of the chute-another one of his conditions, which drew much criticism and resentment from the others. Particularly offended was Mark Dover, who was more qualified. Hiring, developing, and promoting from within was a value that I had always upheld. By abandoning this value, I would lose the trust and credibility that I had worked so hard to establish. I put the entire corporate culture on the line. Everyone was watching, evaluating. Losing trust requires little effort. It's like pulling a thread. Before you know it, the whole garment unravels.

I also forced OPD, Telecom, and Data Source into existence, bringing in three top sales performers from IBM to run them. They knew the product line and the customer set, but they had never managed, and they had no launch experience. Here I thought I had brought in some heavy artillery only to find out later that I had hired a bunch of pop guns. Without my constant coaching, nothing was getting done. I had quadrupled my executive payroll, doubled my own duties, and watched our core business grind to a halt. It all went to hell very quickly.

Once again: every spin-off that you create in your company requires a launch plan and a qualified leader. And if, as I did, you have three individuals launching together with limited experience and paying little attention to costs, you've created a disaster for yourself. How do you get them to have the same vision that you do-or the same drive? This is particularly evident when it's not their company or, for that matter, their dream. I had wrongly assumed that top sales performers automatically possessed such notions, and they would behave the way I did and provide the *lift* and attention to detail required to get the business off the ground. It's not automatic. Believe me.

I made another blunder. I hired the auditing partner from our accounting firm and let Sherry go. We'll just call him Morty. Accounting firms are dangerous if you involve them directly in the strategic planning of your business. They may be close to your numbers, but that's all they're close to. They don't have insight into your culture and tempo or your talent and points of leverage. Morty's advice for me was to strengthen my management team and beef up the back office. We needed a heavyweight on the numbers and better control of our cash. So I hired him.

Taking out Sherry was a terrible mistake. True, the numbers were getting away from her, and she was choking on the new office politics, but she still knew every square inch of our operation. Morty could learn the operation in time, but that wasn't the issue. His personality was. He was a control freak with a bad temper-a number-crunching Doberman. His answer to issues was to yell about them. He had everybody yelling. The daily dose of "F words" that poured out of his office became the norm. I didn't know how to corral this guy. He was unmanageable.

One afternoon Morty invited me to his home for lunch. I went, figuring it was a chance to build some rapport. He had some great leftovers from dinner and insisted that we not waste them. He was an excellent cook and, frankly, a very charming guy when not in the office-the guy I *thought* I had hired. He asked me to grab a jar of horseradish out of the pantry, and when I opened the pantry door, I found what looked like a combination supermarket display and library. Every can, jar, bottle and box was arranged by category and in alphabetical order. I couldn't believe my eyes.

"Are you kidding me? Look at this pantry! How does your wife do this?" I asked.

"Excuse me? I don't let her touch that pantry. The horseradish is on the bottom shelf, right side, two back," he instructed. "When I get done with Computer Options, that's how we're going to look-just like my pantry."

That was the moment I knew I was in trouble. I could barely eat my lunch.

I felt the shifting of power developing. Morty challenged me on every front. He felt compelled to clean house, scrub the balance sheet, and change whatever he didn't like. His weapon was to threaten the high probability of failure unless we changed virtually everything. The other managers' veneration for his opinion became so apparent that the prospect of failure became inevitable. Feeling outnumbered, I resisted retaliation, which provided a safe harbor for Morty. I watched his confidence grow while mine continued to erode.

Pete, once an advocate, started acting very cool toward me, now worried that his coveted number-two position was being threatened by Larry. And the other three managers were clueless, parking themselves at my door like scarecrows. To avoid them, I would stare out the window pretending to be on the phone, only to see their reflections standing there, waiting for me to turn around. *For God sake, get the hell out of my office and go sell something!* I wanted to scream. My patience was shot.

Morty loved delivering bad news about everything-the numbers, the infrastructure, the whole damn business, for that matter. He was the rooster who believed the sun had risen to hear him crow. The management team was shifting their loyalty to him. Larry and Pete had become butt pals, allies of a sort, going to long lunches, and competing about who wore the most elegant suit that day. Occasionally I'd hear them in the bathroom discussing how great dinner was Saturday night only to watch them clam up when I walked in. The signs were all there. Something was up.

I was no longer leading my company. I was following. I felt like one of those cans of soup on Morty's pantry shelf getting put into my appropriate place. In the office, I looked like one of those mindless zombies from *Night of the Living Dead*, shuffling around in a dark, bewildered state. *What's happening?* was all I kept thinking.

You Must Deal with the Misfits

In retrospect, I should have picked one area to expand-the one with the highest potential for growth, lowest barrier to entry, and best alignment with our core business. That way I could have focused and maintained control, with time to hire and develop the right people-preferably from within-at a pace the company could absorb. Above all, we could have planned every detail of the launch. In other words, I should have given my ego a rest, bitten off what I could chew, and maintained good judgment, sensitivity, and leadership. But I didn't.

I learned too late how to deal with organizational misfits. No matter how carefully we recruit and screen, misfits will show up. Quick, decisive action is needed to weed them out. People in the organization always know who the misfits are, as well, and draw negative conclusions about the leader who permits them to remain. Over the years I've seen four types of misfits especially damaging to an organization:

1. Those who don't have the integrity or intellectual honesty to win trust, who don't give recognition to subordinates for ideas and accomplishments, and don't promote an open organization.

2. The "politicians," who always have their finger in the air to see which way the wind is blowing, who are more interested in making the right move than doing the right thing.

3. The "bullies," those who are cruel to their subordinates and sycophantic to their superiors. The Eddie Haskels of the business world.

4. Those who borrow their success from others or ride on someone else's coattails. Oscar Wilde summed it up best when he said, "Their thoughts are someone else's, their opinions a mimicry, their passions a quotation."

When you find these misfits, kick them out-immediately. As Harvey Mackay said, "It's not the people you fire who make your life miserable; it's the people you don't."

Mark Dover resigned one month after Sherry left. He was disappointed that I had let her go and disgusted with Larry, Pete, Morty, and the three stooges-a.k.a. the junior managers. What bothered him most was the culture shift, my tolerance for mediocrity, the sick alliances that had formed, the ass-kissing politics, and the lack of fun in the business. His exit interview was hard for me to hear.

"I loved coming to work, Mike. It was fun, and the people knew what they were doing. Most of all, I liked knowing you were in charge. I felt safe. You're not in charge anymore, Mike. You lost it when you started doubting yourself and believing in those big shots instead. When I first got here, everyone in this company identified you with an expectation of excellence. But you've lost that. Your tolerance of mediocrity has lowered the performance standard for this whole company. You told me once that there is no reward granted for effort, only for results. That you don't find effort per share posted in the annual report. What happened to the guy who said that?"

Now I was scared. I had thrown Sherry away, Mark was leaving, and my core business was collapsing. Remaining were Larry, an unproven VP running an unproven division; Pete, who had lost faith in the business and in me; Morty, a control freak who was ripping out systems as if he was weeding a garden (only now he was ripping out flowers, too); and three junior managers who couldn't lead if their lives depended on it. Everywhere I looked was trouble. My once vibrant company was in deep crisis, facing an enormous meltdown. And it had happened so fast. The only glimmer of hope was Maintenance Innovators, which, thank God, was doing well and had yet to be poisoned by the mess-until we moved everything under one roof.

That, of course, was the crowning blow: forty thousand square feet of office/warehouse with a price tag big enough to choke Godzilla. The move alone cost $50,000. Our rent tripled, and our operating expenses nearly doubled. I'll never forget the picture, forever etched in my mind, of Morty spending the first week after our move setting up the supply center and computer room. Here was my CFO, sweating through his shirt and tie, labeling and stacking boxes on shelves that he had built himself while the company was hemorrhaging cash by the minute. He had found another pantry.

"Morton, what the *hell* are you doing? I asked. "Don't you have something more important to do than this?"

"Hey, if we're gonna grow, we gotta get this stuff organized," he said, heaving a box over his head.

This was a fitting example of the dysfunction and denial that had overtaken the company. Here we were losing our ass, and Morty was slinging boxes around like a UPS driver. Talk about rearranging the deck chairs on the *Titanic*. Unbelievable!

The Skills to Grow

I lacked many of the skills required to take the business from $25 million to the next level-$50 million-let alone $100 million. The *will to grow* is altogether different from the *skill to grow*. Winning organizations are marvelous to watch because they succeed in the face of tremendous odds. It's easy to start a company, but fewer than one percent of them reach midsize-$25 million in sales-so I was right to feel good about that. But, once you reach midsize, you will encounter a whole new set of obstacles. The ultimate winners anticipate these obstacles and manage them courageously, protecting the day-to-day needs of the organization. They have both the will and the skill.

The world does not lack for entrepreneurs. Some 1.2 million corporations were launched in the year 2000 alone, up from five hundred thousand starts twenty years earlier. Nothing seems to stop them, either. In addition to corporations you'll find untold numbers of partnerships, proprietorships, and individuals launching new ventures every year-all of them potential winners.

In the meantime, though, businesses are disappearing in droves. More than three hundred thousand companies declared bankruptcy in 2000, and if you double that, you will be close to the number of companies that simply closed their doors. So, really, business in the United States means small business. The reality is that 999 out of a thousand companies remain small or fail; they either stop growing, or they hit a wall and contract. They simply don't break through. If one percent of these companies did break through and reach midsize ($25 million), the American economy would be double its current size. While conventional wisdom holds that growth is a top priority for all business, the facts say otherwise.

So why does this happen? Why don't these small companies grow or, for that matter, survive? The answer is simple: *They lack the skill to grow*. I believe small companies face five main obstacles to reaching mid-size-which is to say, $25 million:

1. *No Second Idea.* The first idea never lasts. Markets come and go, products come and go. You'd better be searching well in advance for emerging markets in the face of declining ones. If you try to

ride a product horse for too long, it will eventually collapse underneath you (for example, our Series/1 market). You need a stream of product ideas ready to address broadening markets to keep growth turned on. But pick your second idea carefully, get there early, and make sure it is properly aligned with your core business.

2. *No Marketing.* Markets need marketing. In the early stages of growth, marketing is limited to the founder's personal relationships with prior clients and community contacts. I call it the founder's circle (for example, Mamiya Camera and my Chicago clients). The founder's experience and connections provide the initial lift. This usually leads to a great start, followed by a brisk decline. The heart of your market is a long way off. If not fortified, the company drifts. You frequently see this happen with service firms, which fail to substitute the founders' personal relationships with solid marketing programs, particularly when they attempt to expand their business into new territories.

3. *Financially Unprepared.* Growth eats up working capital. The more you sell, the bigger the accounts receivable balance, and your inventory levels may double before you know it. Next, the balance sheet gets out of whack because you spent all your time watching the P&L. Now you're highly leveraged with a debt-to-equity ratio of five to one, enough to frighten even the most aggressive banker. More sales means more salespeople, which means more payroll, putting even more pressure on turning cash. Increased staff means more spending, and before you know it, you're losing money. To get it back under control, you have no choice: Contract or go broke. Growth requires financial stability, careful planning, and a solid control system with microscopic attention to detail. Without it you will run out of cash, and you will stop growing. That's if you survive.

4. *Human Frailty.* Beating the odds is hard work. Many times the founder just plain burns out, unable to either achieve or sustain the cooperative culture or personal motivation to continue the journey toward midsize. The founder can't find stout-hearted managers to help grind through the demands of the day. These are the honest, fair minded people with healthy values, and pride in

their work. Or often owners make the mistake of wanting to do it solo, either lacking trust in people or the skills required to manage them, thereby constraining the organization to the limits of their own energy and capability.

5. *Lack of a Sales Culture.* Everyone in the organization must sell in the early stages. And I don't mean just salespeople. I mean everyone, from the receptionist to the staff to the accountant to the president. Everyone! There is no place for bureaucracy. A strong sales team, well supported by a sales-minded staff, selling solid products in a growing market will win every single time. The minute you burden the early stage company with bureaucratic roadblocks, thus stifling sales, you're on your way to premature death.

Now, granted, Computer Options had made it to midsize ($26 million), and while we were far from perfect, we had gotten a few of these things right. We *sensed* how to cope with the stringent business, financial, and human requirements of a small growing company. But it was at midsize that we sputtered, unprepared for a host of new challenges. We had the will to grow, yes-but the skill to grow, no. I was headed back to the anvil. I still had much to learn.

When the Business Spits in Your Eye

After moving to the new facility, we had a temporary revival. The big shots were all feeling like big shots. They should have. The company had spent about $100,000 decorating the executive offices. The place looked successful as hell. So the illusion actually lifted everyone's spirits-for a while. Now that MII was under the same roof, Bob Erdahl, my partner, got to know the rest of the managers, attended more meetings, and even started wearing a suit to work. I guess the illusion got to him, too.

The renaissance period lasted about a month, until "Dr. Doom" presented the financials after the move. We had lost $120,000 in one month. To put that in perspective, we had to sell $3 million in product to make that up. That was almost a month's production-at least, before Mark had left. Our management meetings began lasting two and three hours. Rarely was a solution presented as we had barely enough time to understand the problems. Erdahl was getting nervous because Morty demanded that MII begin providing badly needed cash to COI.

Things continued to get worse. Morty began evaluating the residual values in our lease portfolio. He was now after a new policy to use a published resource for sizing the residuals. Residuals were the value of the equipment at the end of the lease term. Morty wanted a third party to size them using a predetermined formula. This new policy required that we adjust them down by $200,000. In other words, our books would take a $200,000 hit. He and I locked horns on this matter, causing further erosion of my credibility-not to mention the further erosion of our balance sheet, which would trigger a few negative covenants in our bank agreement. Everywhere I looked I saw trouble. I began to withdraw. Office doors were closed.

Once you begin the painful spiral toward insolvency, people panic and begin to conspire. That's what happened at Computer Options. As the spiral gained momentum, the conspirators became bolder, suggesting a stock position in the company.

"If we're going to bail this place out for you, Mike, we better have some skin in the game. Otherwise it's not worth it to us."

This was the gun being held to my head. So I gave the three VPs stock in the company. I was so frantic for help and felt the company had so little value at that point that I literally gave the stock away. I didn't even ask them to sign a noncompete agreement. My decisions became desperate. I had no one in my camp and little confidence that I could hold this company together.

Ninety days passed, and while I sensed some recovery, we were still floundering. Then the first of a series of Black Mondays began. Now begins the soap opera.

Act I-The First Black Monday

Larry Steelman asked my secretary to set an appointment with me for 9 A.M. That should have been my first warning. We never operated under such formalities. He arrived early for the meeting and wasted no time presenting his resignation letter. He told me he was sorry, he had given it his best shot, but in his opinion it was hopeless. The company would never recover.

"Hopeless?! Ridiculous! You haven't given it enough time, Larry. Besides, you got what you wanted. You got your stock. You're still getting paid. Now you choose to bail out?" I leaned forward in my chair. "What are you up to?"

"Nothing. And I really don't know what I'm going to do. I've been so busy with all this trouble that I haven't given it much thought," he said.

I knew he was lying. "Bullshit. What are you really up to?" I demanded.

He shifted in his chair. "Well, who knows Mike, maybe I'll start my own computer firm. Now that I understand the business, I think I'd be pretty good at it," he said, sounding smug. "By the way, you can either buy out my stock now, or I can just hold on to it. Just make sure you send me financials every month."

My face was burning with anger. I was ready to reach across the desk and punch out the creep. I held my composure. "So let me see if I understand this, Larry. I bring you in here, teach you everything I know about this industry, pay you a fat salary, give you a big office with a fancy title, give you a generous portion of the company's stock for free-and now you resign. In return for my generosity, or perhaps my stupidity, I get a bunch of expensive pay stubs, minimal sales production, no division, and I have the privilege of buying your stock back to help finance your new business, which will be competing directly with mine. Have I missed anything?"

He just stared at me. I had him clear out his desk and leave the building.

I don't know of any other time in my life when I felt more foolish and humiliated. So I swallowed hard on this one and headed to Pete's office to give him the news.

Act II-The Second Black Monday

Pete acted surprised, as if he couldn't believe it. He launched into a Winston Churchill-like oratory, declaring COI a great company worthy of our best effort. We would look back one day and laugh at all this, he declared.

I felt no relief from his remarks. They seemed contrived and uncharacteristic-he was trying too hard. But I needed an ally. It was the kind of need that creates denial. Little did I know that the following Monday morning he would be in my office putting on the exact same show as Larry's. The two of them had choreographed every move. I had no proof, but I knew they were in on it together. My mind immediately went to my customer records and personnel files. These guys had had access to everything. God only knows what they might have copied. One week later they announced the formation of their company and organized a telephone blitz to all of my major accounts.

Act III-The Third Black Monday

The clincher was Erdahl-the blackest of Black Mondays. He walked into my office and placed a certified check for $20,000 in front of me with a letter demanding that I turn over to him my sixty-five percent interest in MII. This one was impossible to see coming. It was almost surreal.

"What the hell is this, Bob?" I asked.

"I suggest you read our shareholder control agreement. It states quite clearly that you are not to transfer COI stock to anyone without proper notice and consent from me. You did not comply with the agreement, so in accordance with its terms, I am exercising my right to buy you out-immediately. This is a cashier's check for twenty thousand dollars. You have two days to hand over the stock certificates."

It was true. The agreement gave him the right to buy me out at the higher of book value or twenty thousand for any unauthorized stock transfers. Since it was a Sub S,meaning your income is taxed personally, we kept MII's earnings close to break-even in the early years to avoid paying unnecessary taxes, even though it was a cash cow. That's why the book value was so low. The spirit of the provision was to protect Bob and me from selling out our interest to some unrelated third party.

"You can't do this, Bob. This is stealing! You know why I gave the stock to those guys. You were in the damn meetings, for crying out loud. You went along with it. If you had a problem with it, you should have voiced it then. But no, you let me set a trap for myself. This is outrageous! We built this thing together, and you know it. Why are you doing this? Who got to you?" I demanded.

"Nobody got to me. Just hand over the stock. You have forty-eight hours," he said firmly.

I told him I would fight to the death on this one.

His strategy was to beat me in the court of public opinion by telling the employees what was going on, thus gaining their support and sympathy. The strategy was working. Being closer to the everyday operations gave him access to the minds and hearts of the people. I was the bad guy. Bob was the poor victim. He went so far as to hold an informal meeting, announcing to the managers that he was the sole owner, that all operations reported to him, and that he was waiting for me to turn over my stock. The nightmare was continuing. I couldn't believe what was happening. I was close to losing everything. I was so overwhelmed that I couldn't mount a defense.

Arriving at work in the morning was like entering a prison. I had told Dawn, "I wish I could hand in my resignation-but to whom?" I walked the corridors and counted the hoards of empty sales offices, each one a reminder of the $2 million in sales that I would never see. And I'll never forget the contempt on the faces of the MII employees or how they snickered as I walked by. I found out much later that at one point my secretary-who had aided the conspirators-kept a sign with an arrow on her desk. Green, I was in a good mood; red, don't go near me. And the VPs actually suggested that I stay out of the staff meetings. "You need to stay presidential, Mike. We'll handle things." Then they would use the meetings to spin their nasty webs. It was torture, the worse kind of emotional pain a person can feel.

You are no doubt asking yourself, "Where were your lawyers through all this, Mike? Or, for that matter, which orifice did you have your head in?" You're right to ask. The fact is the lawyers tried to head me off from trouble on several occasions, but I was forceful, telling them to follow my lead. Lawyers are just lawyers. They're not businesspeople. Their job is to protect you and deliver what you ask for. If they smell a rat, they will tell you so, but the decision still remains your call. They saw me put a rope around my own neck. But I was so lost that *I* couldn't see it.

So here was our current condition: Three executives and recent stockholders had left the firm, two with commission checks, one with a settlement check, and all three with thirty thousand dollars for their stock. Two of them had set up a competitive operation, begun aggressively recruiting my people, and mass mailed my customers. Several salesmen and staff members, including my personal secretary of five years, had gone to work for them-over thirty years of combined experience. I had lost my top salesman, Mark Waldrep, who had been producing $4 million a year. I was being sued by my so-called partner for my sixty-five percent holdings in MII-a company that easily had a market value of several million. I was stuck with forty thousand square feet of near-empty office/warehouse space, the company was losing forty thousand dollars per month, the Series/1 market was all but dead, the bank had called in our note, and my best customers were now phoning me, asking, "What the hell's going on over there?"

I think it was around this time that Dawn's younger brother, Dave drove by the house late one night as he always did on his way home from work. He took his usual routine glance at our house to see if we were still up and noticed that the dining-room light was on, which was rarely the case. As Dave tells it, he slowed his car when he saw me in an unfamiliar pose at the dining-room table: head down, palms pressed against my eyes, sitting before a blizzard of papers and an open brief-case. He described my posture as one of utter despair. He saw Dawn sitting across the table, her hands over her face. "I remember that night," he told me months later. "I was really troubled by it. I almost stopped."

Dawn remembers that night vividly; more so than I do. But I remember it being our lowest point. Dave was our witness. I was ready to give up.

At the same time I had reached one of those crossroads where you're left with few choices. I had been in terrible situations before, but hard work and perseverance bailed me out. I suppose it was ridiculous to think that I could work my way out of this mess, given its severity, but I could hear that voice again in the back of my mind: *You can worry, or you can work. Which is it gonna be, Kerrison?* It's a question I've always known the answer to. It's a voice that never goes away.

Owning a business means continuing to work your ass off even when your company spits in your eye. It might mean starting over from scratch-worse, you may have to dig yourself out first. In any case, you can never give up because eventually you will rediscover your old toolkit, the one you haven't seen in a while. And you'll begin reaching for those old rusty tools that helped you build the company in the first place. You will pick them up, look them over, and say, "I remember you. Where have you been?"

I found no inspiration that night at the dining room table. I felt inept, as though I had never been in charge of anything before. All my old tricks seemed to have deserted me. The only thing remaining was a stubborn determination to keep going and the hope that somehow things would get better.

Just when I thought things couldn't get any worse, they did. Alex finally passed away after a sixteen-month battle with cancer. I never felt so raw inside, so overwhelmed by heaps of bad news. I could see no end to it. Adversity had returned with a (literal) death grip. For years it had tested my strength and my character. In the past, I had always bounced back, becoming even stronger. Having been on prosperity's path for a while, I had also learned to respect the anvil and what it could teach me. But this time I felt different. My whole nature was so inflicted with grief and humiliation that I lost my resolve to fight. The adversity no longer fed an intense ambition.

It was over.

Chapter 12

The Turning Point

Dawn and I got back from Alex's funeral on Saturday night after a grueling three days. Reuniting with our kids brought us relief. On Sunday morning we were back at the kitchen table on in our bathrobes and messy hair. Exhausted and depressed, we sat slugging coffee. We never went to church. I was opening mail and popping Cheerios into Madelyn's mouth-our third child had arrived-while the two older kids were working on coloring projects and fighting over the crayons. Dawn was wiping counters and loading the dishwasher. Everything seemed familiar; it was another routine start.

I came across an envelope from Polly and Kenny Holly. They were friends of ours, not close at the time, but Dawn and I admired them. They seemed to have their act together. We sensed something different about them.

"Good grief, another invitation," I said. "I'm surprised we're still on the list. We've missed the last three parties." I opened the envelope with a vague curiosity and pulled out the card. This was not your normal invitation. It read in bold print:

- *Why do bad things happen to good people?*
- *Is there really a God, or is he nothing more than a psychological crutch?*
- *Is the Bible true, or is it just a bunch of interesting stories?*
- *When I die, is it over, or will I go somewhere else?*

The timing was amazing. Here I was wondering, *What's it all about, Alfie?* and this showed up. At that point, my spiritual life was completely bankrupt. I had thrown in the towel on God. I was your typical Catholic who had fallen away from the church after surviving twelve years of a Vatican-driven education, and after the hammering I had just taken in my business, followed by the inexplicable loss of Alex, I was feeling extremely pissed off at our Supreme Being. *Enough is enough-will you just lay off? Go find somebody else to pound on. I'm sick of you-and your anvil.* Nonetheless, I needed answers to these questions, and I needed them now. We returned the RSVP.

Dawn and I attended a series of discussions held on four consecutive Monday nights, sponsored by Search, a nondenominational Christian ministry. Seventy people attended from every religion you can think of-Hindus, Muslims, Jews, Christians, an assortment of agnostics, and even a couple of atheists. It was fascinating. The discussions were designed to allow an open and free exchange of spiritual beliefs-or disbeliefs. All perspectives were welcome. The only thing that Search asked for was the privilege of sharing the Christian perspective. I loved the intellectual stimulation it provided, and I respected Search for not cramming Christianity down my throat. Each discussion lasted fifty-nine minutes and fifty-nine seconds, starting at 7 P.M. sharp. That was the rule. When the timer signaled the end of the session, people groaned. We were cut off mid-sentence. "Sorry, we'll have to pick up that thought next week," they'd say. The place cleared out at midnight. No one wanted to leave. Each person was searching. Everyone was looking for answers.

Dawn and I joined a Bible study group, made up of seven couples, which was spun off the main group. We originally intended to meet for six weeks to look deeper into the scriptures and make an informed decision about our own beliefs. The group met every Monday night for three straight years. And you didn't miss. Business trips would have to wait until Tuesday. If you were sick, you sat in the back-but you were there. It was one of the most challenging and rewarding experiences Dawn and I had ever had. We found the answers we were looking for, and we found new friends. Somewhere during that three-year period it became clear to me that without a savior, we would all most surely perish.

I had always known who Jesus was-I had been raised Catholic. But until then I had never really made a commitment to follow Him. When I did, the decision changed my life. I'm not suggesting life is perfect now, and God knows I'm sure not. We live in an evil world. The terrible events of September 11 have proven beyond a shadow of a doubt that the serpent sits patiently ready to strike at any time. Why do bad things happen to good people? It's a fair question. The fact is, we live in a fallen world, and we have no way of escaping it. We sit in the comfort of our family rooms gaping at CNN and Fox News, horrified and hurt, looking for answers: *Why? . . . Why?* I try not to ask these questions anymore. I just look to the Redeemer, for I surely can't save myself. The demons are still around, always trying to dig their dreadful talons into my head. But they don't get very far anymore. The Lord fights them off for me. All I have to do is ask him for help. He never lets me down.

I've been warned by friends to stay away from this subject. "Mike, this is a book about business. The two don't mix. As soon as the 'J' word shows up, editors will go nuts. It's the first thing they'll cut," they say. That's fine, I suppose. In fact, I even understand it. But you have to understand something, too. It was Jesus who saved my business-though He had to start with me. Those rusty old tools that I told you about had been put there by Him. And now He's given me a bunch of shiny new ones to use. Yes, this is a business book. But like it or not, Jesus Christ is my new chairman of the board. He calls the shots now.

Just Another Monday

On a Monday morning in the spring of 1987, another miracle happened. This wasn't just some amazing coincidence. This was a real live miracle.

I was on the phone with a client when Lori, my new secretary, appeared at my office door. She had a strange look on her face. (I was so gun shy by then that every time somebody stood at my door, I figured it usually meant more bad news.) Lori's impatience was evident-she wanted me off that phone-so I wrapped up my conversation, took a deep breath, and braced myself for what was about to come. After all, it was a Monday.

"Gosh, Lori, where's the fire?" I asked.

"I'm sorry, Mike, but I thought you should see this right away," she said, handing me a small stack of papers.

"What is it?"

"It looks like Larry Steelman's legal bill. I was just opening the mail, and there it was."

I snatched the pages and began devouring the print.

"Oh, my God! I don't believe it. I absolutely don't believe it," I said.

"What? . . . What is it?" Lori asked.

"Lori, give me a minute, I need to look at this carefully. And hold my calls, will you, please?"

She stepped out and closed my door.

I felt that disconcerting rush of adrenalin when your nervous system starts firing all over the place. My heart raced. I got up from my chair and walked to the window to calm down for a second. After regaining my composure, I slipped back into my chair and picked up the papers again. Clutched in my hand was a lawyer's bill that detailed every single move that Larry Steelman, Pete Jackson, and Bob Erdahl had made over the last four months-a plot to tank COI, steal MII, and go into business for themselves. I had facts, dates, details, and the names of those who attended the meetings. I had known that this coup d'état had been happening right under my nose, but I'd had no proof. Until now.

The legal bill had obviously been sent to our office by mistake. I suppose the notorious trio had left so many different business cards behind at their various meetings that the law firm's billing department got confused. I was convinced it was the hand of God reaching right down and placing that bill on my desk. This was my vindication, my deliverance. I could now begin to fight, to reclaim what had been taken from me. I could feel my spirit filling back up with resolve and determination. I called Dawn to give her the news.

Being a fighter like me, she had one simple message: "Go get those bastards!"

Before calling my law firm, I called theirs. I knew from my own experience that legal bills were prepared from lawyers' notes, which are archived to provide full and accurate documentation to support the bill. I already had enough evidence with the bill alone, but I wanted the notes. I felt my back start to tighten. Lumbar four and five, I think. That's the hunch area. I had a hunch that if I requested the notes-which is not uncommon-and if I remained anonymous, not really stating my name, the law firm would make the same mistake twice.

"Where do you want me to send them?" the clerk asked.

"To the same address as before. Actually, why don't you just courier them over," I said nonchalantly.

One hour later I was holding the lawyer's notes-a stack of the most incriminating evidence I had ever seen. My three execs, with the guidance of their lawyer, had been plotting for months.

As I read through the bill, I began cross-checking the dates of their meetings against their alibis. The deception ran so deep that it made me ill. All of those lies! Why would they want to do this to me? Once you find out the truth about something like this, the relief wears off quickly. Seeking justice gets you only so far.

My own lawyer was flabbergasted. "I don't think I've ever seen this happen in my twenty-five years in practice," he said. "But you need to decide what you want from this, Mike. You need to be wise. Let's not make any moves until we have a plan. In the meantime, send me the notes. If they're in my file, we won't have to give them back."

Above all, I wanted to unpoison the well. I was sick of feeling like an unwelcome guest in my own company. But I'd have to remain patient, letting things play out in due course. Grandstanding my innocence would look foolish and weak.

I went after Bob Erdahl first. Indicating that I wanted to settle our lawsuit for the good of MII, I scheduled a lunch for the two of us at Edina Country Club. He arrived late, armed with arrogance, clearly determined to prevail on what he figured would be a cakewalk negotiation. He entered the pub, sauntered over to the table, and sat down. I greeted him warmly.

"Bob, thanks for coming. Listen, before we order lunch I'd like you to do something for me," I said.

"Yeah, what's that?"

"Pull out your Day-Timer."

He looked confused. "What for?"

"You'll see . . . just pull it out."

He reached into his briefcase and placed the appointment book on the table. He seemed nervous.

"Bob, where were you on June ninth at three in the afternoon?" I asked.

"June ninth . . . Why do you want to know that?"

"Please. Just look." I pointed at the Day-Timer.

His eyes narrowed with suspicion. Reluctantly, he brushed through the pages in search of June ninth. Finding it, he squinted for the answer. I saw a hint of recoil in his gaze. His face was now reddening.

"Well?" I insisted.

"That's none of your business," he snapped, slamming the Day-Timer shut.

"Oh, I think it is." I tried not to smile. I fired another question. "Who did you have breakfast with on June twentieth? I asked.

He broke his stare and began turning the pages, now curious himself about what I knew. Looking derailed, he slowly closed the Day-Timer and folded his hands.

"What's going on here, Mike?" he asked.

"That's funny. I was about to ask you the same question," I replied.

"Look . . . since I'm such a nice guy, let me make this easy for you, Bob." I proceeded to recite chapter and verse every date, time, place, and purpose for every meeting he had attended with Steelman and Jackson for the last four months.

He was visibly shaken. "How do you know all this?"

"That's not important right now. What *is* important is that you understand the fix you're in. Does the term *fiduciary responsibility* mean anything to you?"

We both knew it was a rhetorical question.

"What do you intend to do?" he asked.

"I intend to buy your minority position in MII immediately. I'll give you a fair price and even have you run it for me on a consulting contract until I can replace you. And, of course, I expect you to drop your ridiculous lawsuit and start behaving like a gentleman." I hated the thought of having him around, but at that point I still needed him. "We'll announce all of this later, when I'm ready."

"And if I don't agree to this?" Bob asked.

"My lawyer has already prepared the case. If you're smart, you'll take what you can get." I pulled an envelope from my vest pocket and slid it across the table. "Here's my price. We can sign mutual releases, and you'll be able to walk away from all of this. Otherwise . . . I'm going to fry your ass. You make the choice, Bob. Any questions?"

He glared at me. "No. It looks like *you* have all the answers."

"No, Bob, I don't have all the answers. But I *do* hold all the cards. I expect to hear from you by five o'clock today. Enjoy your lunch." I threw ten dollars on the table and walked out.

Erdahl accepted my offer. I bought him out four days later.

I then immediately filed lawsuits against Larry Steelman and Pete Jackson in Hennepin County. They filed a counterclaim, which I expected. The case never went to trial. My first impulse was to strike out, to hurt them in some way. I was furious. I also wanted to stop the decampment of our people, many of whom had left to work for them. But no matter how strongly you feel about your position, no matter how justified, lawsuits don't work. They are a temporary solution at best.

Two weeks went by and I called a mandatory meeting for all MII employees. Bob Erdahl was present, sitting dutifully in the front row. The mood was edgy, and the employees seemed hostile and insecure. You could cut the tension with a knife. I entered the room and took my position at the front. I was scared. I was the enemy. But it was time to have my say.

"Not long ago I bought out Bob Erdahl's stock in MII. I am now the sole owner, chairman, and CEO of the firm. Bob and I have worked out our difficulties, which you have no doubt been affected by. For that we are both sorry. Bob will remain with the firm as a consultant in his normal duties until we can find a suitable replacement. I know many of you aren't happy with this news. And knowing what I now know, I can certainly understand why. Many of you don't know me very well. Most of you have misjudged me. That's okay. It doesn't matter. What does matter is we have a good company here. And it can get better. So I'm offering you a chance to choose. If you want to stay with the firm, great. You are welcome. If not, I want you out of here today. Simply drop off your resignation letter, and I'll give you a check for two weeks' pay, no questions asked. To those of you who choose to stay, I'm grateful. Should you prefer to leave, I wish you luck. Now, let's go do our jobs."

I was petrified. I thought the whole place might get up and walk out. Out of fifty employees only two quit.

Stop the Bleeding First

I wasn't out of the woods yet. Far from it, in fact. MII was chugging along robustly, but COI was still hemorrhaging, and we owed the bank over $2 million. I was now selling full time, and our little ragtag remnant of what was once an *Inc.* 500 company was doing all it could. I tried to remain positive so that our people wouldn't lose hope. But we were near the end, and I needed to do something fast. With personal guarantees at the bank, I was in trouble. I could lose my house.

Though fearing that Sherry was still sore at me for hiring Morty to replace her, I asked her to come back. I knew she could find a million ways to cut costs and help stabilize the company-plus with her help I could keep selling, just like the old days. I was pleasantly surprised when she returned. Sherry loved a challenge, and having been there at the beginning, she still felt sentimental and protective toward COI. She, Joel (our controller), and I dug in to save the company.

When you're bleeding cash, it's hard to think straight. Don't wait for things to get better. They won't. You must take drastic action. Your business must behave like a trauma center. We holed up in the conference room and examined every single line item of the P&L and balance sheet. We worked around the clock for a week. Rather than selectively choosing what costs to cut, we took the opposite approach: We cut everything and started from zero, adding back only what we needed to run the business. Of course, that's easier said than done, but it creates a mindset-no sacred cows.

When we finished adding back what we needed, it became crystal clear what had to be cut or renegotiated-I was astonished at the pile of wasted dollars that we had been living with.

(By the way, this is a sound exercise for healthy companies, too. You won't get everything cut and renegotiated, but you'll get close. Vendors and lenders want you to survive. That's the only way they get paid. As I learned long ago, you can find tremendous strength in weakness-you just have to find the angle. And you've got to have guts.)

Here's a partial list of what we did: All managers took twenty percent pay cuts for six months (I took a thirty percent cut). They could make it all back, plus more, through special incentives. We lowered sales salaries by twenty percent and doubled the commission rate for six months. Capital expenditures were eliminated for four months, and we renegotiated our long-distance telephone contract, equipment leases, and rental contracts. We eliminated air travel for three months and did purchase leasebacks on our computer equipment to generate cash. We sold unnecessary office equipment and our warehouse forklift. We cut our janitorial service in half. We stopped FedEx and Roadrunner services except for sales contracts. We liquidated slow-moving inventory through wholesale blowouts and offered customers five percent discounts on sales if they paid in advance. We cut office supplies by fifty percent and paid special bonuses to collect old receivables. We increased customer deposits from twenty to fifty percent (no one complained). And by the grace of God we got out of our five-year lease on the forty thousand square feet for a $100,000 penalty. Our new space-less than half the size-from the same landlord saved us $14,000 each month, plus they agreed to finance our moving costs and the penalty.

Two key meetings were needed: one to rally the support of our people and one with the bank. Both meetings were successful. We now had a chance. The bank thought we should cut additional people, asking us to find alternatives for getting the work done. I decided against that for fear of political suicide. These were the people who had remained loyal. "If we're going down, we're going down together," I said. The bank respected my position and dropped the issue.

We found a few more things to cut and picked up another $5,000 a month. The project wasn't perfect, and we did sacrifice much, but we were able to lower our overhead by $40,000 per month. I tried to sell my way out of the remaining losses, and for three months managed to close some of the gap, but I was exhausted and couldn't keep up the pace. We were running on fumes. Something had to happen . . . something! And it did.

The bank called our note. We had ninety days to pay them back.

Avoid Lawsuits

I share all these gritty details with you not from a place of vengeance or some kind of delayed self-pity but to show you what can happen to a perfectly good business. I take no pride in, and I sure as hell don't boast about, the outcome of this fiasco, for in the end everybody suffered. Often the thorns that prick us are from trees that we planted ourselves.

If you sat down with the other side, I have no doubt you'd get a completely different story. Of course you would. You'll always find two sides. Unfortunately, we rarely look at the other side because it may reveal something about ourselves that we don't want to see. We would rather hold on to our anger and remain righteous in our desire to seek justice-to see the other guy suffer. I say to you: Let it go. I wish I had. If you find yourself in similar circumstances, approach it head-on. Get to the negotiating table early. Don't let your pride get in the way, and don't let the situation erode to the point where once sensible, rational people turn to hate and bitterness as their only way of communicating.

Larry Steelman, Pete Jackson, and Bob Erdahl have gone on with their lives, and I would imagine they've been successful. They were talented people. They, too, have learned from this experience. I don't know for sure what was behind their actions. I'm sure in some crazy way they believed they were justified. But that's no longer the point.

By the time the lawsuit had reached its pinnacle frenzy, none of us felt good anymore. You'll find no winners in business lawsuits-except the lawyers, of course. Perhaps they prevent losing, but you don't win, even when you do. And you pay lawyers a ton of money only to find out what the worst of man looks like. So my message is this: Avoid lawsuits. The best ways I know to avoid them are by hiring the right people, moving fast against the wrong ones, being honest and brave, remaining secure in your role as a leader, and, finally, having a heart for fairness. With these attributes you can resolve almost any dispute.

But when all else fails, keep the lawyer handy, and hope for a miracle.

Eating Our Bread in Gladness

This painful experience revealed everything that I needed to change to become a better leader-and a better person. Self-examination comes first. Ask yourself: What things must I change to prevent something like this from happening again in my business? When you ask yourself this question you stop behaving like a victim, and you let go of the things you can't control.

When I first started my business, I was consumed by the Dream. The Dream was the vision of my youth, planted there by the events and people in my life. My Dream was that I would someday be truly special, my name would be famous, my work would be recognized, my marriage would be perfect, and my children would be exemplary. When this didn't happen I felt like a failure, especially in my marriage.

I learned that I would never be happy until I stopped measuring my real-life achievements against the Dream. I would never be comfortable with who I am until I realized that who I am is special enough. You see, if we have succeeded in becoming authentically human, "eating our bread in gladness," and enjoying our businesses and our families that we love, then we don't have to be rich and famous. Being fully human is a much more impressive accomplishment.

In *Seasons of a Man's Life*, Dr. Daniel Levinson sees middle-aged adulthood (which is where I was in 1987) as offering the opportunity to renounce the "tyranny of the Dream" and become successful on more realistic terms. And doing business in the greedy eighties was anything but realistic. Levinson writes, "When a man no longer feels he must be remarkable, he is [freer] to be himself and work according to his own wishes and talents. His principles, not his bank account, become his guide."

The events of 1987 marked the turning point for me as a business owner and as a person. Sometimes in life we have to become less to become more. We become whole people not on the basis of what we accumulate but by getting rid of everything that is not us, everything false and inauthentic. This self-purging also purges our business. We get rid of everything that is not the business-yes, everything false and inauthentic. Now we have a chance to rebuild our business, this time on a profound set of beliefs and principles and faithful adherence to those beliefs and principles.

That's how I went forward: with an organization prepared to change everything if need be-except those beliefs.

Sometimes to become whole, to start over, we have to give up the Dream. And the irony is *that is how the Dream comes true*. With this realization, another miracle occurred. Sorbus, the largest third-party maintenance company in the world, called me.

Chapter 13

Saved by Sorbus

The call from Sorbus in the summer of 1987, expressing interest in buying MII, came out of the blue. We had just moved into our new space, and things had begun to settle down some. I had been spending time at the bank, reviewing our recovery plan and trying to buy time. Now, with Sorbus in the picture, the bank was more than willing to give us an extension on the note.

Most industries eventually consolidate. Big companies swallow up little ones. Two of the largest computer maintenance companies in the world-Sorbus and Decision Data-were competing for market share, buying up every small, successful, third-party maintenance firm they could find. We were on the list. Here's how it happened.

It was late August and I was staying at the Doubletree Hotel in Minneapolis, giving a keynote address for one of MII's seminars. I remember the day vividly. The air-conditioning had failed, and I had sixty prospects melting in their folding chairs. But it played in our favor. They wanted to get in, sign up, and get out. We took on a dozen new clients that day. While I was performing my dog-and-pony show, I suddenly noticed Sherry at the back of the room, frantically trying to get my attention. I wrapped up my pitch, turned the seminar over to our team, and slipped into the hall to find Sherry.

"Sherry, what are you doing here? Is everything all right?" I asked, worried.

"Man, it must be a hundred degrees in here," she complained. Then she got to her reason for being there. "Look, some guy from Sorbus called, looking for you. You weren't around, so I talked to him for a while. They want to buy MII!"

"You're kidding me! He told you that?!"

We headed for the door to get some air.

"In so many words . . . yeah," she replied. Sherry lit a cigarette and took a deep drag. She was shaking.

"So how'd you leave it with him?" I asked.

"I told him I'd find you and have you call as soon as possible." She handed me his name and number. "I'm telling you, this guy was serious."

I rushed to a pay phone to call him-but he had already left for the day, and his secretary said he was gone for a one-week vacation. I was so frustrated I could have eaten the phone. I left a message for him to call me when he returned.

Two days passed. I got the call.

"Mike, this is Jim Barnes from Sorbus. How are you?" he asked.

"Jim! I didn't expect to hear from you. I thought you were on vacation."

"I am, as a matter of fact. I'm in Canada on a family fishing trip. I don't have much time, Mike, but I really wanted to talk to you. Mike, I'm the executive vice president for Sorbus in King of Prussia, Pennsylvania. I do all the mergers and acquisitions for the firm. It's come to our attention that you have a successful small maintenance company serving the IBM midrange market."

"Yes, I do. It's been quite successful," I played it cool.

"This might be a little sudden, but let me get right to the point. Would you be interested in selling your company?" he asked.

"Gosh, Jim, I've never given it much thought, but I guess everything is for sale, isn't it?" I was trying to act coy while my stomach was doing cartwheels. This could be my way out!

We spent time talking about MII, how it got started, our philosophy, and our plans. He was interested in our potential for growth and availability of good people. I shared with him our seminar strategy, which generated ten to fifteen new clients a month. Then I figured I'd better keep my mouth shut until we had a nondisclosure agreement in place. He asked if he could come take a closer look. We set a date two weeks out.

He loved what he saw-so much that he suggested we bypass a letter of intent and go right to a purchase agreement. My advisers felt that I should get another bid and make the situation competitive, so I called Decision Data and found them highly interested. They made it clear that they had beat out Sorbus on the last two acquisitions and urged me not to accept any offer until I heard from them. Turns out, these two giants were fighting each other in the streets to buy up small companies. My timing was perfect.

When a market consolidates, it's important that you pay attention. If you aren't watching closely, you could miss it. Every industry life cycle has an optimal stage for selling a business. The big companies are looking for gangly teenagers like MII. We were the perfect consolidation target: a bite-sized company that a buyer could digest and fit to its own culture and business model.

The biggest surprise to me was the number of maintenance companies across the country that I had never heard of before. Eight of them had already been bought by these two organizations. When you reach the peak of consolidation, you can demand a price of up to twice your company's revenue. The old formula using a multiple of earnings goes out the window. The big boys want market share, and they'll pay a premium to get it. If your company is the right size, and you match up well, you can really score.

I learned that markets emerge, grow, mature, consolidate, and eventually decline. Sorbus bought MII right before the decline. Four months after the sale, IBM reduced their maintenance prices by thirty percent. We would have been out of business. So the lesson is: Entrepreneurial companies must live in a constant cycle of innovation. Don't fight this instinct in search of some imagined stability. It doesn't exist. You must stay alert, focused, and always prepared to launch the next idea. But stay close to your core, and keep your eye on the market. It's easy to get into a hot market. The trick is knowing when to get out.

Another Chance

Sorbus was the high bidder, and we entered into an agreement in late November 1987. The due-diligence process, which was to begin immediately, would be tricky. How was I going to allow them to research every square inch of MII without any of my employees knowing about it? I set up a covert operation in the back corner of COI, using two empty sales offices. My alibi was that the people were there for an audit, which was true enough but also appropriately vague. Poor Sherry and Lori hauled boxes of contracts and reports into these little offices, where we had stuffed the four auditors from Sorbus. I gave them one week to finish their work (they had wanted two), and they were not to talk to anyone but Sherry and me. We took the upper hand, which seemed to play well for us.

Selling MII was strange for me, a clear-cut case of love-hate. Here was a company growing and generating loads of cash for which I felt nothing but contempt. So much damage had been done to my ability to lead it that even though the company was succeeding, I experienced no joy. I guess it went back to a need to purge. This was just one more step.

We had another successful seminar and signed up fifteen new clients. This added another $200,000 to our sale price. We were now holding the seminars in hotel banquet rooms, packing in as many as sixty companies at a time. Sorbus was impressed. I remember Sherry asking if I was sure that I wanted to sell the company, to which I had replied, "I'm not going to look back."

Besides, my new zeal was for the IBM Value-Added Remarketing Program, or VAR. For the first time ever, IBM was using "business partners" to sell their products. I wanted us in the program, which would be tricky since we sold used equipment head to head against IBM. But I had an old friend who headed up a company in Chicago called Datacomp; he had figured out how to get around this problem and became IBM's largest VAR. Datacomp had gone public a year earlier, growing from $35 million in sales to over $150 million in three years. For weeks I studied their annual report and 10K, which spurred me to work harder, aim higher. I was swept away by the sheer velocity of growth they had achieved-and they were operating in my own backyard and in the same market. I was convinced we needed to get into this. MII would be the launch pad.

I told the Sorbus team that we had to get this thing closed before year's end to take advantage of the Tax Reform Act. Their response was that the board of directors at Sorbus would not be meeting until early January, making a December close impossible.

"Mike, there's just no way. It takes sixty days alone to get the final contracts out of legal," Jim Barnes said. "Christmas will slow us down, too. Besides, we have to organize a transition team and prepare all the employee packets. We want this to be professional. We can't just throw it together."

"Look, Jim, I don't want to appear unreasonable, but we either get this done in December, or I'll have to take a pass." I was playing hardball, knowing that he knew Decision Data was waiting in the wings. Jim promised best efforts. The race to the finish line began.

On December 11, I received twenty-five percent of the sale price along with the signed contracts. The closing was set for December 19, which coincidentally was the same day as our company Christmas party. I was in Pennsylvania collecting the final balance and turning over the final documents while Sherry and Dawn were hosting the party until I arrived.

Earlier that day I had called Dawn to inform her that the closing had been delayed and she would have to fill in for me at the party.

"Dawn, you have to go," I had insisted. "It will look suspicious if we're both missing. Everybody will be asking questions about where I am."

"C'mon, Mike, what am I supposed to say? You want me to plaster a stupid smile on my face and go around saying Merry Christmas, congratulations on a great year, oh, by the way, my husband just sold your ass? I mean c'mon. I can't do this," she protested.

Neither of us spoke. I had learned a long time ago that when you're closing the deal the next person who talks, loses. I waited.

"All right, all right, I'll do it. You owe me, buster," she finally said.

Thank God for Dawn. She had suffered through all this, too.

My flight was late, and I hadn't been able to reach my two cohosts to let them know that the deal was done and the balance had been wired to our account. I scrambled out of the airport and headed downtown to the party.

I arrived at about 10 P.M. and began searching the room for Dawn and Sherry. The COI people were on one side of the room, festive but reserved, while across the room Bob Erdahl and the MII folks were raucously indulging in the holiday spirits. *Wow, this was a good decision,* I thought. *They can't even be in the same room together.* I was MII's Benedict Arnold, harboring a secret that would change their careers; I felt a strange, twisted satisfaction from the whole thing.

Dawn and Sherry were huddled in the corner, avoiding everyone as best they could. They spotted me standing in the middle of the dance floor with a big smile on my face. Dawn was clearly relieved to see me, her face pensive but open and imploring. I gave her a big thumbs-up and watched her anxious countenance soften into a broad smile. She could finally relax. We were out of the woods.

Dawn and Sherry had apparently put on a great act. No one suspected a thing. Merry Christmas to all.

We shook a few hands, after which Dawn, Sherry, and I left to go meet Gary for dessert and coffee. We reminisced and laughed about Andrew Stone and everything we had been through over the years plus all the things we had learned about people and money and leadership and stress. We were so relieved, so grateful for another chance to get it right.

Sorbus sent their best team to do the transition. I called an emergency meeting of all my employees for Monday night at five. There I was again, standing at the front of the room in the same spot where I had stood five months earlier. I marveled that we had kept this undetected. We had no leaks. I made the announcement in less than three minutes, at which time I introduced the Sorbus team and turned the meeting over to them. I left the room, having completed my last official duty for Maintenance Innovators.

I felt clean again-fully renewed, restored, and humbled. My little company had brought in a significant windfall. We were able to restore the COI balance sheet, triple our stockholders' equity, and pay off the bank. For the first time *ever* we were able to operate on our own cash flow.

Bob Erdahl approached me after the meeting while I was getting a drink of water.

"So you sold it, huh?" he asked.

I finished drinking before answering. "Yep." I stood there staring at him. I knew he was dying to ask the question. He could only guess what his thirty-five percent would have been worth.

"So what did you get for it?" he finally asked.

I hesitated for a moment. "A lot more than $20,000, my friend. A lot more than $20,000."

Chapter 14

Tubby's Tutorial

Chicago in springtime is electric. Movement and energy are everywhere. Finally out of their winter habitat, people spring into life, ready to take on the world. I was filled with anticipation and hope as I stepped onto the windy sidewalk, primed to add a spark of my own. I paid the driver and headed for Tubby Owens's office at the top of One Financial Place.

Tom (Tubby) Owens was the CEO of Datacomp, the leading computer broker that I mentioned in the previous chapter and one of COI's biggest competitors. His nickname derived from his corpulence-he weighed in at about three hundred pounds. I admired Tubby and his company, and now that they were public I was able to track them closely. He and I had been friends since my IBM days, though Tubby had started a couple of years before I did. He grew his business to $35 million in the first seven years, went public, and was now approaching $150 million three years later. I was determined to know his secret. He had accomplished something I hadn't: He had broken through midsize. To my delight, he had agreed to see me.

One Financial Place is a shimmering gold construction stretching heavenward, competing for space at the top of Chicago's skyline. It is a magnificent building. The revolving door spit me into the marble lobby, where I was immediately struck by the aroma of fresh coffee and pastries. A Dow Jones ticker was sprawled across the back wall, watched by a few anxious souls who had just arrived on the 8:15 train. Businessmen perched on wooden thrones thrashed newspapers while getting their weekly shoeshine. Shops were bursting with frenetic patrons picking up incidentals on their way to the office, and the restaurant windows displayed the theatrical pantomimes of business meetings. I could see and smell the commerce. It was exciting just being there.

I entered the elevator and felt a swift pull up to the fifty-seventh floor. The doors opened into Datacomp's lobby, which I found to be a reflection of Tubby's personality: understated but confident. The lobby was tastefully appointed with comfortable seating, a coffee center with snacks, work surfaces, and private telephone booths. Every detail had been thought through with the visitor's comfort in mind. I was impressed.

Almost immediately Tubby strolled casually into the lobby from the center hallway. No escort for him-another classy touch. And he was on time. *This isn't the way Redfield did things at Itel,* I thought. I walked over to greet him as he approached.

His demeanor was jolly, as always. And as usual he lit his pipe mid-sentence, leaving words and smoke streaming behind him. Seeing me, he quickened his gait, extended his thick, fleshy hand, and said, "Michael, you made it. Sit down . . . sit down. I'll get us some coffee." He approached the receptionist, politely placed his order, and turned to me, saying, "You take yours black as I recall, right, Mike?"

I nodded, impressed again.

He sat down next to me. We chitchatted for a minute, exchanged family stories, tossed wallet pictures back and forth, and sipped coffee. He asked me about Alex and, with concern in his eyes, listened patiently as I told him the whole story. I felt right at home.

"Mike, I'm glad you're here. C'mon, let me show you around," he said, leading me from the lobby.

We strolled through the different departments, and I met a few members of his management team. Tubby took time to explain the functions of each department and how they had evolved. Most impressive was the sales bullpen, which was broken into work centers-small clusters of five or six reps to one administrator, with an equipment center in the middle. Its simplicity was brilliant.

Finally we reached his office, a bright, spacious setting with a classic look-a large oak desk with a blue leather high-backed chair, plus matching oak credenza and conference table. The walls were filled with family pictures, business mementos, and an array of his IBM Hundred Percent Club plaques-all evidence that Tubby had been at this game for a long time. We began our discussion.

"I gather from our phone conversation last week that you've been to hell and back with all the business problems and Alex dying in the middle of it all. What a nightmare," he said.

"It was no picnic, Tom, believe me. I didn't know whether to spit or wind my watch," I said. "Things are better now, though. We're flush with cash, thanks to the MII deal, and while there aren't many of us left, the ones who stayed are terrific. I think we can get it back."

"Hell, yes, you can get it back." Tubby tapped his pipe on the ashtray. "We just gotta figure out how."

"Exactly. And I think the VAR channel"-IBM's new method of product distribution that was an unprecedented marketing move on their part-"is the way to go for us. We're perfectly positioned for it. I think it's a winner. Look at the success you've had," I said.

"Yeah, it's been terrific, but you've got to be careful, Mike," he said, shaking a warning finger. "IBM can change the rules on you in a heartbeat, and if you're too dependent on them, you'll find your ass in a sling."

He proceeded to stress the importance of new business development, finding ways to diversify, and minimizing vulnerability in the event a supplier pulls the plug. It was a comprehensive review for lessons I had already learned.

I sighed and shook my head. "Tom, my biggest problem has been growth. Every time I sneak past that twenty-five million mark, I hit a wall. It all falls apart. I just don't get it. What am I missing?" I asked.

Tubby obviously sensed my frustration. "Hmm . . . I'm not sure. But I'm convinced that it all starts with people. The emphasis should be on them, not on growth."

"That sounds too simple," I said.

"It's not. If you bring in the right people, you've won half the battle. And don't be in a hurry with this, either," he warned. "I gotta tell ya, the most insidious compromise occurs when you're in a hurry, and one of your managers tells you, 'Well . . . he's not ideal, but he's the best we've found so far.' When you hear that-stop! You're better off postponing success than ensuring failure on schedule. Believe me."

"You're preaching to the choir on that one, Tubby," I said, shaking my head. "I've been right on time with failure."

"We *all* have. Don't be too hard on yourself." He torched his pipe with his butane lighter, sending thick plumes of smoke in the air. "Now . . . Mike," he said, puffing in earnest. "Along with good people, you need a growth market . . . *puff* . . . and the right product offerings. But you've got all that. The used-computer market combined with the VAR channel is a powerful combination. You can grow like hell." He leaned forward in his chair and pointed his pipe stem at me. "But not without a plan."

"Now, there's where we've really fallen down," I said. "In the early days we just hit the street and sold our brains out-no planning at all. We reacted to whatever came. It worked for a long time."

"Usually does. But even the most daring and impulsive start-up company had a plan underneath them. You may not have been aware of it, but you had one, too. After all, Columbus didn't just sail, he sailed west. And look what came of *that* impulse."

He stood abruptly and headed out of his office, signaling for me to follow. We walked to the end of the hallway and entered the boardroom, where he flipped on the lights and lowered the blinds. The room was spectacular-graced with leather, maple, plush carpeting, and every audio-visual device imaginable. Executive chairs of royal blue-Tubby's favorite color-provided a soothing atmosphere. He was showing off a bit, but I didn't blame him.

"Have a seat. I want to show you something." He lowered a screen with the push of a button and powered up a projector. The screen displayed his planning model. *(Tubby's complete Business Planning Model can be found in the Tool Kit. His original outline is exactly what I used for all of my business planning.)*

"I think all entrepreneurs start the way we did, Mike. Sell, sell, sell. The hell with planning. Too often, though, the urge to move is so compelling that we fail to completely define what we're trying to do, which is a paradox because that's the kind of behavior you need to start a company." He sat down in the chair across from me. "But if you want to finish what you started, to get beyond midsize, you must have a plan."

I studied his face. "Tom, are you sure you're comfortable sharing this with me? After all, we are competitors."

He smiled and shook his head. "I'm not going to tell you *all* of my secrets. But the way I see it, if you succeed, it's good for the industry. There's enough business out there for both of us. So, no, I have no problem sharing this with you."

I was relieved. "Tubby, I'm all ears."

He leaned back and thought for a moment. "Planning begins with you," he finally said, pointing with his pipe again. "You're the leader. You have to decide what business you're going to be in. There has to be a clear vision-a market-back mentality."

"Market-back mentality. What do you mean?" I asked.

"You need to see the market in your mind's eye-reflecting back at you. What does the market need? Who are the customers? What can I offer them? How will I deliver? You need to recognize the opportunity and then focus." He sat back and thought further. "In your case, the VAR channel is a great fit. But fit is not enough. You need to know what to do and when to do it."

I nodded. "That's where the plan comes in."

"Bingo. If the plan is right, the doing is easy. *If* you have the right people," he added.

I shook my head as I reflected on some of the people I had hired in the past. The best plan in the world would have failed with that cast of characters. *People and planning-opposite sides of the same coin*, I thought.

"Let's take the VAR channel, Tubby. I'm not sure where to start. The list seems endless," I said. "Besides, IBM can't be too happy with my used-computer business. We're a direct competitor, asking to sit at their table. How does that work?"

"Ah, there's a way around that," he said, brushing off my concern. "What you need now is help. You can't do this alone. You need a star to run sales. Someone you can trust. Remember, take your time. Spend hours with this person. You can't be wrong on this one. Then you'll need somebody to run customer support. IBM will insist on it. This person must be able to build the entire customer-service infrastructure. And make sure you charge for your services. Make it a profit center. Let's see. . . . You've already mentioned Sherry and Joel, so I think you're covered," he said.

I had worn a dent into the side of my finger from writing as fast as I could. Nothing was too trivial. "What about IBM? Do they need all this in place before I get approved?" I asked.

"No. They just need to see a plan, which is different from the real plan. You won't have any problem with IBM. Anyway, the real plan begins with the planning model. That's why I brought you in here," he said.

Tubby sipped his coffee and pointed at the screen. "That's our model. Right or wrong, that's what we use. And we don't change it. The line managers do the planning. I never delegate planning to staffers. It's not that they lack the skills, but they lack the experience. They're not in the field."

I moved to a closer chair and squinted at the screen. "So what are we looking at here, Tubby?"

He used his pipe as a pointer. "Okay. See those five colored boxes? Those are the five steps of the planning process. We start with the *planning base:* Where are we today? Next are the *results* required: Where do we want to go? That's followed by the *approach*: How are we going to get there? Then *implementation*: Who will do what? And finally, *review*: How are we doing?" He turned to me and smiled. "Simple?"

I could reason from his remark that planning was anything but simple. The irony, though, was the simplicity of the model itself. It was so clean, so focused. I was engrossed. "So how does all of this work? How do we break it all down?"

"We start with the planning base." He flipped to the next display. "The planning base has four categories. See them up there?"

"Yep."

"Again, this answers the question: Where are we today? It starts with an *internal* and *external assessment*. Internal outlines your *strengths and weaknesses*-external, your *opportunities and threats*. In other words: What do we do best, and where can we improve? From there we identify what markets we should enter and the obstacles we're likely to face."

"How long does this take to complete?" I asked.

"I've spent an entire day just on internals and externals. You have to get this stuff right," Tubby replied. He paused and reviewed the screen. "Once we complete this, we move to *assumptions* and *priorities*. Every plan has them. For example, you must assume that IBM will approve your VAR contract. That one's obvious. And if you don't prioritize things, you're dead because you will always develop more strengths, weaknesses, opportunities, and threats than you can handle. So you shrink the list down to what I call the *critical success factors*. If you make these happen, everything else falls into place."

"Is each manager expected to do this?" I asked, raising my voice slightly to cover my growling stomach. I hadn't eaten since the plane ride.

"Absolutely. Including you." He turned to me and smiled. "Hey, you sound like you're ready for some lunch."

"Boy, am I ever." I said. "Pick out a good spot. I'm buying."

"Oh, no, you're not. When you're on my turf, I buy."

The cab pulled up to Gino and Georgetti's, one of Chicago's finest steakhouses and one of my long-ago favorites. Tubby had invited Bob Pasaneau, his vice president of sales, and Andrew Clark, vice president of finance, to join us for lunch. We collected at the door while Tubby paid the driver, then headed inside.

After the glaring sunlight of the brilliant spring afternoon, the restaurant was as dark as a cave. It took a minute for my eyes to adjust. The tables were nearly filled, and the tuxedo-clad waiters were bustling about, carrying plates of hot food. The air was redolent of sizzling steaks, garlic, and fried onions. Everything was just as I had remembered it. We were seated immediately.

Bob, a twenty-year IBM veteran with a great reputation, was trim, polished, and formal. Andrew, who had come over from Arthur Andersen, was much younger than Tubby and very handsome. I sensed a big brain with this guy. Bob was on my left. Andrew was on my right. I was in good company.

Tubby unfolded his napkin, turned to his sales VP, and said, "Bob, Mike and I have been going over the planning model. We covered the base this morning. I thought you and Andrew could take it from there."

"So now you're on 'results'?" Bob asked.

"Yep . . . we're on results. The part I like," Tubby added with a grin.

Bob got right into his lecture. "What we found, Mike, is that most companies face a big challenge in getting their people centered on a vision. Without one, it's hard to get any result. One of the best ways to bring this about is through a precise *mission statement.*"

Tubby waved his breadstick, interrupting. "That's not something you whip up during planning."

Andrew chimed in. "Correct. The mission statement is built through input and effort from every level of the organization. We think of it as a living constitution that holds our values and beliefs."

"So it's a kind of compass, really," I said, handing the butter to Tubby.

"Exactly. A reminder of where we're going," Tubby said, munching.

Bob continued. "Tubby gives each manager a *goal worksheet* that outlines in broad strokes what he wants the company to accomplish. Andrew, you brought one with you, didn't you?" Bob asked.

Andrew reached for his vest pocket and pulled out a worksheet.

I examined it carefully. "Let's see . . . you have sales revenue, gross margin, return on assets, capital expenditures, headcount. You've got all kinds of stuff on here," I said.

"Yep, it's comprehensive," Bob said. "And there are no rules here, Mike. Every company can design their own objectives-their own worksheet, too, for that matter. This happens to be what we look for."

"You can take that with you, Mike," Tubby said. As I refolded the sheet of paper and tucked it into my pocket, he leaned forward and tented his fingers. "Mike, you have to set the big goals. That's your job. Then each of your managers has to figure out his or her part in supporting those goals. Keep this process open and interactive. To get the best result, you need a collaborative effort."

Bob summed things up. "So once we know where we are-the *planning base*-and where we want to go-the *results required*-we can now go to approach-how are we going to get there?"

I was anxious to hear what Bob had to say. The "how" part had been my weakness.

Suddenly the waiter arrived to take our order. I hadn't even looked at my menu.

"Get the salmon and the chop salad, Mike," Tubby suggested. "It's the best in the city."

I handed back my menu. "Done."

The waiter took everyone else's order and dashed away.

Bob picked up where he had left off. "The *approach* is really the guts of the plan. Here we deal with strategies, organization, and marketing programs." He explained that strategies are the ways, means, and hows, combined with detailed methods by which you can achieve your goals. It's about being different. What Tubby called *formidable competitive advantage*."

Andrew put in, "In the old days planners could rely on a bunch of carefully linked action items to leverage what they were good at-their core competency. Today that won't work. Competitive advantage is too fleeting. Markets are too unstable. Look at the VAR program, for instance. IBM could pull the plug tomorrow. But until that time there is a ton of money to be made. You get in, you get out. And don't fall in love with your market. It won't love you back forever."

"Andrew is right, Mike," Tubby said. "Today's competitive advantage is created through *unpredictability*, not *sustainability*. You must manage like it could all end tomorrow, and you'd better have your next idea ready to go-or at least started. That's how you get your edge . . . and keep it."

"When you say the word 'strategy,' what do you *really* mean?" I asked. "I think I know the answer, but I want to hear it from you."

"Strategy creates competitive advantage," Bob said. He grabbed a crayon from the glass on the table and began drawing an outline for me on the paper tablecloth. (At Gino's, more than a few business deals were written this way.) Bob was in his glory, having been the mastermind behind much of Datacomp's strategy. "Competitive advantage comes in many flavors: cost, value, price, speed-things like that. Or you may decide to grow, hold, milk, or get out of a market. Maybe you need to acquire something, build something, divest something, or restructure. All of these are the elements of strategy. It tells you what you have to do to be excellent. Both inside and outside."

"And if you can't be excellent, get the hell out," Tubby said.

"Here, here," Bob agreed. "One last point: While the tactics are important to your success, they are less important than the overall strategic direction of the firm. I can tolerate some mistakes in tactics provided that the strategy is sound."

We were interrupted by the approach of two waiters carrying four sizzling plates. My mouth began to water.

"Okay, boys, here's our grub," Tubby said, rubbing his hands together and looking very pleased. "Let's enjoy this. We'll pick up our discussion over dessert and coffee."

We dug in.

The teamwork and mutual respect between these gentlemen at the lunch table was extremely apparent. The entire experience was refreshing. I couldn't wait to get home and roll up my sleeves. I was determined to have this, too.

Over coffee and dessert-my choice was the most amazing strawberry shortcake I had ever seen-we got back to talking strategy.

Andrew picked up the ball. "Next is *organization*. To get the work done, you must be organized. When you think about it, there are several organizations in your business, Mike. We define an organization as a group of people working together toward a common goal under a single leader." He smiled. "Does that make sense?"

"Yes it does. It's a bunch of little teams, isn't it?" I asked.

Andrew nodded while sipping his coffee. "Yes. Like a bunch of clockwork wheels all working together to make things tick. And to be effective, those teams need to understand the goals of the organization, what part they play in attaining them, what part the others play, and what part this guy plays." Andrew pointed at Tubby.

"Yeah, I'm the big wheel, they're the little wheels," Tubby quipped, and we all laughed.

"Now all you have to do is put together an organization chart, define the work, and assign the positions," Tubby added. "Then you can function. The clock starts ticking."

Bob leaned forward to pour more coffee, saying, "The only thing I'd add to that is: Always try to put an individual's goals into the position description itself. For example, I put the quotas, headcount, margins, marketing budget, and territories right into the position description for our regional sales managers."

"What's the rationale behind that?" I asked, still feverishly writing down everything they said.

"It transforms their job into something precise, something measurable, and it's fully owned. The closer the accountability approaches the doer, the better the performance," he responded.

I sat back taking it all in. It made so much sense.

"Now, Mike, I want to warn you about *committees*," Tubby said. "They are the unwilling doing the unnecessary, and they breed like rabbits. Committees are good for one thing: gathering and dispensing information. That's it. And they don't make decisions, managers do. Hell, if Columbus had had an advisory committee, he'd still be at the dock. Don't ever forget that. If a committee makes a decision and they screw up, who do you hold accountable?" He grinned. "Get the picture?"

I reflected on the committees I've had in the past. Tubby was right. Then I asked, "Marketing has to be part of 'approach,' too, doesn't it?"

"Hold that thought, Mike," Bob put in. "I need to get back to the office for a meeting. We'll talk marketing in the car, Okay?"

I arm wrestled Tubby for the bill. Tubby got his way.

We strolled leisurely outside, where we were met by a warm breeze and the heat radiating from the sidewalk. The late-afternoon sun was powerful but soothing as it fanned its golden rays between the buildings. It had been a *good* day . . . a *good* day. Gino always had a Lincoln Town Car waiting for his best customers. We climbed in and headed back to One Financial. Tubby sat in the front, resting his head on the seat back for a quick snooze. I took the middle of the back seat between Andrew and Bob.

Bob never missed a beat, picking right up where he had left off. I was amazed by his energy.

"All right. Marketing. That's an easy one, once your goals are defined. Marketing is the stuff that breathes life into your strategy. When I say 'stuff,' I'm referring to the *marketing mix*-mass mail, advertising, telemarketing, blitz days, seminars, trade shows, partnering . . . whatever you want or whatever you can afford. But worry about that later. For starters, zero in on a consistent set of messages that support that edge you're looking for, pick your marketing programs, and then deal with the budget later. Got it?" Bob looked at me, seeking agreement.

"Got it," I responded.

The car pulled up to One Financial. I literally threw a twenty-dollar bill at the driver, determined to beat Tubby to it.

"Tubby, wake up. We're here," I said. I gave him a push on the shoulder.

He roused himself, opened the door slowly, swung both feet around, and hauled himself out of the car. "God I'm exhausted," he said. "Must have been the crème brûlèe. Sugar low."

We scurried into the building and caught the waiting elevator. As we rode up to Datacomp's floor, I thanked the threesome for their hospitality and the unselfish gift of their time. This was an impressive team.

The elevator doors opened on the lobby. Bob and I shook hands, and he dashed into his meeting. Tubby, Andrew, and I headed for the boardroom.

"Okay, let's see if we can wrap this up," Tubby said as we reached the room. "What time is your flight, Mike?" He stretched and yawned.

"Six-thirty, I think," I said, searching my briefcase for my Day-Timer.

Tubby switched on the overhead light and said, "All right, we gotta hustle. Andrew, take it away."

Andrew nodded, sitting at the head of the huge conference table. "There are two more parts to the planning model that we haven't covered: *implementation* and *review*. As Tubby told you earlier, Mike, it all comes down to people. That's what implementation is made of-people doing their jobs. It's a beautiful thing to watch when a thousand little daily tasks, done by people, all come together to achieve a goal."

"I'd like to see that day again," I mused.

"You will," Andrew promised. "Okay, you got your goals, you got your organization, your strategy is clear . . . now you have to delegate authority and responsibility down the line. *Implementation*-this is where the work is done."

"That's how you get leverage, isn't it?" I asked.

"Exactly. One plus one equals three. But that equation is quickly reversed if you're not organized or if your people don't know what to do or when to do it."

Tubby interjected, "You want to move every decision to the lowest possible level, where the best information and the most experience is available for making it. This is the purest form of *decentralization*. The productivity explodes."

"How do you handle crossover situations?" I asked. "Say a department manager needs resources that he or she doesn't directly control. Now there's conflict. What happens then?"

"Good question," Tubby said as he turned toward the door. "Sounds like you've seen that one before."

"More often than I care to admit," I responded.

"With the staff it's easy," Andrew said. "Usually no crossover is needed. Managers with direct profit responsibility have a different situation, though. For them to succeed, they must have control over, or at least have access to, sales, shop functions, human resources, finance, things like that."

Standing in the doorway, Tubby added, "Yeah, and if you don't give them that control, they're handicapped. They can't control their destiny. This is where abdication creeps into the picture. You're not delegating, you're throwing it over the wall. Dangerous practice, Mike. Real dangerous." He slipped into the hall.

Andrew handed me a booklet that outlined the *compensation systems* of Datacomp. "I'm going to let you browse this for a while. This was one of my first assignments. Tubby wanted the compensation plans coordinated to pull the company together. As you know, money is a great motivator, especially for salespeople. We pay a lot of money to the sales force after the company achieves a certain level of profitability. The cost curve tends to be flat, while the profit curve-once you're beyond break-even-is steep. You'll notice that these plans have personal and team rewards. If you have one star making all the money in a department while the rest are floundering, you have a problem." He smiled. "I'll let you look this over while we take a break."

I was getting tired, and my back was starting to hurt. We had been at it for nearly six hours. I walked to the window and looked out over the Chicago landscape. The authority and prosperity on view out that window filled me with awe. Despite my fatigue, I was excited and motivated. Everything seemed fresh and new. I knew I could make it work. I walked back to the elegant boardroom table, plopped down in my chair, rested my head on the table, and closed my eyes.

"All right, that's enough. Wake up!" Tubby flopped a three-ring binder on the table.

I had been out cold for half an hour. I sat up now, blurry eyed and embarrassed. "Wow, I can't believe I went out like that! Sorry." I rubbed my eyes and pulled up to the table. Turns out, Tubby had told his secretary to close the door and let me sleep.

"Don't apologize. I do it all the time. I think it helps, don't you?" he asked. I nodded still rubbing my eyes.

He handed me a cup of coffee, and we got down to our final round of business.

"The last piece of planning I want to talk about is *control*. You're the boss. Strong initial control will assert your prerogatives, and you'll be respected for it. Later on you loosen it. This shows that you have faith in and respect for your subordinates," Tubby explained.

He opened the binder and began showing me his reports. "The reporting system is the feeder for this control. And you need a *control cycle*-the time it takes to conceive, document, approve, implement, and assess the results of a decision. These should be short intervals-say, every quarter."

I smiled. "You know, Tubby, this is beginning to make sense. It all fits together. Your company is properly controlled when your team is selected and trained, they know what to do, when to do it, and what's expected. In fact, they can track their own progress against these reports to spot problems early, while there's still time to do something about it."

"Hey! You could teach *me*," he said, beaming proudly like a teacher who had just watched his favorite student win an award. "And, Mike, that's when *your* job gets exciting. You're watching others succeed under your leadership. It's a wonderful feeling. I read somewhere that the safest way to make your fortune is to help people see that it's within *their* best interest to promote *yours*. I think that's *the essence of leadership*." He stood in front of the whiteboard at the head of the conference table. "Now for a few housekeeping items. The meetings I hold . . ."

Tubby went on for another half hour, talking about how to conduct a good meeting, the importance of an *early-warning system*, managing from one piece of paper, and the emphasis that he placed on getting results. I had caught my second wind and could have listened to him for hours more, but we were out of time.

My old friend sat down in the chair beside mine and lit his pipe with precision. "So there you have it. But remember, it still comes back to people, Mike. The results will always be traceable back to the individuals who make up the organization. That has always been true, and will never change."

"I think that's where I've made most of my mistakes," I said wearily.

"Well, look . . . give yourself a break. So you made some mistakes. So what? Look at the education you got. You're a good leader, Mike. You were on the right track. You made some bad hires, that's all. So now go find yourself some stars, plan well, and build your company around them. You know what to do. As for midsize-trust me, if you do these things, you will blow the numbers away." Tubby smiled.

I sat there staring at him, almost in a trance, letting his words resonate within me. I had been given a lesson in leadership by an expert. What a kind and generous gift he had given me!

Gathering my things, I went to say good-bye to Bob and Andrew, then headed for the elevator with Tubby as my escort. I turned to him and said, "I'm immensely grateful to you, Tom. You've provided an excellent education. I can't thank you enough." I gripped his hand firmly.

He patted my shoulder and smiled. "Glad I could help, Mike. Do it for someone else sometime."

I smiled back. "I will."

Chapter 15

Rebuilding the Business

I was determined to get the Value Added Remarketer application approved by IBM. Without that, not much could happen. Industry-specific software was the component required by IBM-no software, no approval. I either had to buy a package or cross-license one. But which one? And in what industry? I examined the list of industries that IBM was weak in. One of them was telecommunications.

I had an idea.

Throwaway Code

By June 1987 we were positioned to enter the IBM channel, and it was finally time to get the golf clubs back out. I hadn't played the entire spring. Summer in Minnesota is spectacular. It's the only justification for living here. People like to joke that we only have two seasons: winter and July. But they're wrong. We have three: winter, July, and August. Nonetheless, people from all over the country come here to camp, fish, hunt, golf, and hike. I guess I came to work. But I have to admit, I was now a lot more relaxed. Thanks to Tubby, my work suddenly had a sense of direction and purpose. I wasn't going to blow it this time. And I wasn't going to work forever, either.

I was hard at it, trying to ignore the beautiful day, when the phone rang. It was Mike Campion of IBM, returning my call. He had been eager to get us into the program, but there were a few hurdles.

Jumping right in, I asked, "Mike, what about telecommunications? I found a company in Denver that's willing to cross-license their software to us."

"Telecom! That's perfect. We're dying for packages in that area. If you can put it together, I'll get you in the program. Guaranteed," he promised.

Mike Campion was a savvy veteran. He had built a career walking on the edge. Brokering used IBM equipment didn't bother him a lick. He knew we could move a bunch of iron for him. Numbers-that's what he wanted. And he didn't care how we got them.

The IBM channel strategy was poorly aligned with their direct sales force. The purpose of the channel was to significantly broaden IBM's sales coverage in the midrange computer market and establish themselves in new industries. The strategy was working brilliantly, but the two divisions hated each other. The channels were slowly replacing the direct IBM rep-or so they thought-leaving them threatened and vulnerable. The directs were forced to sell at list price, while the big VARs (like Datacomp) were receiving up to forty-seven percent discounts. With both sales forces calling on the same prospects, it was just a matter of time before the shit hit the fan. We'd be fighting in the customer lobby, for crying out loud. But that's the way Campion liked it: right on the edge. Personally, I found the edge a bit steep for my liking.

"Tell me about this software, Mike. What does it do?" he asked.

"It's called Call Analyzer. It integrates the System/36 and System/38 with the phone system, collecting raw call data. Once collected, the software distributes cost by department, identifies waste, locates abuse, and catches billing mistakes from the phone company. It's powerful stuff," I said.

"Sounds like a no-brainer to me. I'll submit your application as soon as it's ready. And hurry up, we need you."

The beauty of Call Analyzer was that any company with a phone system was a prospect. This wasn't a vertical telecommunications package, it was horizontal-fitting every industry. We could sell it everywhere. I was able to negotiate a price of a thousand dollars per package under an exclusive remarketing agreement-a cost less than two percent of the hardware price. With our deep discounts, the customer could buy the software, throw it away, and still save a ton on the hardware.

Throwaway code was precisely what the IBM directs detested. "These channels aren't adding value; they're brokering new boxes," they said. But Campion would laugh them off. He loved it. We were his value-add pit bull. We'd win every lobby fight.

In midsummer 1987 IBM approved our application and special price bid for the System/36 and System/38. We received a forty-two percent discount. The street price was eighty-seven percent. We looked to make twenty thousand dollars on each sale. And when we combined a new processor with used peripherals, we could make thirty thousand-twice what we had made on the Series/1, even during its heyday. I called Tubby to give him the news.

"Congratulations, Mike, that's terrific," he said. "Now, go build your team. By the way, keep your eyes and ears open. IBM is getting ready to announce their long-awaited System/38 replacement system."

"Yeah, I know. All I keep hearing about is this Silverlake . . . Silverlake . . . It's everywhere," I said.

"Silverlake is the code name," Tubby explained. "I hear it's a whole new architecture. Anyway, it's going to be a huge announcement. The word is it runs System/36 and System/38 software without modifications, so Call Analyzer should be grandfathered in on day one."

"Boy oh boy, Tom, this is going to be a bonanza, isn't it?"

"You got it, sir. Squirrel it away as long as you can."

Selecting the Team

Bob Solfelt, one of IBM's top marketing managers in the Des Moines office, was introduced to me by a friend. Unlike many of his colleagues, Bob saw the benefits of the VAR channel, and rather than fighting the VARs in the lobby, he invited them in. "The direct reps get seventy-five percent credit for a VAR box, so why fight it?" he declared. "The other managers are caught up in some ridiculous pride thing. They think if they don't sell the box direct, it'll reflect poorly on them. That's ridiculous. I figure: C'mon in; the more salesmen in my patch, the better." Bob had posted some enormous numbers with that philosophy.

I invited him to Minneapolis for an interview.

We sat in my office on the day of our meeting. Bob was about six-three, handsome, with piercing blue eyes. His confidence was so apparent, it was almost intimidating. But I wouldn't be fooled this time as I had been by Larry Steelman. Bob wouldn't be fooled, either, for the rumor mill had spread far and wide throughout IBM about Steelman, Jackson, and the MII fiasco. *Lord only knows what he's heard about me,* I thought.

Three hours later we were wrapping up the interview. We had gotten into everything. Most of all, he had wanted my side of the story. When I had finished telling him everything that had transpired, he shook his head in amazement.

"Wow, Mike, this company must have nine lives. You've been through a lot. I imagine you're better for it, however. The good Lord had his hand on you."

His remark opened up a whole new discussion. We were both

Christians. Bob was a spiritual person who tried to live his faith. I was now learning to do that myself, having just renewed my faith after Alex died. It was grace that carried me through-a kind of force that infused my life, providing yet another chance. Grace is the gift that sits and waits for you on the side of the road until you finally recognize that it's there. It's the free provision you get when you're out of gas-and maybe a little out of your mind. Bob was right. God's grace had been with me through all of it.

Bob had recently lost his father so we had much in common, and we liked each other. He was from Minneapolis, and his mother was now alone up here. COI looked like a perfect fit for him. I shared my vision for the company, and he believed in what I was trying to do.

Two weeks later he accepted a position as a marketing manager for COI. I found it refreshing to hire a manager who didn't insist on either a fancy title or a salary "becoming to an executive." I was filled with enthusiasm.

Next, we hired Mary Gerber to run client services. She was one of IBM's top system-engineering managers, with a sterling reputation. Mary was also a tougher sell than Bob. If she had cut herself, she would have bled IBM blue. Naturally, she came from the same branch as Pete Jackson, so I had a few objections to handle. But she knew Bob well and respected COI, even though we had competed vigorously over the years. What finally won her over was the dream of building a business from the ground floor, giving her control over the entire service business. She saw it as the chance of a lifetime.

The table was now set. Bob ran sales, Mary ran services, Sherry ran operations, and Joel ran the numbers, giving me time to plan, train sales reps, and unearth the next idea. I wasn't going to get caught flat-footed this time.

I wanted a lean organization, too. *Hierarchy* makes organizations sluggish and creates redundancy. Layers are filters and funnels. Hierarchy creates less control but the illusion of more. The software business was changing so fast that we needed agility and adaptability to remain competitive, so we established lean, self-directed work teams. This eliminated distortion. Remember playing telephone when you were a kid, and you'd whisper a message to the kid next to you, and so on, until the message reached the last kid? By the time it had gotten to the end of the line, the message was completely garbled, and everyone would roar with laughter at the outcome. Well, it's no laughing matter in business. As it is, you're going to get some *intentional* message distortion. It's human nature to cover your ass somewhat. It's not out of disrespect that the message is distorted but rather a manager's disdain for vulnerability and a need for self-preservation. So I removed the layers, thus minimizing distortion, and I stayed close to my people.

The planning process took about six weeks to complete. We followed Tubby's model to the letter. We were ready for explosive growth, but IBM had been signing up VARs all over the country, which made me nervous.

"Don't worry about it, Mike," Mike Campion told me. "We're gearing up for Silverlake. We want the biggest sales footprint possible on announcement day."

"Fine, but if it gets too crowded out there, prices are going to suffer. I hope you guys know what you're doing. We need twenty-five percent gross margin to cover the client services overhead," I explained.

VARs were now responsible for supporting the IBM operating system and providing a 24/7 technical help line, functions that previously had been handled by IBM. This new department, which Mary designed to provide brilliant service, was labor intensive and costly. The other VARs being brought into the program weren't doing squat for client support. I could see it coming: low-budget operations that would whore up the market with cut-rate machines. They would squeeze one or two years out of the program, then move on. The gray market was about to begin.

Silverlake Turns to Gold

In April 1988 IBM announced the AS/400 (a.k.a. Silverlake). For a company with a no preannouncement policy, they had done a masterful job of letting this one leak out, creating gargantuan market anticipation. It was the biggest product promotion in IBM history, with fanfare everywhere-TV, radio, major newspapers like the *Wall Street Journal*, billboards, mailings, and product demonstrations at major hotels across the country. It was mind-boggling. I was invited to Miami, where IBM hosted at the Fountainbleu Hotel-a spectacular kickoff meeting for its channel partners. IBM spared no expense. Attendees were treated to laser shows, gourmet food, rock bands, and other smoke and mirrors. You name it, they had it. We were so pumped up that I thought we would explode, and as Tubby had predicted, Call Analyzer was immediately authorized on the AS/400. We were free to start taking orders.

People ran for the telephones at the break. I went to my hotel room and for a solid hour took orders from my best clients. I phoned Gary at Mamiya Camera. "Just send me an order letter and ten percent for now Gary. We'll figure out the contracts when I get back. But get the order in fast. You remember what happened with System/34 deliveries."

"I'll put it in the mail today, Mike," Gary promised. Call me when you get home."

By the end of the first week we had sold $850,000 worth of AS/400s. The frenzy was beyond description. Bob and I hired salespeople for six straight months, many of them ex-IBM reps. The order rate surged, and by the close of our second quarter, we booked over $15 million in sales. Mary was running at full throttle, hiring and training technicians to support our increasing install base. Sherry was writing new procedures almost daily to deal with the complexities of sales support, inventory, and backlog management, and Joel, besieged by numbers, was trying to keep up with reports and cash. The place was nuts. But, boy, was it fun.

"How long can we keep this up, Bob?" I asked. "If we screw up services, IBM will have a cow. These machines need to go in clean or we're dead." IBM did a post-installation review with each customer, verifying the installation of our value-add software and the adequacy of our support. We had a lot at stake.

"You're right, some of these machines are going in sloppy. We better slow down so we can speed up," Bob said.

Mary developed a system-assurance procedure to be used with each installation. It was so good that it became the model for the IBM region. Our client satisfaction ratings were stellar, thanks to Mary and her team. She organized "Professional Days" at our office, inviting our best clients to an all-day roundtable discussion focused on how to improve our products and services and strengthen our business relationships. The discussions were a huge success and doubled our sales volume with existing clients.

By the end of our first year in the program, we hit $35 million in sales and had installed over a hundred systems. We now had fourteen salesmen, ten systems engineers, and a host of administration, accounting, and warehouse people. Our productivity was staggering, thanks to a strong back-office support team that allowed us to generate over $800,000 in sales per employee.

We were exhausted.

IBM nominated COI for VAR of the year and sent us on a four-day all-expense-paid trip to Bermuda. It was hard to remain humble. But I remembered where I had come from, and Tubby's warning lingered in my mind: *"You need to manage your business like it could all end tomorrow."*

Compliance

We began planning our second year, shooting for $70 million. By this time Bob and Mary had developed some middle managers. Filters and funnels were a worry, but we needed the span of control. I wanted no more than eight direct reports per manager. Sherry and Joel held the lid on people costs by automating everything they could. The challenge now was opening two satellite offices, one in Chicago and one in Milwaukee. The critical factor, of course, was finding the right branch managers. Once again: people.

The market demand for the AS/400 had softened slightly to a more predictable pace. As I had feared, IBM brought some screwballs into the program who provided marginal services and were low-balling prices at seventy-five percent, putting pressure on margins. We were still getting eighty percent, but every deal was now a dogfight. I told my reps to avoid the discount buyer. If they come for your price, they will leave for someone else's. In fact, we decided to increase prices in the face of the discounters-and guess what happened. Our win ratio improved. Price creates perception. When you give your products away, the assumption is that they must not be worth much. Furthermore, price is usually the excuse you get when you lose business, but it's rarely the reason.

To make up the margin shortfall, we packaged the main system unit with used printers, CRTs, and third-party disk drives, which didn't make IBM too happy. We also put a big push on operating leases, looking to build a portfolio to maintain better account control. When you own the lease, the client can't do anything without your knowing about it. We got "last look" on every deal.

We found our branch managers for the two satellite offices and continued to build the sales force. The business model was working, and our quarter-over-quarter growth was a staggering twenty-five percent.

We faced three problems. Gross margin was still slipping, operating overhead was creeping up two percent per quarter, and the leasing business was eating cash. Joel was beginning to sputter-which I guess was the fourth problem. We were still profitable, but it looked as if $70 million would produce only slightly more earnings than $35 million. This is a typical phenomenon in fast-growth companies. When you are gobbling up market share, you usually lose ground on operating costs. The prime culprits were increased interest expense (due to leases, larger inventory and growing accounts-receivable balances), sales expense (due to a growing sales force), training costs (required for new software releases) and space costs (to house our expanding work force and physical inventory). We were blowing out walls, building cubicles, buying audio visual equipment and bigger copiers-you name it. At some point you have to regroup and seek optimization. We either had to increase sales productivity, raise prices again, or lower overhead. The easiest solution for us was to get more out of our sales force. Easiest, yes; best, no. You have to go after all three.

Tubby called me with a warning about a compliance department that had been formed-a kind of IBM police force. IBM was now requiring the VAR software to justify the purchase of the AS/400. In other words, they wanted the software to drive the sale, not the service and price. They had discovered that most VARs were now selling AS/400s with throwaway code-hence the gray market. We were within the letter of the agreement but not the spirit, according to IBM.

Now seething, I paced behind my desk as far as my phone cord would let me. "This is bull crap, Tubby," I said. "Call Analyzer was always a minor part of the software mix. IBM knew that going in. They're changing the rules on us. How can they do this?"

Tubby was unsympathetic. "They can do anything they want, Mike. That's the whole point. It's their game and their rules. When you hitch a ride in someone else's wagon, that's what happens. So grow up. I warned you about this," he said.

"I know, but I feel used. They built this massive distribution channel, capture a huge market share, and now they're putting us out to pasture," I complained.

"Time for the second idea, remember? It wasn't raining when Noah began building the ark," Tubby said. "Besides, you got a good meal off of this one. And it's not over yet. Unpredictability versus sustainability. We talked about this. You'd better get used to it."

I saw the handwriting on the wall. The compliance team was starting to breathe down our necks on every deal we made. IBM routinely called our clients to interrogate them on the merits of Call Analyzer and whether it justified the sale. Bob and his sales managers were spending more and more time coaching the client on what to say when IBM called rather than selling new systems. It was exasperating. We had no clue where this program was going. In the meantime we kept growing like Jack's beanstalk. I began looking for another market.

The Software Era

The ads were everywhere. System Software Associates (SSA) was one of the first companies to convert their software package to pure AS/400 native mode. "Native mode" is a technical term for software rewritten to take advantage of the enhanced features of the AS/400-a huge undertaking for SSA. Roger Covey, the founder of SSA, had written the original package at his kitchen table. Now nearly ten years later, he was a recognized leader in manufacturing control systems, and he had built a $90 million publicly held firm.

Bob and I were in the car on our way to Flagship Athletic Club to work out. We made a lot of good decisions running side-by-side on the treadmill. I reached into my briefcase and handed him a brochure that I had received in the mail that morning.

"Bob, look at this. They use affiliates to sell their software-that's where the money is. This hardware business is just too unpredictable. All they want is price, price, price. Packaged software is the next wave. What do you think?" I asked.

"I don't know, Mike, selling software is tough. We're not geared for it. Our people don't have the skills," Bob replied.

"So we'll teach them. Besides, I've sold software. So have you. Selling is selling. I think we should check this out," I said.

Bob grinned. "Hey, I'll look at anything that makes money. I'm just saying it's gonna be hard, that's all. But you're right, we should probably look at it."

After our workout I called SSA's headquarters in Chicago. I was astonished to find that Rick Halperin was the vice president of sales for the company. The last time I had seen Rick was the day I resigned from IBM, nearly ten years earlier. I was afraid to call him, once again feeling assailed by self-doubt-a familiar reaction that I thought I had licked. I finally dialed his number.

He answered with a brisk, "Hello, Rick Halperin."

"Rick, this is Mike Kerrison."

"Michael Kerrison! Ya gotta be kidding me! How the hell are ya?" came the effusive reply.

I was relieved by his enthusiastic tone. The last time we had talked, he had sounded more like a dial tone. I asked him about his wife and family, and then he asked me about mine in turn. I caught him up on my four kids.

"Wow, you've been busy." He paused. "Gosh, this is a surprise, Mike. What's the occasion?"

"Actually, to come right to the point, Rick, I want to sell your software," I said.

"Software? You're a hardware jockey," he said, chuckling.

"True enough, but we're thinking of making a change. Too many of us in hardware these days. It's becoming a commodity. No differentiation, low margins-it stinks, actually. Besides, I cut my eye-teeth on manufacturing software, remember?"

Rick laughed. "I remember. You were good at it, too. Why don't you come down to Chicago so we can talk about it? You'll need to convince Bill Lyons, though. He runs the affiliate channel. Hold on, I'll see if I can patch him in."

He got through to Bill immediately and told him who I was and that I was interested in being an affiliate.

"Really? Well, the timing could be good," Bill said. "We're having trouble with the Minnesota territory." Then he added, "In fact, we're making a change, but we're pretty far down the road with someone else, I'm afraid."

I spoke up. "Bill, don't do anything until you talk to us. We've been putting in computer systems for ten years up here, and we're one of IBM's leading VARs. This year we'll do $70 million. I believe we're exactly what you're looking for."

Bill chuckled. "How can I say no? C'mon down."

I called a special meeting with my staff to discuss the challenges of becoming an affiliate for SSA. The team had a cool reaction to my proposal.

Mary stated her objections first. "Why couldn't you find something a little easier, Mike? We'll need to cross train everyone in the company. And the start-up curve will be enormous. It's gonna eat our time and our pocketbook. I don't think we can pull it off."

Her words were sobering.

"Bob, what do you think?" I asked.

"You tell me what we're selling, and I'll sell it. But I think Mary's right. Our people may not be able to make the transition." He turned to Joel and asked, "Joel, can we afford this?"

As I said previously, Joel had been sputtering for some time, trying to keep up with the growth. Because of this, I was worried about our inventory balances and cash flow.

"I'm out of cycles, Bob," he turned to me and said, "We need to get ready for the audit, Mike. If you want to keep booking leases, our line will have to double next year. This software game is an awfully big move. I'm uncomfortable with it."

"Yeah, well, all the more reason to get in it. It's hard. Besides, how comfortable are you going to be when IBM pulls the plug on this channel, and we have nothing to sell?" I asked. "A bunch of people will be standing around with nothing to do-and we'd be to blame for it."

I looked from face to face. Their concern was evident.

"Look, gang, I'm not gonna jam this down your throats, but face it, software is the future, and so are services," I said. "Hardware is getting faster and cheaper. Before you know it, someone will figure out how to run their business with a network of PCs. There's no money in this anymore. If we don't make the transition now, we could be out of business in two years. So you'd better start thinking about how to pull this off. We'll talk about it again in a week."

I was concerned. The company was so wrapped around the VAR axel that I wasn't sure we could pull ourselves off of it-or if we even wanted to. But one thing was for sure: The train was coming. If we weren't careful, we'd get run over again.

Bob and I went to Chicago and did a fabulous job of convincing SSA to sign us up. With the increasing pressure from IBM's compliance board, the decision was getting easier. But first we had to get through our audit. I wanted to be sure we were on solid financial footing before making any major moves. For some reason I just didn't feel comfortable with the numbers. I put SSA on hold.

Things quickly got dicey.

We hired Peat Marwick for the audit. Big accounting firms made me nervous, but since we were going for a $5 million line of credit, the bank insisted we use one. My worst fear came true when they found a major discrepancy. We had been on a consigned-inventory plan with IBM, shipping nearly $6 million per month. This terrific plan allowed us to have product on hand without paying for it until it was sold. At the end of each quarter, IBM did a physical count, compared it to the last count, and billed the difference. The accountants found that our inventory was off by $1.5 million-which explained why cash had been tight.

I called Joel into my office to discuss the bad news. "How did this happen, Joel?" I asked.

"I'm not sure, but I think it had to do with the commingling of our inventory with IBM's. When we did our physical assessment, we either double-counted or didn't count at all. I just don't know which. Boy Mike, I feel awful about this!"

"Here we go again," I muttered. "Joel, we have to find that inventory. Can we pay IBM when they come in next week?"

He just stared at me. I had gotten my answer.

"Keep this between us for now," I said. "Let's not worry the others till we have to."

I knew that Joel was in over his head, but he had been so loyal during all the trouble, I didn't have the heart to let him go. Besides, I was within a few weeks of hiring a new CFO, someone with the experience and background to take us to the next level. I felt like a heel, but I knew better. I couldn't let my personal feelings for Joel cloud my judgment or diminish my objectivity. If I didn't act now, I would put my leadership in jeopardy and the whole company at risk.

Dave Faidley started as our new CFO right after Thanksgiving weekend in 1988. Joel agreed to stay through the audit and help with the transition. This would give him time to find a new job while we faced some significant challenges. Dave was a grinder-a realist. He was also the kind of person who never panicked. Easygoing yet intense, he was a curious mixture of Iowa farm boy and Big Ten basketball player. Dave played to win. He understood all the issues, and he quickly brought control to the organization.

A control system is nothing more than a loop of critical business information. Dave set our control cycle for ninety days, which minimized distortion and allowed me time to correct faults of the plan. He was able to isolate the relevant and meaningful control points, and he always provided a written explanation with the numbers. And once again, it was on one piece of paper. Any more than that and you have distortion again.

The Peat Marwick auditor was a weasel. This guy behaved like a covert spy, digging around in the company to see what he could find next. Unfortunately, he didn't have to look far to discover the $1 million of unguaranteed residuals on the books. He was like a dog with a bone, digging and yipping and salivating all over those residuals. The pressure was building. Inventory was now off by $1.8 million, the residuals were under attack, IBM compliance looked like the Gestapo, and now IBM wanted a $2 million payment that we couldn't make. I felt as though I was in a shit storm without a hat. *Don't panic . . . just think . . . just think*

. . . there is strength in weakness; you just have to find it.

Monday morning I got busy. I called SSA to tell them I needed another couple of weeks to decide. They were disappointed but gave me the time. Wanting to keep the bank apprised, I set up a meeting with them to warn them about some of the issues we faced. Now I had to face IBM. How was I going to dance around a $2 million payment?

I looked for every excuse possible to avoid calling Mike Campion. But it was time. I dialed his number and gave him the bad news.

"What do you mean, you can't pay us?!" Mike yelled. "Ya gotta pay us, or give the equipment back."

"I can't. I don't have the money right now. And I have no equipment because I sold it all. Look, Mike, we have a major problem, and we need some time to straighten it out," I said.

"We have a problem? What do you mean, we? You have the problem- and it's $2 million dollars. That's not a problem. That's a disaster. You're going to get me fired!" Mike was shouting into the phone.

"Now, relax. You're not going to get fired. Just work with me on this, and everything will be fine. I just need some time," I said. What I *really* needed was another miracle. But I had already gotten more than my fair share of those.

"I'm going to have to bring Dale Carr in on this one," Mike told me. "The minute you miss that payment, it'll hit his desk anyway. We're better off preempting this whole thing."

"I think that's a good idea," I agreed.

A Line in the Sand

Dale Carr, IBM's regional manager, was a classic-right down to his pinstripes and forty-pound wingtips. He had been with Big Blue since the System/360 had been announced. Standing nearly six-four, he cast an enormous shadow from the early winter sun streaming through our lobby. He had a pretentious, self-important look on his face-the old "I'll- show-this-guy" look.

Good grief, not another jerk, I thought. I had heard all about the infamous Dale Carr, the ass kicker. I led him and Mike Campion into our conference room and offered them coffee or a cold drink.

"Do you have any tea?" Dale asked.

Oh, brother, a prima donna, too, I thought.

"Uhh, tea . . . of course . . . tea." I began searching through the coffee cabinet. "Would you like some sugar in that, Dale?" I asked with a hint of sarcasm. "Maybe it will sweeten you up a bit," I said under my breath.

"What was that?" he asked.

"Oh, nothing. Just talking to myself." I smiled.

Dale had a long face, bulldog jowls, and baggy dark circles under his eyes. His rumpled suit had a hint of dandruff on the collar. *This guy is overworked,* I thought. *The corporate ladder has claimed yet another hapless victim.*

I handed him his tea, which he sipped as if wondering whether I had poisoned him. The thought had occurred to me. Mike Campion sat there like a chump, the pose of an underling who had no doubt been scolded on the drive over. He was on the edge, all right-the edge of a cliff.

"So, Dale, how's the VAR channel going?" I asked casually.

"Apparently not very well for some of us. When am I going to get paid?"

OK . . . small talk's over. "Well, Dale, that's what we're here to talk about. We have-"

"No! No! *I'm* here to talk, you're here to listen," he corrected, holding up his hand like a traffic cop.

Shit, I can see this is going to be a real treat.

Campion shifted nervously in his seat. I sat back comfortably and crossed my legs.

"You have the floor," I said, holding open my arms magnanimously.

"For starters, we're eliminating Call Analyzer. It's not a system justifying value-add. That's a requirement from now on," he said.

That made me furious, but I didn't react. I already knew where the line in the sand was. "Go on," I said.

"I don't know where that leaves us," he said. "Without Call Analyzer, you have nothing to sell. But the bigger problem is your payment." He opened his briefcase and pulled out a stack of computer printouts to justify his case.

"Dale, put those away. I know what we owe you. And we intend to pay you. But we're going to need time," I said.

"You're out of time. You know the terms of the contract. Payment is due one week after we take the physical. It's been over a month. You have until Friday. If we're not paid by then we will take you out of the program, and file suit."

He was really revving up-showing off for Campion.

"You're not listening," I said. "That's not going to happen. Besides, I don't respond well to threats." I turned to Campion, who was nervously training a curl on the side of his head. "Mike will you excuse us for a minute, please? I'd like to talk to Dale alone."

Mike looked at Dale, who tightened his lips and gestured with his head toward the door. Campion slipped into the lobby.

I leaned forward in my chair, looking into the face of my opponent. *Strength in weakness . . . strength in weakness. Talk the language he understands.* "Look Dale, let's get a couple things straight right now. For starters you haven't done your homework. IBM is an unsecured creditor. The bank has first position on every single asset in this company. If you throw us out of the program now and sue us, you will be cutting your own throat. We'll fold up like a pup tent. While you're filing your lawsuit, I'll be filing for bankruptcy. And if that happens, you won't get shit-except maybe a pink slip from your boss. With your pension looming right around the corner, you can't afford that. So wise up. If you can't bite, don't show your teeth. Leave us in the program long enough to pay you back, and give us some time to find something else to do."

He glared at me. "You're bluffing. You won't file for bankruptcy."

"The hell I won't. My lawyer told me I'd be in and out of court in ninety days, with you off my back permanently. Would you like me to call him?" I stared him down.

He leaned back in his chair and folded his arms. "Hand me that phone."

I placed the conference phone in front of him.

"I need some privacy."

I left the room.

Fifteen minutes later Dale opened the door. Mike and I shuffled back into the conference room like two defendants returning for our verdict.

"Okay, what do we have to do to work this out?" Dale asked.

Bingo, I got a chance.

Two weeks later we had a settlement agreement providing time to pay IBM back and time to start our software business with SSA. Over time we paid IBM every penny we owed them. Another era had ended, and a new one was about to begin.

Chapter 16

More Ups than Downs

A great way to silence a room full of bankers is to stand up and tell them you missed four out of five covenants, took a $1 million hit in inventory, and an auditor is writing down half your residuals. Believe me, that gets their attention.

The audit was finally completed in February 1989. Dave Faidley and I had spent much of our time arguing with a stubborn Peat Marwick about the value of our residuals-a battle that we would lose. We arrived at Norwest Bank armed with a presentation designed to soften the bad news. We figured with the SSA deal at hand and the IBM mess now behind us, there was reason for optimism. We had figured wrong.

Tim Flynn and his cohorts from Peat Marwick had insisted on being in the meeting, no doubt to cover their ass. My account manager at the bank, Paul Eaton, escorted us into the formal boardroom on the lower level, which enshrined a table big enough to seat fifty people. The mood was immediately darkened by low lighting, heavy wood, portraits of dead bankers, and red high-backed chairs. It was a cold, clammy dungeon.

"What's the occasion, Paul?" I asked. We've never used this room before."

"Oh . . . some of the other executives want to sit in on this," he said nervously.

Dave gave me a sudden glance and mouthed the words "Oh, shit."

We were all huddled at one end of the table-me, Dave, Tim Flynn, and his lackeys. Minutes later the bank's executive vice president, Dick Boles, and a few unidentified bankers entered the boardroom. Their faces were sober. We exchanged the usual intros and pleasantries, took our seats, and the meeting began. I made the most convincing presentation of my professional career. What was really rotten financial news actually sounded pretty good-to me, anyway.

"This is an outrage! This is malfeasance!" Dick Boles exploded, slamming his notebook on the table.

I momentarily froze, then turned to Dave for support. Dave had a look on his face as if he needed a dictionary: *I know what an outrage is, but what the hell is "malfeasance"? That sounds bad.*

I soon recovered and decided to press. "Dick, I don't understand. We don't agree with the auditors-our residuals are good. They have value, but I can't prove it until the leases renew," I said.

"That won't do," he snapped. "You owe the bank over $2 million, and we need to get paid back immediately. Your company is no longer bankable."

Tim Flynn sat there, letting us twist in the wind. I'm not sure what I expected, but one thing became clear. Some bankers and auditors run for the hills when the chips are down-or at least that's their initial reaction.

"Dick, if I have to, I'll sell the lease portfolio, and our balance sheet will fall right back into line. But it will cost us dearly if we're forced into a fire sale. We'll lose thirty to forty percent," I said. "Look, the bank has never given us credit for our leased assets. If you put even half the residuals in your calculations, we will meet every covenant you have for us."

Dick would not budge. "If you have to slow down sales, collect A/R, wholesale inventory, and liquidate leases, then do it. We want this note closed in sixty days," he declared.

I was pissed. Packing up my stuff, I headed out the door with the others. No one made eye contact. I could feel their disapproval. They just didn't believe in those residuals.

Late that evening Dave, Bob, Sherry, and I were sitting in my office licking our wounds when the phone rang.

"Mike, this is Paul Eaton." His voice was low and shaky. "Are you going to be able to get out of this? I mean, this is going to be career altering."

"Are we talking about my career or yours?" I asked.

He was silent.

"Paul, what is it you are trying to tell me?"

"I'm trying to tell you that I'm going to lose my job. You guys floundered on my watch. If you go down, I go down," he said.

"So we're in this together." I thought a moment. "If I get us out of this, you have to turn Dick Boles around. He's far to severe on this one,"

I said. "And I'm getting a new auditor. I fired Peat Marwick after the meeting."

"You get this done, and I'll take care of Boles," Paul said with conviction.

A few weeks later I sold the entire lease portfolio to Sun Data in Atlanta. They paid us cash on the barrelhead, and as I predicted we took an $800,000 hit on the balance sheet but generated over $2 million in cash. I guess sometimes you have to take a beating just to stay in the ring. We knew there was another round to fight. We paid down our note and much to my satisfaction, renewed and eventually deepened our relationship with the bank. I was determined to win them over. Never again were we challenged in this way. We became their model client and earned a merit badge for Dick Boles. Ours was the one war story that he loved to tell.

After that miserable experience I decided to study accounting. I had Dave teach me everything. Never again would I be at a disadvantage when negotiating with auditors or bankers. I would always know more than they did. To run a business you must know where your cash is, how your balance sheet works, and all the nuances of your business cycle. I liked hanging out with the sales force. It's where the fun was. But I learned to devote an equal measure of my time to the bean counters. They will save your butt.

If you put your mind to it, you can overcome just about any obstacle. Tell the truth, tell people what you're going to do, and then do it. Most of the time they are with you. I had learned the hard way once again. But then I remembered: Business is just plain hard.

Change Can Be Painful

We learned that the business had to keep changing to survive. Change became our friend. It had to because change was not going to change. The organization was constantly reshaping, shifting, flexing, restructuring, downsizing, and now reengineering to capture another booming market: software. I no longer fought this imposing force. If we resisted change, we would meet oblivion. The inference is that if a company doesn't progress through change, it will regress. We had faced uncertainty with the VAR life cycle, which could have easily led to uncertainty in the company life cycle. But one major difference exists: the company life cycle is controllable. It need not decline. If you're alert, you're already spinning the new web-restarting the cycle.

SSA, our new partner, used affiliates to sell its products across the globe. What I liked best was their dependence on the affiliate sales channel. They had no sales force of their own, which provided a balance of power-unlike the relationship with IBM, which always had the directs to fall back on. But the SSA business model presented the biggest challenge our company would ever face. We had always been a hardware reseller in a horizontal market. Now we had to become a solution provider in a vertical market.

Consider the differences:

1. Our sales force would shift from a national horizontal territory to a five-state vertical territory: manufacturing.

2. The sales cycle would expand from one month to six months or more.

3. The sales force, normally self-sufficient, would now depend on a pre-sales specialist to provide product demonstrations and customer surveys.

4. The installation cycle went from two weeks (at the most a month) to as long as eighteen months.

5. Post-sales support would shift from a quick-fix customer hotline to onsite engineers who would become an extension of the customer staff.

6. The number of transactions flowing through the accounting staff would shrink by eighty percent, with the average sale rising from $80,000 to $400,000.

7. Training was tedious and expensive given the demands of the software industry, unlike hardware sales, which required only thirty days for training.

8. Our people would now work in teams to accomplish a goal, whereas in hardware the workers were more or less autonomous.

9. Competitive advantage was now achieved through customer intimacy, and operating excellence, versus the hardware model which was driven by market coverage, speed, and price.

10. Managers would now have to be product specialists with talent in molding and managing teams, versus the old model where managers merely had to grind volume and be rapid-fire problem solvers.

We had to learn these new skills fast to have a chance.

SSA was exploding. Their Business Planning and Control System (BPCS-pronounced *bee*-picks) was recognized as the natural replacement for a whole class of manufacturing software. They were winning early adopters and rising to the top of the charts. This new product, now hooked to the AS/400 wagon, had unleashed a vortex of market demand. IBM was our friend again.

We had to reengineer fast and become a learning organization, which put tremendous pressure on our managers. This requirement for frequent and dramatic change caused painful dislocation for our people. Nearly one out of three couldn't make the transition. Senior management was excited about the new opportunity, but that enthusiasm didn't carry to all of our people. Many on Mary's team had to be let go. She didn't have the stomach for it, either, and eventually left herself.

Change can be painful. When it damages careers, emotions like grief, anger, and depression come naturally, making it hard for people to buy in and be productive. But the strong ones turn to mobility, not mourning, and reposition their career. Encouraging this behavior became the new job for our management team. We all had to learn new things. And we did.

We started growing again.

The lesson is this: People are not like parts in an erector set. They do not regularly or easily reconfigure themselves, nor are they crazy about such reconfigurations being imposed upon them. The organization can slip into chaos if it is continually recharting and redirecting. The paradox, though, is this is exactly what survival and sustainable growth requires. So find the people who can handle it, and make it part of your culture.

Bulwarks of the Station

By our third year in the program, we became the second-largest affiliate in the country, winning awards for our significant sales contribution. Best of all we had built a consulting practice that was now contributing $1.50 of revenue for every software dollar sold. The other affiliates were generating only thirty to forty cents. We became the model by which the others were patterned. What we couldn't accomplish as individuals could be easily accomplished as a team.

By 1994 we had built an organization that was heaped with expertise in manufacturing processes, implementation, software development, training, and hardware planning. Our customers depended on us for their survival. Price was rarely a factor, which contributed to our significant profitability. We had finally become a trusted business advis-er, an extension of the client's board of directors. Once again my job had changed-I'd gone from top salesman to owner/operator to man-ager/builder and now to leader/visionary. This was new territory for me.

I spent much of my time in the field, talking to executives. I was now an ambassador, determined to strengthen our client relation-ships, look for ways to improve, and above all search for new oppor-tunities. The team was strong, with Bob still running sales, Dianne Frisbee running implementations, Dave Van Meter running program-ming services, Dave Faidley running finance, and Sherry running operations.

Though I preferred being in the field, I still wanted to remain close to the day-to-day operations. To accomplish this I began signing all the accounts payable checks. This drove Dave nuts, but he came to understand that this was my security blanket-my microscope, allow-ing me to get a close look at where our money was going and why. Occasionally I would see something that I didn't understand and decide to investigate. When you track a check back to its inception, you touch every step of the decision-making process and can evalu-ate how the process is working. The checks by themselves won't tell you much, but what happened before they were cut will reveal the truth about the effectiveness of your operation. I caught a lot of mis-takes this way. I also caught people doing things right-and told them so. This simple procedure-signing checks-was a terrific *diagnostic tool* and coaching aid. My advice is to do it.

Dianne Frisbee and Dave Van Meter were superstars whom I had promoted from the field. This seasoned team stayed above the fray, saw the forest, stayed out of the trees, and eschewed fire fighting in favor of fire prevention. They were more unflappable than charis-matic, more disciplined than personable, attached to priorities, not details, and they were cool-headed even when they didn't see eye to eye. These were the bulwarks of the station, allowing me time and space to seek opportunities and watch for the next train, for both would surely come.

Opportunities and Threats

Carlisle Plastics was our biggest client-and the most demanding. They wanted a Freight Management System (FMS) integrated to a

Business Planning and Control System (BPCS), which SSA didn't offer. So we decided to build one for them. Carlisle and COI together developed a package that was fully integrated to BPCS, filling a gaping hole in the system. We found hundreds of prospects worldwide that needed this functionality, and SSA had no current plan to develop it. By default, we had become a software developer. After installing the system at Carlisle, we began an aggressive campaign to sign up the SSA affiliates to remarket our freight system. Soon we were taking orders and installing FMS throughout the country.

Roger Covey, SSA's founder, caught wind of our success. Realizing the gap in his own product line, plus the significant demand for this application, prompted him to approach us. He wanted to buy FMS, invest in COI, and make us a certified software-development partner. After a thirty-day negotiation, we sold FMS for seven figures, and SSA bought ten percent of the company, with the requirement that we change our name to SSA North Central. This unprecedented move set the stage for SSA to buy out its affiliates and go direct. We felt it was a marriage made in heaven.

By late 1994 the industry was showing discontent with proprietary hardware platforms. Clients wanted open systems, requiring all software companies to rebuild their packages to run on the new client server platforms. Only the companies with deep pockets could risk such an undertaking. It would cost SSA millions, but Roger Covey jumped in with both feet. SSA was well positioned with $500 million in sales and a ton of cash. Their stock had reached an all-time high of $42 per share, making it simple to do a secondary offering if necessary. I could see nothing stopping them, and as a certified development partner, I could see nothing stopping us, either.

SSA completed the development of their new software in sixteen months, their aggressive timetable assisted with a rapid-application development tool. A huge kickoff meeting was held in Chicago at the Nikko Hotel. Customers, affiliates, hardware providers, software developers, accounting firms, consulting houses, and media were invited to the celebration announcing BPCS/AS-the "AS" standing for Advanced Systems, an object-oriented technology designed to run on any hardware platform. Even though the market hadn't achieved widespread adoption, SSA was among the first to enter this new paradigm of computing.

We began taking orders for the new system, slow at first, but gaining momentum. More training was required, but as a development partner, we had the inside track. Early reports began to roll in on the software. In short, *it didn't work*. We found bugs everywhere. Bad news traveled quickly. Sales slowed. Green dollars turned into "blue dollars"-nonbillable service time spent fixing broken code, hence the nickname.

The size and scope of the problems were beyond the reach of SSA's research and development team and field support.

I gathered my team in the boardroom. Their mood was dark, something I hadn't seen in a long time.

"What should we do?" I asked my management team. "We're selling software that we know doesn't work. Our clients are running their businesses on this junk. Any ideas?"

"We'd better do something, or we're going to get sued," Dianne said. "Our customers have invested hundreds of thousands of dollars, and they have nothing to show for it. We are in trouble."

"Bob?" I asked.

"She's right. I'm not making friends out there delivering something that doesn't work."

"Hey, look, guys," Dave interjected. "I don't mean to be a crab ass, but we better find something to sell quick if you want to keep making payroll. We have over a hundred people out there who are counting on us."

"All right, all right. Give me some time to think about this," I said. "I'll get back to you soon."

Having been through this before, I didn't panic. We had time to react. I planned a trip to Chicago to visit Roger Covey.

Thirty-Seven Weeks of Hell

Roger's work schedule was booked the following week, so rather than wait, I got on a plane and visited him that weekend at his home. His home was in the city, and like Roger, the house was unusual-a old warehouse converted to an eclectic design of sharp angles, high ceilings, lofted bedrooms, and an open-pit cooking center. I had heard that the front door had been brought in from a castle in Scotland. It was bizarre but impressive.

As always, Roger was accommodating and friendly. Greeting me warmly at the door, he led me to his study. He was relaxed and attentive-a side of him that I hadn't seen before. "Mike, you seem panicky. What's going on?" he asked.

"Not panicky, Roger. Concerned," I replied. "I believe we'll get through this, but I can't risk going it alone. It appears that without immediate assistance from SSA, we could get sued. We can't afford it, and I won't allow it. We've worked too hard."

"Why don't we just buy you out, Mike?" he offered.

He sat motionless, watching me squirm. Roger always worked fast, but I was completely unprepared for that suggestion.

"You're kidding. Right?"

He wasn't. "That way you don't have any risk," he said. "And I don't run the risk of losing you." Roger smiled. "You can't tell me you haven't been talking to other software companies." His intelligence was good. We had been approached.

He studied me through the large frames that slid down his nose. Roger Covey was an odd assemblage of geek and visionary-Ichabod Crane with a PC. He was skinny, pasty white, and spoke in a high-pitched squeal. At his office his laugh pierced SSA's sprawling hallways. This was followed by serious walks, head down, hands clasped behind his back, sometimes holding a cigar. One moment he'd be chatty and animated, brewing some genius idea. The next moment he'd be withdrawn, moody, and liable to bite your head off. His genetic code was thoroughbred technician, but he had an affinity for sales guys. He studied them, bemused by their approach to life. He wanted to be like them, be respected by them. That's probably why he and I got along so well. He always told me things that he rarely told others. And he always told the truth.

"Now's the time to sell, Mike. I'm not sure how long the new architecture can be supported through affiliates, anyway. The world is changing. The software is too complex. Why don't you think about a price and let me know?"

I couldn't believe how sudden this was. Here I had gone to Chicago to work out a problem, and now I was facing the prospect of selling out. I wasn't ready for this, and I had no idea how the others would react. The thought of selling the company was intriguing. For the right price I could retire, which under the circumstances was tempting.

I flew home, met with my managers, and laid out our options.

"We can continue business as usual, which will clearly lead to more trouble in the field. Serious trouble I might add. We can find a new software relationship, which will require us to start over. We can get out of software and just provide services, but we would have to fire half of our staff. Or . . . we can sell."

My team stared at me with shocked looks.

"Would you *actually* consider selling?" Dave asked.

"For the right price . . . yes," I replied. "Look, business as usual is dead. One lawsuit and we could lose the whole thing. And I'm not anxious to start over with another software company, either. Our people couldn't take it, anyway. Here's what I propose we do. Break the services organization out as a separate company. SSA's a minority shareholder, so they can't prevent it. We sell only the components that SSA needs. That way we get a return on what we've built, and we pave the way for a future business: *professional services*. I think I can get Roger to go along with it."

We debated for a long time. But in the end I convinced them that this was the best course of action for both the good of the company and our people. We formed a new services firm which we called North Central Consulting-NCC-and moved about thirty people into this organization. We were now in position to negotiate.

I flew back to Chicago.

Roger and I agreed on a price in less than fifteen minutes. He was so swamped that he couldn't afford to quibble. We shook on it and began preparing the contracts and arranging due diligence. The entire experience was surreal. This was not like most company sales. It was so fast, so easy. I didn't even have time to get excited. On the cab ride home from the airport, exhausted and hungry, the adrenalin rush sliding into quiet contemplation, I began to realize the huge dollars that were on the way. I started to get excited. And with NCC up and running, I would still have something to do. The only catch was that I was required to stay with SSA to assist with the transition-a reasonable request.

The sale was structured as a stock-for-stock transfer. I was the sole owner at the time; however, Bob Solfelt had earned significant incentive stock options, affording him a handsome pot of his own. The SSA stock that we received in the sale had to be properly registered with the Securities and Exchange Commission before we could sell it. We were promised that this procedure would take no longer than six weeks.

Bob and I waited anxiously for registration, fearing that the price of the stock could drop during that time. As with all software companies, the stock was subject to large quarterly swings. Investors have always been fickle about technology. The strike price in the deal was $17 per share. Every dollar below that would cost us $400,000. Six weeks came and went. No registration. I called SSA's legal council, Kent Israelson, to begin applying pressure.

"Kent, what's going on?" I asked. "You told us our demand registration had been filed and that this would take no longer than six weeks. You said it was a simple routine. It has now been two months. This is not right. You have our company, and all we have is a bunch of paper that we can't sell."

"Relax, Mike. It shouldn't be much longer," he said.

"It better not be, Kent. If this stock starts dropping, we're gonna have a real problem."

"I can't control the stock, Mike. And I certainly can't control the SEC. Just be patient. Everything will be fine," he said.

The stock began to drop. Now Kent was avoiding my phone calls. I was getting scared. Eight weeks went buy, then ten, then twelve. No registration. Bob and I were frantic. We both had taken a serious pay cut after the sale, which would have been fine had we been able to cash out our stock. We continued to operate the company and assist with the transition, in direct conflict with our better judgment. We were trapped.

SSA put out a press release, announcing a delay of their annual report. They had had a dispute with their auditor. The details of the dispute were sketchy at first, plunging the stock to $8 per share. It turned out that SSA was under investigation by the SEC for allegedly booking over $35 million of fictitious business in the third and fourth quarters. When the story broke, the stock plunged to $3 per share, and a stockholder suit was filed against SSA, its board of directors, and its senior officers. Bob and I were devastated. SSA had our company, and we had nothing but a bunch of worthless stock certificates, meaningless jobs, and devoured paychecks.

After thirty-seven weeks the smoke finally cleared. SSA negotiated a settlement with the SEC and the shareholders, then hired a new accounting firm that eventually certified their financials. Bob and I finally registered our stock, which had rebounded somewhat. We got out at $9 per share-a fifty percent hit on the sale price of the company. We ended up with less than book value.

Sixteen years of work-down the drain.

With no job and no company, I had little choice but to accept a position as general manager of global marketing for SSA. NCC couldn't support us. It was too small. The irony was that I spent most of my time in public relations trying desperately to prop up SSA's tarnished image. They were losing market share, and many of their best people left to go work for competitors.

Once my stock was finally sold, I turned in my resignation to Roger. I intended to return to NCC, get back on my feet, and somehow reclaim my old company. But a tight no-compete clause had me tied up.

I walked in Roger's office unannounced and quit.

"Mike, you can't quit right now. It would look bad. I can't lose any more executives. Stick around until after the financing is complete," he pleaded.

SSA was days away from closing a financing deal worth $100 million. The company's survival was at stake. This was my opening. Roger needed me.

I unabashedly exploited the situation.

"Look, Roger, if I'm going to help you, you'll have to help me," I said. "I want my company back. I'll pay you for it-not much mind you, but I want it back. I got killed on this deal, and you know it. I didn't build this thing for sixteen years just to end up with a few table scraps. So that's the deal. Take it, or I'm out of here today."

"All right, you can buy it back. But we need a complete release on both sides. I don't want any more trouble. Agreed?"

"Agreed."

We shook on it. It was done.

Roger got his financing, and two weeks later North Central Consulting bought back SSA North Central (formerly Computer Options). The whole thing seemed crazy. I knew the situation was going to be highly sensitive. You don't just throw people around as if they're beanbags. One minute you're sold, the next minute you're bought back. So I gave our people a choice: They could either stay with SSA or join NCC. Their decision to return was made easier when NCC was named a development and implementation partner for SSA, allowing our company to pick up where it had left off. The partnership was part of the negotiated settlement between Roger and me. All but a few of my people returned.

Battered by the storm but still afloat, we were finally liberated, back on the open seas. For the first time in years we were no longer dependent on a partner or supplier. We could set sail wherever we wanted. But where should that be? And what route should we take? Wherever we were going this time, I wanted to get their fast. I was getting tired.

Chapter 17

Leading NCC

Perhaps you've questioned whether you have what it takes to be a leader. Well, if you have willing followers, you're a leader. It's as simple as that. Leaders lead. The good ones don't even declare themselves "leader." They don't have to. They just start moving in a certain direction, pulled by a vision. This vision is so compelling, so ideal, and so clear that they feel as though they can reach out and touch it. And they want others to see it, too, believe in it, and forge ahead with them so that together they can achieve something great. A leader's enthusiasm is infectious. His or her mere force of will, like a strong current, pulls people along.

At first, the vision is clear only to the leader, but soon others also begin to see it because the leader is constantly painting a picture for them, with attention to every detail. The leader inspires them to think how great it will be when they all get there. The leader challenges others to reach down deep and contribute their best to attain the vision. When this inspiration takes hold, the organization is transformed. Willing followers go beyond themselves, no longer just knowing what to do but also why they are doing it. They see where they fit, where they add value, and the payoff that's in store for them. They begin thinking like leaders themselves, with a sense of resolve, focused on the same destination. The vision is no longer just the leader's; it belongs to everyone.

This creates an explosion of momentum, a kind of corporate "Aha!"- a quickening effect for everyone on the journey. The leader can begin to hand over the reins to some of the other leaders because he has done his job preparing them. The team can now carry on the rest of the way while the leader begins to scout ahead for the next adventure.

Look, I don't mean to be dramatic, but these are truly the images that

I conjure up when I think of leaders. People have been trying to define leadership for years. They say, "I can't describe it exactly, but I know it when I see it." It's easier to illustrate leaders by what they do than by what they are.

Sharpen the Vision

NCC borrowed two hundred thousand dollars from Norwest Bank. Our relationship was so strong at that time that they didn't bat an eye. They just gave us the money. This brings me to another point: Bankers are required business partners. But they're quirky, and they're high maintenance. Build a relationship with them. The key to a good relationship with your banker, which took me a while to understand, is no surprises. Tell them everything-good and bad-and tell them early. Bring them to the office at least once every quarter. Go through the numbers, share your vision, and get them on your team. They have to believe in the vision, too.

NCC was small in early 1995-fewer than forty people, but they were all very talented and motivated. Looking back, I was still stuck in the SSA mess and traveling to Chicago every week, so I was providing marginal leadership at best for NCC, which you can get away with for a while if you have good people. But you can be an armchair quarterback for only so long. Eventually chaos sets in. Other leaders emerge within the organization, pulling it in several directions. People get frustrated and confused. They wonder who's in charge.

Vision was never the problem. I knew *exactly* what I wanted NCC to be. The return of our SSA folks, combined with NCC's original core group, provided everything we needed. I wanted to build a diversified consulting team, doing hard projects-the hardest, in fact, the ones no one else wanted to do or even *could* do. We would serve only midsize companies because we understood them, they were willing to pay for quality, and we could develop relationships with their top executives.

I saw it all.

I saw fast growth and fully engaged people who understood the big picture. I saw career paths with personal and corporate goals perfectly aligned. I saw divisions, or work centers, tendering specific talents and specialties. These centers would be cooperative and synergistic, creating unique solutions for clients.

I saw all ages, all religions, and all races working for the company. I saw comfortable working conditions, tasteful but understated. I saw casual but professional dress, a departure from the pinstripe days-except for my sales force, who would remain in pinstripes. I saw managers leading and leaders managing because they needed to do both and do both extremely well. I saw celebrations and birthday parties and kickoff meetings loaded with fun and excitement. I saw two hundred consultants, big enough to be a force in the market but small enough to remain personal and agile.

I saw goals clearly defined, fully understood, and supported by carefully crafted plans. We would provide recognition for our people, a "Wall of Fame" for overachievers, and a bell to ring each time a salesperson brought in a new account. I saw a carefully designed recruiting process, hiring only the best and brightest. I saw a disciplined back office that knew how to run the numbers and report the facts as they were happening. I saw strong financial performance and an ever-increasing return on investment for the stockholders.

I saw a business strategy supported by a mission statement and a set of guiding principles that people took pride in-principles so compelling, goals so worthy of our best effort that the people would *manage themselves* to achieve them. I saw happy, not just satisfied, clients, absolutely delighted with the business relationship. I saw managers who were trusted and respected because they were competent and fair. I saw recognition from our community as well as competitors, acknowledging our market leadership. And it goes without saying that I saw the best sales team in the industry.

I could go on, but I won't. Just believe me that somehow this time I knew it could be done. You create your vision in your mind first. The details may be fuzzy, but through collaborative discussion and synergistic thinking, the vision becomes more realistic, more actionable. This collaboration is first done one on one, between you and your subordinates. The leader can't be hampered by a group discussion at this point. That would contaminate the vision. So you work alone at first, picking up a few bits of wisdom from each member of your team, all of which serves to sharpen the vision.

Flesh out the Vision

One afternoon Dave Van Meter came to me deeply concerned.

"Mike this is a mess. I know you've been tied up with SSA, but we're starting to fall apart. We have two completely different cultures that we've slammed together. Half of the company wants to do leading-edge stuff, and the other half-the SSA folks-are stuck in the old legacy systems. I sense resentment between the two groups, and there's an us-versus-them thing developing-which I'm finding ironic since the SSA people were here first, and they're the ones being alienated. People are confused, Mike. No one seems to know where we are going. I thought you should be aware of this."

It was sobering to hear, but I knew he was right. As I've said all along, the first order of business is the launch. You have to establish a cash flow if you're going to survive. We borrowed the money, and the bank was counting on us to launch this thing successfully. This is when a leader must be strong and willing to do whatever it takes to get the company off the ground. Now I had to get off my ass and inaugurate this vision because Dave was right. The company was spinning around.

The first thing I did was pull the resumés of every consultant in the company. I then asked each manager to summarize the resumés into their chief areas of expertise because I wanted to see what we were good at-or, more accurately, what we knew how to do. We had forty-five consultants at that point, and we were adding three new people a month. But who were we adding? And why?

Then I asked each manager to research the market and come to agreement about what they thought were the top five technologies being used today. I wanted leading-edge stuff but not at the exclusion of our bread-and-butter technologies, things that we could always depend on. Next, I had the managers overlay the expertise of our people against these five technologies-connecting the dots, so to speak.

An interesting picture emerged. We ended up with eight fast-growth segments, and we had at least three people skilled in each one. But eight seemed like too many, so I cut it back to six. I wrote all six segments up on the white board, then locked the door for two days so that I could create an organization to fulfill the vision that was in my head.

I wrote down the names of each consultant under one of the six segments, sifting through the organization to select those individuals who precisely matched our segments. A new organization was taking shape, one that allowed for the expression of individual capabilities and a chance for them to respond to the challenge. And if they did, I would support them and recognize them and promote them. This would create the motivational climate I was looking for and ready them for the next challenge. I can't tell you how many applicants told us in the interview that the primary reason for seeking new employment was a need for "more opportunity, more challenge." It was rarely just the money.

A fairly even distribution emerged, although we were thin in a couple of areas. While I liked the diversity, I was afraid of breaking up the SSA people for two reasons: (1) They were already traumatized by the sale, followed by its undoing, and (2) they were profitable and working on some lucrative long-term projects. So I killed one of the inadequate segments and added a segment exclusively for the SSA folks.

These segments now needed names. I went back to my managers for ideas, only to have them ask, "What are you doing in there?" To which I'd respond, "Nothing, nothing at all." They smiled and shook their head. Twenty-four hours later I had names for all six segments, which I decided to call Centers of Excellence (COE).

The names given to these COEs were Application Solutions, Enterprise Solutions, Advanced Technologies, Engineering Solutions, Client/Server Solutions, and Project Management. Each Center of Excellence became a stand-alone business unit, responsible for revenue contribution, profitability, and growth. Each would also be responsible for innovation (business development), and people development, and all were designed to anticipate and meet future challenges. Technology changed so quickly that I wanted each COE to adopt a grassroots approach to finding new opportunities.

Next I selected leaders for these Centers of Excellence. But I hadn't figured out what to call them. The word *champion* always seemed to creep into any conversation concerning technology. I'm not sure why, but people would say, "He's a champion at that" or "She could champion that cause." So I called them champions, departing from the conventional wisdom of calling them tech managers. Who wants to be one of those dull-sounding drones?

I now had a clear picture of our business units and their mission. But I was worried about unity-a person's loyalty to the entire enterprise, not just to their Center of Excellence. In other words, I didn't want six separate companies. I wanted one company, united by a set of guiding principles and a common vision. I wanted people to have pride in their COE and have a sense of competition with one another. That's healthy. But I also wanted them to support one another and be one another's cheerleader. How could I accomplish this?

First, I looked to the compensation system to inspire that unity. We would devise a way where fifty percent of management bonuses would be tied to the attainment of COE goals, and fifty percent would be tied to overall corporate goals. It wouldn't do us much good to have three superstar centers only to have three that were mediocre-or worse. And I was concerned that each center would be competing for people resources. Large client projects needed expertise from more than one center-sometimes up to four. I didn't want managers hoarding resources to protect their revenue, and I certainly didn't want them hiring people when another unit already had what they needed. That would be crazy. But I've seen this happen before, and it is always caused by misalignment of company goals and personal compensation.

Second, I looked at the sales strategy. Did I want a dedicated salesperson for each center, or should I split the reps by industry? Or maybe I should go with territories, allowing the sales force to have all centers in their bag. This was a tough one. Without a dedicated sales force, it would be tricky to hold a champion accountable for growth within his or her center. This would give them an out: "Hey, I don't have my own rep. Gimme a break." And salespeople sell what's hot or what they're most comfortable with. I decided to go with territories, allowing the salespeople to have everything in their bag to sell. But there was a catch. Their quota assignment required them to be balanced performers: They had to sell all six centers. I packed big incentives into their plan to drive this behavior. Salespeople go where the money is.

From the White Board to Reality

This vision was now scrawled all over my white board, and I was beginning to like what I saw. I brought Dave Van Meter into my office. Dave was not a yes-man or a know-it-all. Above all, he wasn't political. So I knew I could trust his reaction. This is an important step in fleshing out your vision. Up till now you have been operating alone. And as I said before, you must. But at this stage you need a sounding board, someone who gets an early peek at what you're doing. Choose wisely. This person should challenge you and force you to think more clearly. You must take this step before going any further.

Dave loved most of what I had come up with and offered to design the compensation plans when the time came. "What I really like is the focused recruiting we can now do," he said. "The centers define the exact skills we need. We won't be stuck with these oddball skill sets that we can't sell. Now you can assign quotas to the recruiters and have them specialize on certain technologies. They'll know where the bones are buried."

"Exactly! And think of the synergy we'll have between the sales force and the recruiters. They'll need one another to make their numbers," I said.

"Absolutely. But something's bothering me here."

"What's that?"

"Each of your champions is a huge revenue producer today. The minute you put one in charge of a Center of Excellence, you've lost that revenue. That would be about eighty-five thousand dollars a month. You know how it is with new managers, Mike. They get their stripe, and then they think they don't have to work anymore."

That brought me up short. "Gosh, that's a good point." I thought about it for a moment. "Maybe we can devise a scheme for them to work their way out of the field. In other words, they have to keep billing until they reach a certain revenue threshold within their center. Anyway, we're getting ahead of ourselves. We can work all that out in planning."

Okay, I'm going to stop with the minutiae now. But you get the picture. I took a mob of consultants with no rhyme or reason and began to give them order, though not just any order. It had to support the vision. Think of an artist who visualizes a finished painting is in his head. He now has to choose the right colors, the right texture. The approach must have a certain order. Leaders are like artists.

Once you illustrate your vision, the business structure to support it, and the people you can count on to fulfill it, you're ready to open your door and start selling it. The first place you go is to your team. But you do it one on one. You need that intimacy, that free exchange of ideas. And if you have objections or concerns, you can handle them more easily. You will also get loads of new information to refine the vision.

After that, get your team together, preferably offsite, in a comfortable and professional atmosphere, and make your formal presentation. This is one of the most important presentations you will ever make, so pull out all the stops. This meeting will set the tone and the direction for your company. The goal is quite simple. Your team must see the exact vision that you do, and they must believe in it as much as you do. Then organize your team around this new purpose-a purpose so compelling that they work relentlessly to achieve it. I'm not sure it's realistic to believe that everyone will carry the same passion as the leader. But they must be committed to the vision and willing to do their part to make it a reality.

And that's what I think leaders do.

Chapter 18

Putting it all Together

North Central Consulting (NCC) caught a tidal wave-two of them, in fact. The first was the Y2K craze. Remember? Every company in the world was scrambling to make their software Y2K compliant by December 31, 1999. They thought they were facing doomsday. The second was e-commerce, an explosion of Internet applications. This market was the forebearer as well as the pallbearer to the rise and fall of the dot coms. Between these two markets there weren't enough technical resources on the planet to meet the demand. Consulting firms that had the right people-and enough of them-were the big winners. You could name your price. The average billing rate climbed from $65 to over $130 per hour. Profitability surged, and NCC surged with it, thanks to our business model, which handled the hypergrowth beautifully.

But how long would it last? What would happen to all those consultants after the Y2K bubble burst? The work would grind to a halt, that's what.

I calculated we had a three-year window to build the company, after which time we would sell it or go public. That was the plan. By June of 1998-the probable peak of the Y2K frenzy-we would have to be ready to exit. By then the big consulting firms would be gobbling up the little ones, all of them in desperate need of resources. I expected a mass consolidation at premium prices. It was beginning to look just like MII, only five times bigger.

They Needed to Want Us

NCC's cast of characters started with none other than my nephew, Marc Strazzanti. He had grown up wonderfully and was so much like Alex-charismatic, funny, bright, and Italian through and through, right down to his bushy black hair and heavy beard. Maybe it's in the genes, but this kid was a natural salesman. I was determined to make him a star, a promise that I had made to Alex and Lindsey years before.

Marc was my top salesman, crushing his quota year after year. Alex would have been proud of him. Bringing in Marc was like bringing in my own son. His loyalty was never a question, nor was my commitment to him. He knew he would have to perform at a high level to escape any assertions that I might be showing him favoritism. And he did so.

Another surprise was the discovery of Erica McClean. At age twenty-six, she was beautiful, athletic, young, and amazingly driven. She had been an All-American volleyball player in college and a straight-A student. Erica started as an administrative assistant for our first recruiting manager, who washed out quickly. Seizing the day, she became our best recruiter and within six months was promoted to director of recruiting. Dawn, who had helped out with recruiting during the early stages, spotted Erica and told me to keep an eye on her, telling me, "She has something special." Erica hired and trained seven full-time recruiters, who together produced fifteen new consultants per month. When Erica and her team got done with you, you were no longer the recruit, we were. She was a star.

It's not about age, folks. It's about desire, inspiration, and perspiration.

The rest of the management team-one of the finest I had ever assembled-was led by Dave Van Meter, vice president of professional services; Brad Duhaime, vice president of advanced solutions; Pat Voelker, vice president of sales; and, of course, Dave Faidley, vice president of finance. The secret to managing these high achievers was to state what to do and when to do it-but I had to avoid diligently any assertions of *how* to do it. They had to figure it out themselves. Otherwise I would fall into that old trap again, demoting myself from leader to doer, which would stifle both them and our growth. In other words, I had to get the hell out of the way.

I finally discovered that high achievers must always be viewed as logical candidates for an upward move. These people want broader and more rigorous challenges and opportunities. They want the results to speak for themselves. Sink or swim is their way of life. When they perform, keep moving them up, and expand their duties. Otherwise they'll get discouraged or, worse yet, quit. If they aren't performing, and the situation is left unchecked, everyone will know it, and you'll be signaling to the entire organization that it's okay to miss expected results. That's how we now ran the railroad, with neither malice nor pity. And the organization grew, filling its ranks with the best and brightest. Tens were hiring tens. Once it starts, you can't stop it. The locomotive steams ahead.

The turnover in the industry was extraordinarily high, around thirty-five percent. Ours was half that. People with technical skills were extremely hard to find, and companies were paying a premium to get them. So the personnel function-responsible for recruiting, procuring, or pirating the individuals that we needed-rose quickly to the top of the charts. At one point we were paying our employees $3,000 referral bonuses to find the right skills. But we needed something more to attract them-and keep them. *They needed to want us.* If all we had to offer was a high salary, we would eventually lose them, anyway. Our business model and corporate culture both needed the rudiments to attract and keep the best.

Here are a few examples of what we did:

1. We offered a competitive salary, comprehensive benefits, and hefty incentive bonuses, tied directly to client-satisfaction ratings. Consistently high ratings plus tenure earned points that, for example, could be converted to tuition dollars to be used toward job-related education at the university of their choice. The consultant's desire to be leading edge paved the way for this incentive and promoted positive relationships with clients. It was a perfect integration of personal and corporate goals.

2. Our business model provided opportunity for personal-skill enhancement, challenging projects, expanded industry knowledge, and rapid advancement. With multiple Centers of Excellence (COEs), our consultants could swing in and out of different technologies and industries with each new project, finding variety, recompense, and challenge.

3. We started NCC University, an inside COE providing advanced technical education for our people that mostly had been taught by insiders. This cross-pollination of skills enhanced the job experience for both teacher and student.

4. We established an "office hotel" concept, whereby consultants could check in and have at their disposal a personal computer, educational tools, internet access, research materials, a comfortable meeting area, and privacy. They had state-of-the-art resources to use, and the company saved a ton on space costs.

5. We had an award and recognition program that regularly honored people for high achievement. Accomplishments were posted for everyone to see. Win reports and technology briefs were published, which were used for marketing while showcasing our successes.

6. Our annual kick-off meetings were vibrant, thematic, clever, and, most of all, fun. We reported the company numbers quickly and set the stage for the upcoming year. I always gave a keynote address, but once finished I turned the meeting over to my managers, who presented the numbers. Once people knew everything was solid, we went directly to recognition, awards, and bonuses. We had skits, talent shows, door prizes, and some of the finest motivational speakers in the country. We celebrated our people.

7. We established a formal orientation process for each new employee, regardless of position. I wanted everyone to know the history, values, goals, and opportunities within the organization. Orientation took two days, during which time newcomers were treated like royalty. They hit the ground running.

8. We did the little things, too. Our reception area flashed a scrolling Power Point presentation, promoting our mission, values, and occasional job openings. We posted announcements, birthdays, anniversaries, new babies, new employees, and significant new business that we had won. We included a picture of each new person and a bio on his or her talents.

All these things and more created a culture committed to excellence and innovation. Technology became art, not just the drudgery of writing code. We had no room for bureaucracy or unnecessary controls designed to minimize and eliminate risk. Our people knew the boundaries, and as long as they stayed within them, they were free to experiment. We encouraged risk-taking. If a person made a mistake, so what? Just fix it, learn from it, and share what you learned with others.

Our corporate culture never allowed for criticism of an individual for being "too ambitious," "too aggressive," "too impatient," or "too demanding," provided he or she was a good thinker-fair-minded, and straightforward with others. I've seen companies use these labels to criticize their people, but they characterized exactly the kind of people we wanted. People who are too easygoing, willing to compromise their principles to avoid conflict, and more interested in being liked than getting things done came under fire at NCC. These people create a mushy and political work environment that makes it impossible to build a strong team or achieve outstanding results.

Of course, primary to all of this was the client, who paid our salaries. We never let anyone forget that. The only sustainable competitive advantage any business has is client satisfaction. Actually, this is a far too modest goal-heck, every customer expects to be satisfied. We wanted them to be delighted plus highly referenceable-an extension of our sales force. So we had to create a business model that would hold these essential values within its very makeup. We needed a model that would attract seasoned and inventive people with years of experience as well as the young mavericks who had something to prove. We wanted irreverent, out-of-the-box, transformational thinkers because the world of technology was changing so quickly. This model and blend of skills delivered a customer-intimate approach and held the keys for our phenomenal growth.

What were some of those keys? We started offering our clients a cost-containment feature in their contract. Most clients feared hourly contracts, since they were so open-ended. Project costs could get out of control quickly, with no guarantee of quality. They also feared fixed-price contracts because they were fattened up to protect the consulting firm against overruns. Both of these approaches are fraught with risk. We created a better approach. We called it the "Phased Bid Method." This approach, supported by our COEs-the backbone of our company-facilitated the coordination and packaging of expertise to deliver the best solution at the best price while allowing our clients to maintain control over their own destiny. The objective was simple: win/win, which leads to long-term clients.

This method broke the total project down into smaller projects or phases. Each phase could be priced separately, tightly, and at its completion would have discrete deliverables for clients to accept or reject, thus preserving quality and giving them some control. The client had the choice to continue with us to the next phase, or fire us and bring in someone else. We were held accountable every step of the way. If there was an overrun on the phase (which could happen), we would bill the overrun at fifty percent of the contract rate. This allowed us at least to cover our cost, with the client also getting a break. At no time would any phase surpass a fifteen percent overrun.

If it did, we would suspend all charges. It provided protection for both parties plus preserved quality.

The trick to making this model work was tying the consultants' compensation plan to the project phases and *client satisfaction index*. Every two weeks, when we billed our clients for our services, we requested that they complete a client-satisfaction index-ten simple questions. The results of the index, combined with the size of the project billings, determined the consultants' bonuses. This *integrated business and compensation model* was a huge success. The clients were delighted, the consultants were motivated, and NCC excelled. Some consultants were able to increase their earnings by thirty percent. With all the repeat business we were getting as a result of this model, we were glad to pay it.

Personal Goals and Company Goals Came Together

We were actively seeking funding to accelerate growth and take more market share. Raising capital wasn't actually a necessity, we figured, but with only a three-year window, the company had to grow fast. Next came opening offices in Milwaukee and Chicago, and we wanted to start a new COE specializing in CAD/CAM applications, which was another booming field. To do this safely we needed more cash. We had built an integrated business model, and it was working. I wasn't going to put things at risk by running out of money. I had already been down that road. We had several funding options available to us.

Dave Faidley and I were sitting in his office on a Saturday morning. I brought the doughnuts. Dave always looked like a lumberjack on the weekends: unshaven, John Deere cap, dirty blue jeans, and long underwear under his flannel shirt. I chuckled at the sight of him. He was not exactly the CFO image. But he was good at what he did, and I trusted him. We had been through a lot together.

He leaned back in his chair, straightened his cap, and stared at the ceiling. "Mike, what do you think we should do? We can take the mezzanine financing deal-one and a half million dollars to be paid back over five years with interest and warrants. Or we can do the venture-capital deal for one million in equity. Or we can just go back to the bank. They've already agreed to a credit increase."

I thought for a minute. "The bank bothers me because secured debt is always subject to covenants that are likely to be rigid. That could be too restricting, given how fast we want to grow. As for the mezzanine, that's a little pricey in my opinion. We'll pay three points over prime, plus they get stock warrants, too. So . . . I don't know. What do you think?"

I asked.

"I think I like the venture deal. It's pure equity; no strings."

"C'mon, Dave, there are always strings with outside investors. You know that."

Dave pulled his cap over his eyes and yawned. "Well . . . maybe . . . but what else is there?" he asked.

"You're not going to believe this, but I think we can raise the money internally," I said.

"*Internally*?! Are you kidding me?" He sat upright in his chair. "Haven't you had enough trouble with internal shareholders?"

"Different time, different place, Dave. Think about it. The benefits are enormous. We'll present it to them just as we did to the venture guys, and just as professionally. We'll bring in legal to answer questions, and the accountants should be there, too. We'll even invite the bank. I'll put a pitch together that will knock their socks off. We can raise the million internally. I'm telling you. It will work."

"With internal financing, there's a bunch of things to consider, Mike," Dave countered. He ticked them off. "No-competes, shareholder agreements, covenants, shareholder rights, full financial disclosure, increased legal and accounting expense, more staff required, more record-keeping. I mean, it's complicated."

"Dave, I don't railroad things anymore. You know that. But this is perfect! Absolutely perfect timing. We gotta do this. Call Dave Byron"- he was our lawyer-"on Monday. Let's see what he says."

I had a good feeling about it, and after another half hour of debate, so did Dave. I've always believed that when personal goals and company goals come together, you release an energy within your organization that's unstoppable. The company will belong to everybody, so they'll all *act* like owners, looking for ways to increase revenue, lower costs, cut corners, improve quality, delight customers, develop products, streamline processes, make money-and all the while having fun. Everyone would be investors, not merely employees, all pulling in the same direction. If we did this right, the payoff would be phenomenal.

The managers supported my idea and helped me create the presentation. We called all of our employees together on a Tuesday after work (Mondays had never been good for me). We provided a tasty buffet dinner and set the stage. Every detail was worked out, every number checked and rechecked for this key presentation. What I wanted to impress upon them first was that we had several options available to finance the business, but *this* was the one we wanted. We wanted our people to share in the dream. The target was simple: fast, profitable growth, followed by a sale or public offering in three years.

The second impression I wanted to make was that we were well beyond the start-up phase. We hadn't just laced up our sneakers, we were winning the race. The business model was working, the market conditions were ideal, and we had the best team in the industry-who attacked obstacles, found solutions, outsmarted competition, recovered from mistakes, knew how to have fun, and had a killer instinct.

On their one year anniversary, all employees were invited to invest. They were entitled to buy up to four units of stock. A unit was ten thousand shares at $1.00 per share. The charter shareholders would also receive one stock option at $1.50 per share equal to the same quantity purchased in the initial round, in effect doubling their holdings.

The reception was overwhelming. An astounding eighty percent participated. Some people took out second mortgages on their houses to buy their units. I personally invested $400,000 to demonstrate my commitment and belief in the organization. We raised $1.5 million, only giving up fifteen percent of the company, which was consistent with the valuations arrived at by the venture capital people. The bankers and auditors were thunderstruck. They had seen private placements before, but they had *never* seen a large employee base write out a check to buy stock in a private company. One of our lawyers said, "If it wasn't a conflict of interest, I'd invest myself."

The Business Life Cycles

As I expected, the company exploded, achieving ten consecutive quarters of double-digit growth, and in 1997 we were ranked by *City Business* magazine as the second-fastest-growing company in the state of Minnesota. Our rate of growth far exceeded COI the year it had made the *Inc.* 500. For the first time I could clearly see all the life cycles of the business taking place, and the management disciplines required to deal with it.

Let's review:

The *first* cycle is the launch. Moderate planning followed by action. Remember, this creates lift. You will need enough working capital to cover the launch period. The cash is out there-go find it. Your goal is to generate a cash flow in the first ninety days. Begin sorting through the conditions in the market. Spot the opportunities and align the company to exploit them. Pick and shape your team. Configure a flexible organization with the necessary checks and balances. Turn the team loose, and grab whatever market share you can. Worry about substance, not form. Most of all: Act!

The *second* cycle is stabilization. You are off the ground. *Poof!* Now you must pick your spots in the market. I call this preplanning, fleshing out the vision. Who are you and where are you going? As the leader you must shape a business model, enlisting help and gaining support from your team. This model should integrate the personal goals of your people with the business goals you have established, with everything supporting growth and profitability. Don't etch it in concrete, though, until you complete your detailed strategic planning, and make sure everything is focused on delighting clients.

The *third* cycle is strategic planning. This you must do while you are operating. Planning is tedious and time-consuming. Use Tubby's planning model outlined in chapter 14. (You'll also find it in complete form in The Toolkit.) Complete the plan, and introduce it to your entire organization. Roll out the vision, set the culture, outline the rules, and steadily gain the hearts and minds of your people. Focus your human-resource policies on personal growth, reward, recognition, and advancement. Your people are your number one natural resource. Feed them challenges, encourage innovation, allow them to make mistakes, and honor them for their successes.

The *fourth* cycle is sustained growth. The company must be profitable-unlike the travesty of the dot com companies. The quickest way to bye-bye is no profits. Sustained growth comes from solid plan execution, healthy cash flow (which is only achieved through profits), and a corporate culture devoted to delighting the client. Everything must be weaved together to allow this to happen naturally. You made a smart plan, now work it-and measure everything. I received a report every Friday that I called the Critical Success Report. It summarized accounts receivable, accounts payable, daily sales, headcount, new hires, terminations, average billing rate, gross-margin percent, gross-margin dollars, capital expenditures, top-ten clients (measured by revenue), size of bench (consultants that were not billing), birthdays, and anniversaries. I watched every move. If the indicators were okay, I didn't interfere. When I spotted trouble, I started coaching. I was still calling the plays, but I let my team run the ball.

You must be careful in this phase. When you're experiencing the euphoria of explosive growth and huge margins, it's easy to get sloppy. High tide covers a lot of rocks. But low tide will return soon enough, and if you've neglected the basics, instead of floating on the high seas for the long haul your heavily laden ship will be hung up on a pile of rocks you never saw coming. Stay on the high seas-full steam ahead, in fact-but keep the radar on, and watch where you're going. Fat margins are your friend, but they can also be your enemy.

After twenty years I had finally figured out how to build a corporate culture that truly aligned precisely with the value commitment to customers. We realized that customer value and exceeding their expectations was the ultimate measure of our success. That's the only way to turn on growth and keep it turned on. This customer credo was sewn into the very fabric of our company. Our employees were proud that their customers could count on them, and they were rock-solid on delivering what they promised. They got up in the morning, got right, and got going with a sense of purpose and direction. As the leader, it's your responsibility to remove every obstacle that blocks the value commitment, and you are obligated to provide the necessary tools so that your people can do their job. Then and only then can you demand performance.

I had no need to micromanage; all of our consultants knew and freely accepted their responsibilities. They became heroes for our customers, providing solutions that had once been only a vision. My job got easier and easier. I simply rounded up our heroes and carried them around on my shoulder.

In 1998 we entered the *fifth* and final cycle: the exit strategy. Just as I had predicted, the industry began to consolidate. The big guys had to protect and expand market share through strategic acquisitions. We still wanted to go public, but it seemed we might have missed the window. It appeared that acquisition was our best bet.

We received a call from Whittman-Hart, a high-flying publicly held consulting firm out of Chicago. They had opened an office in Minneapolis that was struggling. NCC was kicking the crap out of them. Our name had hit their radar screen as a key acquisition target. Within thirty days we had three other companies interested in buying us, which didn't hurt the bidding process. But we liked Whitman-Hart. Their business model and values were similar to ours, and they had an excellent reputation. They also offered us the best deal.

After several visits, extensive negotiations, and burning gallons of midnight oil, we reached a final agreement. The sale was structured as a "pooling of interest" (a tax-free exchange of our stock for theirs).

Having been through hell and back with SSA, we insisted that the stock be registered, enabling it to be freely tradable on the day of the sale. Pooling deals are terrific because you are not taxed until you sell your stock. You can hold the stock if you want, allowing it to appreciate at full value. This flexibility was particularly attractive to our people. The numbers were staggering.

On July 7, 1998, we hit the grand slam. Several individuals became instant millionaires, and every single one of our shareholders nearly doubled their money. Four days later Whittman-Hart announced a two for one stock split, doubling everyone's holdings. Whittman's stock then doubled again six months later. Some of our shareholders received a four-to-one return by the time they cashed out. If you follow the math, an employee who had invested the maximum of $40,000 (four units) in NCC, received $80,000 in stock on July 7, which was worth $160,000 six months later. It was unbelievable. It all finally came together. After twenty years of trying, it *finally* came together.

In Closing

Staying in the Boat

When I'm asked for the secrets of my success - and I hope they are not a secret anymore - I often say I have three: Pray a lot, never give up, and live your life with your eyes open - so you don't miss it. This may seem like an oversimplification, but for me it's true. I finished what I had started, I stayed in the boat, and without prayer that never would have happened. I would have given up. I found out later in life that this level of spiritual commitment, when combined with seeing and accepting life on life's terms is what paved the way for my demanding business career. And I believe the reciprocal is true: my business - even with all the headaches - taught me never to give up, humbled me before God, and opened my eyes to a world that I still struggle to understand. A world that even now continues to throw me in the air as I strive to land on my feet. A world that I'm glad to be a part of.

I'm sitting in my office right now, trying to figure out how to close this book. It's late-about two, I think. My eyes are burning and my back hurts. But I keep at it. I look around and see my books on the shelf-the ones with the coffee stains. A few are still open and lying on the floor. My Epson printer hums in the silence, reminding me that I'm a business guy, not a writer. My eyes drift to the picture, and I chuckle. *I must tell my readers about the picture.* And then I wonder again, why did I write this book? Did I share everything I wanted to? Do I have any last-minute advice I need to give my readers? Was I too preachy, too long winded? Did I confuse them? These are just questions, I guess. Perhaps fears.

What I've imparted on the preceding pages is almost everything I know about starting and building a business. I've tried to be encouraging because that's my nature and because I love business. And I want you to love it, too. But you must understand that if you're not willing to work your ass off, then you have no business starting one. That's just the way it is. But if you do start a business-and I hope you do-never, never, never give up. You'll find as I have that success is nothing more than going from failure to failure without losing hope. Eventually you'll get it right. So embrace your failures, for *they* are your true teachers. Success teaches us little; it's just the way we keep score.

Now, about that picture, or should I say sketch? It has hung on my office wall for over fifteen years, a picture that is truly worth a thousand words. Most people think it's quite silly, even ugly. I don't even remember where I got it. But I love it because I feel like I'm in the sketch. The sketch is of a stormy sea; the sky is dark and angry, with lightning crashing into giant swells of water. Waves are churning and reaching into the heavens, blending the two into one. Sharks circle in the water, their fins piercing the steel-gray surface. Danger is everywhere, and there is no land in sight, no safe harbor. In the middle of this spectacular storm is a fisherman in a tiny boat, perched perilously at the crest of the highest wave, his net thrown onto the water. Wrapped in foul-weather gear and fisherman's cap, his face punished by the rain, he pulls his oars against the elements, his resolve to make his catch is etched on his face.

My eyes have drifted to this silly picture during times of great despair and great triumph. For me it has become a rousing symbol, a reminder, a friend. At the bottom of the picture is a simple caption that sums it up perfectly for the entrepreneur-at least it does for me. It reads: Famous last words . . . I've always wanted to run my own business.

Starting and building your own business isn't about making money, getting famous, or obtaining power. It's about staying in the boat. It's about outlasting the storms. It's about trusting God. Eventually the skies will clear, the waters will calm, and your nets will be filled. And to your delight you will discover that others were in the boat with you the whole time. Because in the end you have finally figured out that your business-your boat-is about enriching the lives of people: your employees, your clients, your loved ones. And in so doing, you enrich your own. And that, my friend, is the biggest payoff of all!

So what are you waiting for? Go find yourself a boat, climb in and start rowing. And remember - keep your eyes open.

The Toolkit

"Rusty old tools that will always work"

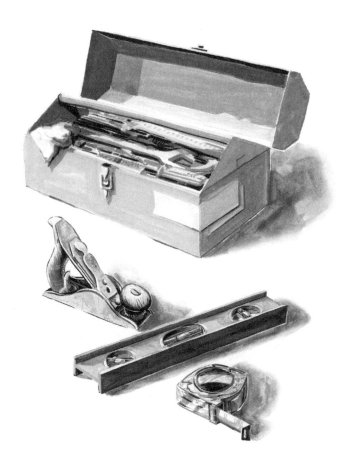

Selling Tools

Without Selling, You Have No Business

All right, let's talk shop for a minute. I know that I've made a big deal about selling as if it's the only thing that counts in business. True, lots of things count, but selling is the heartbeat of the business. Everything depends on it. Everything flows from it. The fact is, without selling, you have no business.

Nothing happens until something is sold. This axiom is older than dirt. Nonetheless, nothing could be more profoundly true. You can give me people, products, services, plans, money, and prospects, but without sales, I have nothing. Conversely, you can take everything away from me, and let me keep my sales force, and I'll be back in one year. If you want to start a business, if you have a dream, you'd better learn how to sell. Sure, you can find somebody to do it for you. It's called building a sales force. That comes later. Initially, though, you're the salesperson. You have to make it happen.

Selling Is a Professional System

What exactly is selling? I can tell you it's not signing contracts and taking orders. Selling is a professional system, made up of *repeatable, logical,* and *visible* steps. It's also a dynamic system, where the sales professional can *package, refine*, and *adapt* his or her selling approach to fit the environment or situation.

Mastery of a professional selling system requires many skills besides selling skills. It requires people skills, strategy planning, product knowledge, industry knowledge, competitive knowledge, organizational skills, territory-management skills, and time-management skills. You can make an okay living in sales merely by collecting a few of these. But if you want to become an expert, the highest of achievers, you must master all of them. Combine these skills with the desire to win, and you have a breakaway performer.

Selling is Like a Bicycle

A bicycle in its simplest form has a front wheel, a back wheel, and a frame. Imagine the front wheel representing the *relationship* side of selling, where people, strategy, and selling skills are required. The back wheel represents the *product* side, where product, industry, and competitive knowledge are important. The frame represents *infrastructure*, where organization, territory, and time-management are necessary.

The front wheel (relationship skills) takes you and your prospect where you want to go. The back wheel (product skills) provides the power to get you there. And the frame (infrastructure) holds everything together during your journey. You, the rider (salesperson), make it all go-first with training wheels and over time with mastery if you're willing to work hard. Salespeople have to work only half a day. It makes no difference which half, the first twelve hours or the last twelve.

Why is it so important that you have these skills? Simple answer: As a business owner, you will be selling yourself, your company, your products, and your people every minute of every day, whether you like it or not. No matter where you are-with a client, in the office, at the bank, at a church picnic-you will be representing yourself and your company. You will be building relationships and establishing your reputation everywhere you go. You will never know when one of these relationships could turn into a client, employee, investor, banker, board member, or important reference.

It also takes one to know one. Great salespeople are hard to find. Most of them are imposters who ride a great unicycle. If your guard is down, you'll end up hiring one. So you'd better be able to recognize the good ones when you see them. And when you do, you must convince them that your company is where they should be.

Many excellent books have been written on the art of selling: *Power Base Selling* by Jim Holden, *Strategic Selling* by Stephen Heiman and Robert Miller, and *Spin Selling* by Neil Rackham are three of my favorites. And then there's Tom Hopkins, whose books such as *How to Master the Art of Selling* should be on every executive bookshelf. I love reading these books because I love selling, I love salespeople, and I love helping them get better.

My Own Amalgamation

Over the years I have developed my own selling system, an amalgamation of my IBM training, seven years of carrying a bag, countless refresher courses, a shelf of well-digested, dog-eared books on selling, and two decades of owning a business. During that time, I constantly looked for ways to improve my selling skills, and I developed my own sales curriculum and personally trained all of our reps, a practice for which I was often criticized. "You don't have time for that, Mike. You have a business to run," I'd hear. But my critics were wrong. Not only did teaching sharpen my own skills, it gave me a close look at the strengths and weaknesses of each rep. It allowed me to establish an insider language with my reps-saving time, diagnosing problems clearly, and forming lasting relationships. Teaching also established trust and helped with goal setting, compensation, and, above all, retention.

I don't have a fancy name for this amalgamation. Perhaps that will be my next book because I can barely do the subject justice in a few short chapters. Nevertheless, I'm going to try.

I'll begin with the front wheel, which centers on the *structured sales cycle* (Tool #1). These steps and tactics are visible, logical, and repeatable. Since the front wheel takes you and your prospect where you want to go, we'll spend some time analyzing *buying behaviors* (Tool #2), giving you a handle on how prospects make decisions. You will find four different types of buyers in this section.

I won't spend time on the back wheel (products) because each company is different. But remember: High achievers know their product line. They can't afford to rely on support personnel to do this for them. It's too risky. That's not to say that support people aren't important. They are. My point is that you are handicapped if you are solely dependent on them to help make your sale. Learn your product line.

Next (Tool #3) we'll pull it all together with the frame (infrastructure), where I'll describe ways to leverage your *time, territory,* and *talent.* And finally (Tool #4) I'll share with you ways to understand and hire *breakaway performers.*

These articles are not meant to load you up with a bunch of impressive sales jargon or CliffsNotes solutions to be used on your next call. They're about fundamentals, with the assurance that once you understand and perfect these fundamentals, you and your sales force will always achieve extraordinary results.

Tool #1

The Structured Sales Cycle

Selling has a definite structure or cycle. To make a successful sales call, you must always know where you are in that cycle. And you must obey the rules of the structure without appearing canned or rehearsed but rather authentic and polished.

Let's look at the first step of the cycle:

THE OPENING

The opening is simple, but its importance is often overlooked. When meeting your prospect, give your name, company name, and a brief description of your core business. Keep it crisp, keep it professional, and speak clearly. Don't be in such a hurry that you confuse the prospect about who you are. I can't tell you how many times I've watched a rookie salesperson open the call with questions, jumping right into the pitch without properly introducing himself, the company, or, for that matter, me. I have literally stopped a call so that I could introduce myself to the client. There we were, staring at each other across the desk, listening to the salesperson blabbing endlessly, with the prospect clueless about who I was or why I was there. It happens.

Everyone feels tension when meeting someone for the first time. But if you blow something as simple as an introduction, the tension will skyrocket. That's why it is so important that openings be delivered in a professional but casual manner, not coming off as canned or stilted. Just relax as if you were talking to an approving friend. And for God's sake-smile!

Avoid the coldest of cold calls. Many openers meet disaster because the salesperson has no knowledge of the prospect other than the company's name. Do your homework before the call. Know something about the company, the industry, and, if possible, the person you are calling on. "Yeah, but somebody will screen me out if I ask for this information," you might say. Yes, sometimes. But you'd be amazed at what a typical self-important screener will tell you about the company or the boss if you simply ask.

That's the nuts and bolts of the opener. Now, immediately following the opening is the:

IMPACT STATEMENT (IS)

This is a commanding statement meant to have an instant impact on prospects. It gives them a reason to keep listening. Never break this rule. Whether it's making money, saving money, saving time, improving life, or whatever, let them know what you are offering. And don't be vague. If someone called you and said, "I've got a product that saves time and increases sales," you'd have a marginal interest at best. But consider if they said, "I've got a product that is absolutely proven in your industry and has helped hundreds of sales reps increase their personal income by fifty percent-meaning more sales for your company and more fun for your sales team. Would you like to hear how they did it?" See the difference?

The best way to add strength and credibility to your IS is with references. Mention two or three of your best clients, with a brief statement about the value or savings or something that you provided them that made a powerful impact on their business. These statements should be precise, targeted, and memorized. When I was selling, I had a half dozen statements rehearsed and perfected.

Once again, you want a uniform flow and tempo when delivering your lines, but you don't want to sound canned. A good way to do this is to rehearse in front of a mirror, without over rehearsing, which is the point where they do sound canned. The key is making an impact, giving them a glimpse of something that you know they need. This is your bait. Here's an example of a solid Opening followed by an Impact Statement:

"Mrs. Collins, my name is Milt Hearne from IBM's General Systems Division. Thanks for taking my call this morning. I know how busy you are, so I'll get right to the point. [rapport and empathy] IBM has installed affordable products in hundreds of manufacturing companies just like yours. These companies have doubled their shop floor productivity, cut inventory by fifty percent, and reduced scrap by forty percent. The impact on earnings has been magnificent. We've become their trusted business adviser, and with your permission, I'd like to pay a visit and show you how we did it. Maybe we can do it for you, too."

This is not far from what I used twenty-five years ago. Nor is it different from what I would use today. These techniques are timeless. Now read it again, only this time pretend you are talking to your best friend.

Even in a world of voice mail, which I know is frustrating for every sales rep, you can leave a powerful message through a well-constructed IS. The odds of getting a return call are increased substantially.

Now, during your Opening and IS you need to:

BUILD AND MAINTAIN RAPPORT AND EMPATHY

Much of this is established through a proper introduction. Consider the example above. Right out of the gate, I thank her for taking my call and show her respect with a pledge to get to the point. This puts her at ease. Being a *trusted business adviser* demonstrates closeness in the business relationship. I ask for *permission* to see her, which gives her some control. And, finally, I want to come for a *visit*. Visits are for friends. These are subtle but effective ways to build rapport.

When you do make that visit, though, realize that this is a new person you've just met. Treat the prospect like a new friend. Don't be sugary and sappy. Just be yourself. After the opening and impact statement, get to know this person a little. Usually you can spot something that will identify personal interests. Ask a few questions about those interests, and help create a relaxing atmosphere.

After some comfortable small talk, you are ready to proceed. Be empathetic and sensitive to your prospect's time and needs by outlining your purpose for being there and what you plan to do with your visit. Ask for agreement to your approach and whether there's anything they would like to cover that you may have missed. This kind of empathy builds trust and shows our respect for their turf. Laying out the call demonstrates that you are in control and you have a plan. It now becomes your mutual meeting, an opportunity for both of you to benefit.

The opening, impact statement, and empathy portions of the call don't take long and flow smoothly. Up till now you really haven't been doing any selling. You've been earning the right to go forward, positioning yourself for the most important part of the selling cycle, which is:

QUESTIONING AND LISTENING

One of the major victories in the selling cycle is getting the prospect to admit pain. We all struggle with this admission, especially to someone we don't know very well. And you'll find no shortage of pain in American business today-eroding market share, sliding margins, poor customer service, high inventories, invalid information, high turnover, etc., etc. If you know what questions to ask, and if they're asked in the right sequence, you *will* find pain. But identifying pain-or weakness or vulnerability-does not guarantee a sale. The fact is, most business people live with pain because they don't believe a solution exists.

Through a series of skillful open- and closed-ended questions, a salesperson can probe deeply into this pain and steer the prospect toward a solution. Solutions begin with a vision shared between you and your prospect, which is realized through the use of your product or service. Once the prospect sees the solution, action usually follows. By helping to identify the pain and then the solution, you increase the odds that you'll get the business because prospects buy from people they like.

Questions push pain buttons, elucidate facts, identify decision makers, build understanding and trust, uncover competitors, determine needs, surface objections, and above all, close deals. Is there any wonder about their importance? If we know our prospect (front wheel) and the industry (back wheel), we will ask questions that we already know the answers to-like having the answers to a test.

The other half of questioning is listening. That's why we must prepare our questions in advance of the call. If we don't, we become so wrapped up in asking the right question that we fail to listen to the answer. That's why God gave us two ears and one mouth.

Let's look at questions more carefully. You will find two types-open-ended and closed-ended. Open-ended questions probe for details, needs, and the position of the buyer's attitudes, feelings, objections, and-plain and simple-whether you're winning or losing. These questions get the prospect talking. If you're doing all the talking, not only are you not selling, you are losing.

Closed-ended questions usually have a one-word response, like *yes* or *no*. Their purpose is to pin things down, seek agreement, set the record straight, or confirm something. I use a simple model for designing questions for a sales call. It's called FIND-a euphemism and acronym rolled into one. *F* stands for *facts*, *I* stands for *issues*, *N* stands for *needs*, and *D* stands for *dreams*. You can easily structure your questions around these four categories.

Some examples of *fact*-finding questions are:

- **What is your most popular product line?**
- **How many warehouses do you have?**
- **What integrated software system do you use?**
- **How many executives are on the committee?**

As you can see from these examples, the answers will have a tendency to be superficial and closed-ended, but that's okay because you're looking for facts. Facts provide orientation and focus for you and the prospect, and that's what you want.

Questions that raise *issues* might look like this:

- **What's the most serious problem your company faces with customer service?**
- **Why has your delivery system been failing?**
- **What are the weaknesses in your management reporting system?**
- **Where does your sales force need to improve?**
- **What problems in your department keep you awake at night?**

The answers to these questions, which are open-ended, provide the golden nuggets you need to formulate a solution. But hold off on the solution. Let the prospect first feel a little more pain. Remember, if you are talking, you are not selling. So be patient, manage your tension, and move on to needs.

Questions that identify and clarify *needs* could be:

- **Once we solve this problem, how will it impact your growth and profitability?**
- **What outcome do you see with a better customer-service procedure?**
- **What would happen to your office productivity with this new work station layout?**
- **What does your company need to do first and why?**

These questions are not rocket science. They are designed to steer the prospect into your solution. Remember the bicycle? These are front-wheel questions, taking you and your prospect where you want to go. If you ask these questions skillfully, you'll feel as though you're on a tandem bike, with the prospect doing the steering. You just have to keep pedaling. (Sorry for the pun.)

I see a small, very subtle difference between issues questions and needs questions. Questions that identify *issues* are structured without a solution in mind, whereas questions that identify a *need* assume that a solution is in place. Needs and issues are simply opposite sides of the same coin. Issues identify pain, while needs identify solutions. It is important that you make this distinction in your mind so that your prospect, too, can see the distinction.

Overlooked questions to prospects are the *dreams* questions, often holding the keys to getting the business:

- **If our system cuts your time by thirty percent, will that get you home for dinner once in a while?**
- **You've described very well what a new system will do for your company, but what will it do for you personally?**
- **What are your dreams for your business, and how can we help you attain them?**

Every person on earth has dreams for his or her life. That's why people work so hard to fulfill at least some of them. Your job as a salesperson is to help them tap into those dreams and renew their commitment to them. If the prospect sees you and your company as the means by which those dreams come true, you've got yourself an order. *Do not leave out this important step.* Nothing will build more trust than simply acknowledging their dreams.

Questions must be prepared in advance of your call. I mean scripted word for word. If you try to wing it, you will fail. And the order in which you ask them must be intrinsically tied to listening. If you listen empathetically, you will know what to ask next. You must listen with your whole mind and body-hear it, sense it, feel it. One more thing: Don't confuse *scripted* with *canned*. Nothing causes discomfort or reveals rookie status more than hearing you struggle through a canned assimilation of words that are not your own. Salespeople are often actors, taking on a role. Learn how to deliver your lines. I used to practice mine in front of a mirror until I liked what I heard and saw.

O.K. You have gathered your golden nuggets. Now it's time to:

SUMMARIZE

Right before you summarize what you've learned, you must ask one more simple question, a final probe. "Mr. Prospect, before we move on, is there anything else you want to tell me-anything that we overlooked?" You will be amazed at what follows. When I thought we were done, I've had prospects dump on me for another half hour. Be patient, manage your tension, and let him talk. This is the stuff you need.

The summary distills and organizes the information. If you misunderstood something, this will flush it out and keep the prospect engaged. The prospect is becoming your coach, helping you to achieve a deeper understanding. As you untangle the information, giving it order, you will be able to lay before him his world of facts, issues, needs, and dreams-like holding up a mirror. Through the summary you can reshape the information in such a manner that will later fit your solution more effectively. The summary will also reopen the prospect's wounds. This is good. You want pain.

Once you've delivered a solid summary, seek agreement. You and the prospect must be on the same page. Until you have agreement on the issues, you can't proceed. Another tip is to create a written shorthand because the prospect will spill faster than you can write. If you know shorthand, great. If you don't, invent one. This way you can listen closely, jot notes, and not miss anything.

You and the prospect are now on the same page. You have your notes in front of you, and you are ready to deliver the:

SALES PRESENTATION

The sales presentation links your product with the prospect's pain. And they must be inextricably linked. You aren't providing just any old solution, you're providing the solution, creating a marked advantage over your competition. Define your products carefully; tie the solutions to the critical concerns. Demonstrate savings, productivity, qualitywhatever you can. Look for the customer's reaction. Check in with him, ask him what he thinks. "Are we still on the same page?"

Product knowledge is paramount in the sales presentation. You must shine at this point. You are becoming the trusted business adviser. Not only will he be evaluating your products, he will be evaluating you. The customer will be thinking, *Does he know what he's talking about? Can I trust him? Will his company stand behind him? Where am I exposed?*

Will he deliver? That's why the back wheel is so important.

After your presentation, don't go to the close. Go to another summary. But this time summarize benefits. You are now relieving pain, creating hope, building trust. This is the stuff the close is made of.

Now you're feeling momentum. You want to wrap the deal up, but it's still too soon. Again you must manage your tension, and give your prospect a nudge with the:

TRIAL CLOSE

Now you're looking for a baby "yes." You're searching for which way the wind is blowing. The trial close is an unthreatening technique used to determine if the prospect is ready. The best way to do this is to ask for his or her opinion about your solution. Here are a couple of examples:

> *"In your opinion, based on what you now know about our products, will this approach resolve your inventory problem?"*
> and:
> *"In your opinion, will the other executives want to go forward with this?"*

I like these two questions. People will always give you their opinion, and they will be frank. An opinion is not the same as a commitment. They can give their opinion, and even tell you what you want to hear, but it's only an opinion, not a commitment. There's no risk.

Look at the questions again. If you remove "In your opinion" from the question, can you hear the difference? The question becomes more direct, more confrontational. You are going for the throat. The trust that you've worked to establish will deflate like a three-day-old helium balloon. When you're in a position of high trust, you must be careful and sensitive. You need the answers to these trial-close questions. If they're all green-light answers, go right to the close. But that rarely happens. The prospect needs further validation, more evidence. Even if he is thinking a big "yes" on the inside, he is still going to test you with a baby "no" on the outside. These are called:

OBJECTIONS

I don't think of objections as a "No" but rather a "Not yet." I'm never afraid of objections. In fact, I welcome them because usually on the other side of an objection is an order. But to get to the order, you first need to handle the objections. Objections are the reason we need salespeople. Without objections, you could find far less expensive ways to sell products and services than maintaining and supporting an unnecessary sales force. But the old maxim is true: Nothing happens until something is sold.

Objections are a natural part of every sales cycle. Great questions and a quality trial close will surface them every time. First we need to know if the objection is real or not. Sometimes it's a smokescreen designed to knock you off the trail or test you in some way. Many salespeople launch right into a response without knowing what the objection really is. Again, you need to manage your tension. To surface the real objection, you must ask skillful questions designed to clarify and miniaturize what the prospect is really objecting to. Once you think you have it, restate the objection in your own words. This gives you a chance to restructure the objection into something that you can more easily overcome. Next, seek agreement about exactly what the issue is; then and only then are you ready to respond.

Let me give you an example. First I need to set up the call situation:

I am a salesman for a leading CAD/CAM software company. I've had a solid call so far. The sales presentation went well, and I'm getting buying signals. I'm ready to move to the trial close. Let's see which way the wind is blowing.

Mike (salesman): Jeff, now that you've gotten a close look at what our clients have achieved with our software, in your opinion, can a fifty-percent decrease in design cycle time be achieved? (A trial close.)

Jeff (prospect): Well, maybe not fifty percent, but I can certainly see time savings. In my opinion, a bigger benefit would be design quality. Frankly, this is where the engineers have been asking for help. (A baby "yes.")

Mike: Well, why don't we give them what they want and begin accruing the benefits immediately? I can have the software out here next week. (Another trial close-only this time more direct)

Jeff: Next week? Are you kidding? I have four projects going right now. There is no way I could tackle this-even if I wanted to-and expect to see my family again. I'm already working Saturdays. (An objection-is it real or just a smokescreen designed to knock me off the trail?)

Mike: Jeff, I understand completely the need to be home with your family, and I want this solution to be a source of relief, not added pressure. Let me ask you this. If you had the resources to install the system now, would you do it? **(Always cushion the objection, show empathy; seek to clarify with further questioning.)**

Jeff: No. **(He's hiding something.)**

Mike: Really? I'm confused. A moment ago you said the engineers were looking for quality improvement. What am I missing? **(This question will flush out the real objection)**

Jeff: Well, yes, I did say that, and I meant it. Here's what you're missing, Mike **(Now it comes out).** *Our MIS director is leaving the company. Few people know about it, and we haven't found a replacement yet. It could take months. In the meantime I've been assigned his duties in addition to my own. I barely have time to come up for air, and everybody's on my back because things are falling through the cracks. I can't add another project now. Maybe in six months.* **(He's overwhelmed, stressed, and trying to delay the decision)**

Mike: And I suspect the engineers are feeling really ignored, right? **(Further clarification; create more pain, and seek more ammunition.)**

Jeff: You got that right. But what can I do? **(The door is open. Manage your tension.)**

Mike: Okay, I think I understand the problem. You see the advantages of our software, and you would probably go forward today if you weren't so understaffed, burdened by too many projects, and working Saturdays. Are we together? **(I've restated and reshaped the objection to fit my solution, and I continue to build trust through empathy.)**

Jeff: Yeah, I think so.

(I am now ready to handle the objection.)

Mike: Well, Jeff, I think we can make this easy for you. Not only can we make the engineers happy by getting them started now, but we can also free you up from some of these other projects and keep you home on Saturdays-maybe even on the golf course. It's going to be eighty-five degrees this weekend. **(I'm setting the hook. Will he take the bait?)**

Jeff: Oh, don't even go there. Besides how do you propose to do all this? **(He took the bait.)**

*Mike: As I described earlier, Jeff, our project managers are trained in a variety of technologies, not just engineering. We simply need to assign two managers to your account for the first three months. Not only will they nail the CAD/CAM installation, but one of them can help you manage your other projects. Everything will speed up. People will be smiling again, you'll be a hero, and you can play some golf. (**A dream.**) And furthermore, I'll put our most experienced project managers on your account (**product knowledge needed here**), for added protection. What do you think, Jeff? Will this work in your opinion? (**Another trial close.**)*

*Jeff: Hmm! It might work. But now I've doubled my project management costs. (**Another objection-a real one this time.**)*

*Mike: What's it costing you to have these projects slipping? That can't be very comfortable. Besides, if you move now, I can probably give you the second project manager for half price. And with your MIS guy gone, your payroll costs are down. Jeff, this solution is perfect. It fulfills all your concerns. Let's not wait, we can make this happen. (**A hard trial close.**)*

Jeff: If I do this, I'm holding you responsible.

*Mike: You should. That's my job. I won't let you down. Why don't we go over the agreements and wrap this up today? (**In his eyes, I've gone from salesman to trusted business adviser. At this point the close is very natural because I have earned the right to ask for the order.**)*

Jeff: Ah, what the hell. Let's do it.

Objections spring from four different positions. These positions are central to what lies between where you are and getting the order. And as I already said, you must always know where you are in the cycle. The four major positions are: No trust, No Need, No Help, and No Hurry.

No Trust

If a prospect doesn't trust you, you will never get the order. He is objecting to you, not your solution. This is why establishing rapport and empathy is so important. Only through trust do you transform from salesperson to trusted business adviser. Trust is earned by taking the time (without shortcuts) to listen to and truly understand your prospect's requirements as well as by knowing your products and your industry better than your competition. Trust is also earned by conducting yourself as a professional. The prospect is looking for an adviser, not a best friend, so don't get too folksy. No one trusts a schmoozer.

No Need

Sometimes there really is no need. These are the times you walk away with permission to stay in touch. But prospects almost always do have a need; you just haven't found it yet-or they just don't see it. Finding need is different than creating need. When finding need, the prospect has a need and knows it, but he's unwilling to reveal it to you. Your job is to keep pressing until the prospect cries uncle and fills you in. That's how you find need.

Creating need happens when the salesperson takes the prospect through a discovery process: The prospect has a need but doesn't know it. Good questions will identify and create undiscovered needs. Once the prospect realizes that a need exists, the solution must be understood. This is fulfilled in the next step, the sales presentation.

No Help

Often the need is well established, but the prospect doesn't see how you can be of help. He continues to feel pain, even after you present the solution. The breakdown occurs in one of two ways. (1) You never fully understood the need, or (2) your sales presentation missed the mark. The remedy is to ask more questions. That is the only way to reestablish the need and pick up the scent again. When you think you have it, redeliver your solution, summarize, and continue the cycle.

No Hurry

The toughest objection is the foot-dragger. Everything is right, you feel the momentum, and you close. Then the prospect says to you, "Oh, there's no hurry; we can't do that now." You must keep your composure in these situations. It's easy to destroy whatever trust you've established by getting agitated with foot-draggers. How dare they put you through all this and not give you the order?

This happens when the prospect has no authority to make the decision (shame on you for not qualifying this earlier!), or he or she has authority, but you've missed a hidden objection, which tends to be more personal rather than business in nature. A good example of this is Jeff (in the scenario given above), who was freaking out because his MIS director was leaving, and he was already overworked.

One last piece of advice: Always anticipate in advance of every call every single objection that you're likely to get. Know them, rehearse your responses, and go into the call prepared. Your confidence will soar if you take the time to do this. Objections are your friends, not your enemies. Once you understand what they are and how to handle them, you are on your way to becoming a great salesperson. An excellent way to develop these skills is through an "objection clinic." Get your sales force together and have them fire objections back and forth at one another. It's both fun and a great way to see different styles and techniques.

So, you have successfully handled the objections, and you are now ready to enter the final phase of the structured sales cycle, the:

Closing

This is the easiest part of the call, though people who don't understand selling would call it the hardest. By now you are getting obvious buying signals. If they are *not* obvious, you have work left to do. Perhaps an undiscovered objection is lurking in the bushes. A failsafe way to flush things out of the bushes is to seek agreement with one last summary of the benefits. Then ask, "Before I go further, is there anything on your mind that we may have missed?" This is a clearing question, getting everything on the table. You've earned the right to ask, the prospect is ready, and the process is free and easy from here forward.

I like an assumptive close. This approach has no trace of confrontation. It's like asking a friend what movie he or she wants to see tonight—it already assumes that you're going. Closing is just that simple, that natural. Be prepared for additional objections always, but at this point, any objection usually has to do with the terms of the deal and is not about the deal itself. In fact, it's really not an objection at all but negotiating, which when handled with grace and empathy will usually lead to the order.

Summary

The structured sales call works. It works for both short- and long-term sell cycles, with simple and complex products, with senior executives and middle management, on the phone, face-to-face, in groups, and in any industry. I need you to understand this point: The structured sales cycle is universal. You do not have to learn four or five different ways to sell, depending on the industry or product or whom you're calling on.

You have to learn only one way, and if you learn it well, you will have it your entire career.

Selling is like a golf swing. It's hard to learn, but once you do and provided you work at it, you can repeat it over and over. And even though golf allows fourteen different clubs, you basically have only one swing. Such is the case with selling. You have many different prospects and industries, but only one structure.

The Structured Sales Cycle

Opening Approach
- *Give Name*
- *Company Name*
- *Briefly Describe Core Business*
"Keep this crisp and professional, speak clearly."

CLOSE
"You've earned the right."
"Very Natural Process."

Impact Statement
- *Powerful*
- *Makes Them Listen*
- *Use Refrences*
- *Precise/Net*
"Prepare & rehearse up front."
"You need several of these. Memorize them."

Trial Close Again
"Solid Buying Signals."

Quickly Seek Agreement Again
"Things should start getting warmer. Buying signals are strong at this point."

Empathy
- *Sensitive to his time and needs*
- *Show you care*
- *Outline for him what you plan to do*
- *Ask for agreement to your approach*
- *Proceed to Q & L*
"Try to identify his buying style at this point."

Cycle within a cycle
Objections should be handled with more questions to reveal the actual objection.

Objection Handling
Objections:
No Trust, No Need,
No Help, No Hurry
- *Never a "No" just "Not Yet"*
- *Stay Calm*
- *Anticipate in Advance*
- *Prepare Your Answers Ahead of Time*

Trial Close
- *Non Confrontive*
- *In your opinion will this work?*
- *Looking for a baby "yes"*
- *Wind Blowing?*

Questions & Listening
- *Child buys so get them emotional*
- *Closed Questions, Open Questions*
- *Must Flow Well*
"Prepare all questions in advance of call."

F acts
I ssues
N eeds
D reams

Sales Presentation
- *Demo or Explain Features*
- *Define Benefits*
- *Get a Reaction to "So What"*
- *Know Product*
- *Summarize Benefits*

Summary
Mr. Customer this is what I have learned from you today.
"Don't rush to this until done with Q. & L."
"Seek Agreement."

Tool #2

Buying Behaviors

There are a few things you must know about people and their patterns of buying behavior.

Can you actually put people in a box and have that box represent who they are? Of course the answer is no. But we need some way of sizing up the people who we are calling on, a way of understanding how they think and how they make decisions. If we have such insight, we can adjust our own style to meet theirs. The sales call then has a higher probability of success. It is not a perfect method, but it provides a logical model for determining a person's style. I call this the *buying behaviors* of people.

To use the model in your selling, you must accept the premise that the world has four different buying behaviors: the *aggressor*, the *analyzer*, the *emotive*, and the *harmonious*. We begin differentiating these four patterns of behavior by measuring how reactive they are or how declarative they are.

Think of the "reactive axis" as the degree with which people control their emotions. Some people are *task oriented* (high control), others are *relationship oriented* (low control). Think of the "declarative axis" as the amount of effort a person is willing to put forth to influence or persuade others. Some are in *tell* mode (high influence), others are in *ask* mode (low influence). We have all seen these different patterns of behavior, but we usually don't recognize them-or at least we haven't labeled them. Think of your friends when you go to a party. Are some of them quiet and laid-back, asking questions and taking things in, while others are telling stories and jokes and carrying on? A party is not directly comparable to a business setting, of course, but it's useful to get you thinking this way. Even at a party you approach these people differently.

The same is true in selling. Let's create this model that's the means by which you can recognize the different patterns. If the reactive axis runs north-south and the declarative axis runs east-west, we now have four boxes to place people in. Examine the following diagram:

Buying Behaviors

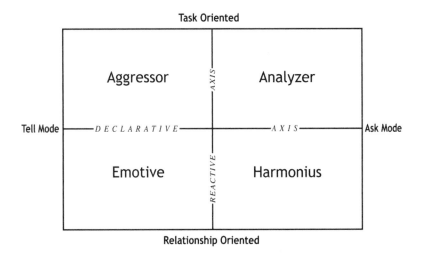

DECLARATIVE AXIS - Perceived effort to influence or persuade others. Take charge buying behavior.

REACTIVE AXIS - Degree with which one controls their emotions when in a buying situation.

Let's look at aggressors first. These people are assertive, always in *tell* mode and usually controlled and disciplined in their approach to things. Aggressors need to be in charge. They tend to be very disciplined about time, and they are decisive. They want the facts, they want them quickly, and they don't want your opinion, or anyone else's, for that matter. Aggressors are not afraid to take risks, and they like to stay on task. They are interested in one thing: getting to the right decision. They don't care to be your pal because they're not relationship oriented. Just give them the facts, save the rhetoric, and they will make the decision.

Analyzers also like control and show little emotion. Never get in a card game with an analyzer. This person is the supreme poker face. Although disciplined about time, analyzers will allow you to answer their questions, and you should expect a lot of them. They want to know everything, and they will be as patient as necessary to get what they need before making a decision. As a result, an analyzer is a slow decision maker and will not be rushed. The primary difference between an aggressor and an analyzer is the way they approach risk. Even with all the facts, the analyzer will do anything to avoid risk. And while the aggressor wants facts only, the analyzer only wants opinions. "What does so-and-so think about this, and how did she arrive at that?" Analyzers are the picky ones; they'll drive you nuts if you don't know how to handle them.

Emotive people are talkers and very animated. Their hands and arms are always moving, and they are not good listeners. Since they are not disciplined about time, they will waste their own and yours to boot. The good news is that they will make a decision-usually without having all the facts, again because they don't listen effectively. They're also not afraid to take a risk, but to minimize their risk, they are really banking on you. The relationship-do they like you and trust you?-is crucial to their decision. The old expression, "Given a good product at a fair price, people generally buy from people they like", is most applicable to the emotive buyer.

The harmonious is the most dangerous of all behaviors. Harmonious buyers want to make a friend of anyone who calls on them. Since they are undisciplined about time, they will spend an eternity talking sports, golf, family, church, you name it, with no intention of buying anything. When they do get down to business, you will find them dependant on other people's opinions, so expect a lot of questions. They are not risk-takers and will do anything to cover their butts. After all, they want everybody to like them. Furthermore, they will take forever to make a decision. You can't push them-good buddies don't push each other. What lies underneath their need for relationship is their insecurity about their decision. You are ultimately the means by which they get their butts covered, and they will leave your ass out to dry to cover their own. Harmonious buyers, like analyzers, remember everything.

Distilling Down

How can a salesperson best influence these four individual buying behaviors? Why does it matter that we know something about them? Because we can now bend our behavior to theirs. Salespeople must be pliable and adaptable to the current environment. But what are they adapting from? In other words, what is *their* natural behavior? If you're an aggressor calling on another aggressor, you will blend nicely. You see the world the same way-you connect. If you are an analyzer (yes, analyzers can make great salespeople, too), you'd better adjust your style a bit, or you will drive an aggressor nuts.

Let's look at this more closely.

The aggressors want facts. They can make their own decisions. So a salesperson should provide options for aggressors, let them choose. Also let them talk. Aggressors talk themselves into things. This is how they process information, by grinding through it quickly. Let them be in charge of this process. This is what they need. Eventually they will buy. You don't have to push an aggressor. Once he sees the solution, he'll move quickly. He will act because he sees no risk, only reward.

The analyzer also need facts. Since they are skeptics by nature, you must show them proof. "How do I know this will work?" is a typical question from an analyzer. The best way to prove something to analytical buyers is to take them to a customer site. The reference sell is perfect for them: They must see it to believe it. They want to step back and think about it for a day or so, only to come back with more questions. They will take whatever time they need, and they will not be pushed. If you push, you will lose them. So be patient. Wait for them. They will get there.

Emotives buy from people they like. If they don't like you, or more importantly, if they don't trust you, they will never buy from you. In fact, they'll buy an inferior product from an inferior company strictly on the basis of the relationship. They, too, like to talk, so let them. But occasionally they need prodding to keep on track because they don't see the world as a bunch of tasks like the aggressor or the analyzer. Eventually they will get down to business after they are comfortable with you. Since they are decision makers and unafraid of risk, they will respond well to a good summary and trial close. If you are buddies, you will get the deal. Lastly, keep a healthy supply of perks around, like ball games, golf trips, theater tickets and the like. It can't hurt. But that usually comes later.

Harmonious buyers need reassurance to help support their decision. "Boy, I don't know. I'm going to have to think about this" is a typical response from a harmonious buyer when encountering a trial close. The more references you can provide, the better. They need you to spell it out, to draw pictures. Harmonious buyers, too, need to see it to believe it. Give them time, and keep giving them strokes. They are not decisive. They are afraid of risk and usually not very confident in their decisions. So when you get the order, reassure a harmonious buyer once more and get out of the office fast because buyer's remorse is just around the corner for them.

A good way to simplify the application of the model, is to combine it with the four main reasons people object. Once again, those are: No Help, No Need, No Trust, and No Hurry. *(see Buying Behaviors Chart, Page 245)*

The aggressors will object because they see *no help*. They may still have a problem; they just don't see how you solve it. Remember, aggressors are very confident people, and until they see a solution-which can only happen when they have all the facts-they will see no help.

The analyzers will object because they don't see *the need*. Of course they don't. Otherwise, they would have to do something about it, which would mean making a decision-something they prefer not to do. Remember, they're the picky ones. It's easier for them to put on blinders so they never have to see the need. No need, no decision. Without a decision, they can keep analyzing, which is what they love to do. Get the picture?

The harmonious buyers are in *no hurry*. They will acknowledge need and, for that matter, see how you might help them, but they don't act. They lack the confidence to act. So rather than saying no, they say not yet. They are never in a hurry, and they will procrastinate as long as they can. The only thing that speeds up a harmonious buyer is CYA-"cover your ass."

Finally, the *emotive buyers* object because they have *no trust*. They will acknowledge their need and even show a desire to act, but without trust you won't get the order. This is a tough objection to handle because it's usually a smokescreen covering up the real issue. After all, it's hard for somebody to say to you, "I don't trust you." So you must be sensitive and willing to ask vulnerable questions. If done the right way, the expressive will open back up, allowing you to redeem yourself, reestablish your trust.

Summary

Understanding buying behaviors and how they impact your sales call is enormously important if you want to be a professional salesperson. Your ability to influence people and speed the sales process is tied directly to these skills. Is it realistic that after five minutes with a person, you can shove him or her into one of the four boxes? Of course not. But over a period of two or three calls, particularly in a complex sale where you are selling both high and wide within an organization, meaning you're calling on executives down to lower-end managers and across many departments you will develop a sense about each person. You can now shape your style to fit theirs. Not change your personality, mind you. That would be crazy, if not impossible. What I am talking about is approach, style-an adaptive behavior. You don't approach an aggressor with a smile and a handshake as you do with a harmonious. He would think you're being rude and presumptuous. And don't dive straight into a pile of facts with an emotive. He wouldn't listen to them, anyway. He might want to talk about golf or his daughter's first dance recital. See the difference? Remain who you are, but make sure you adjust to the person you're selling to. You need every advantage you can get.

I'm not a psychologist, nor have I formally tested these theories. But I can tell you this. I've been using buying behavior techniques throughout my career. They have always worked for me and my sales teams. The top achievers swear by it. Remember the bicycle? Buying behaviors puts a navigation system on your front wheel. After you gain experience with the various patterns, you're selling on autopilot, and it becomes tremendous fun. When that happens, you will never work another day of your life.

Buying Behaviors

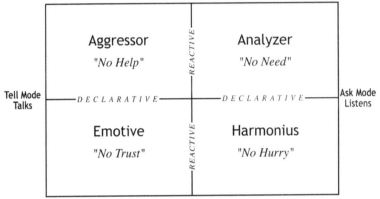

Task Oriented • Control

	REACTIVE	
Aggressor *"No Help"*		Analyzer *"No Need"*
DECLARATIVE		DECLARATIVE
Emotive *"No Trust"*		Harmonius *"No Hurry"*

Tell Mode / Talks (left)   **Ask Mode / Listens** (right)

Relationship Oriented • Emote

DECLARATIVE AXIS - Perceived effort to influence or persuade others. Take charge buying behavior.

REACTIVE AXIS - Degree with which one controls their emotions when in a buying situation.

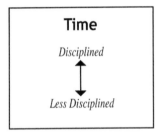

Time

Disciplined

↕

Less Disciplined

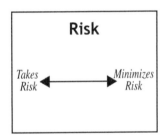

Risk

Takes Risk ↔ *Minimizes Risk*

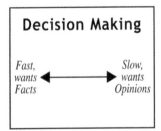

Decision Making

Fast, wants Facts ↔ *Slow, wants Opinions*

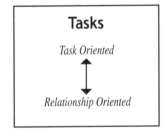

Tasks

Task Oriented

↕

Relationship Oriented

How to Approach Different Buyers

The Aggressor Needs:
- Lots of options to choose from
- Hard Facts
- To Talk
- To Take Charge
- To Be Allowed To Buy

The Harmonious Needs:
- Support
- Time
- Pictures Drawn for Him
- Reassurance
- Strokes
- References

The Analyzer Needs:
- Cold Hard Facts
- To Be Shown
- To Eliminate Risks
- Proof
- To Cover His Butt
- Time

The Emotive Needs:
- Rapport
- Trust
- Prodding
- To Talk Through Issues
- A Relationship

Tool #3

Time and Territory Management

The goal of the sales manager is to hit his numbers month after month, year after year. How? Hire the best reps, train them properly, give them the tools they need to be successful, and define the opportunity in their territory. Help them plan their work and ultimately work their plan. These are the principle elements of territory and time management.

Time is a salesperson's number one natural resource, and also the only resource that isn't renewable. If you waste it, it's gone forever. How much time do salespeople really have? "Oh, I have a whole year to make quota. I'm going to take a breather," I hear salespeople say at the start of a new year. But when you beat last year's results, all you really did was set this year's performance bar. So you'd better get moving, or you'll blow the first quarter and be playing catch-up for nine months. Besides, do you really have a year? Let's take a look at that.

There are 365 days in a year. How much of it is selling time? Let's see:

One year		**365 days**
Now Subtract:	**Weekends**	**104 days**
	Meetings	**12 days**
	Education	**8 days**
	Vacation	**10 days**
	Holidays	**11 days**
	Personal Time	**4 days**
Net Selling Days		**216 days**

Before we even get started, we're down to 216 days to do our job: selling. Let's assume we want to sell twelve new accounts this year. And if we assume a thirty-three percent win rate, we will need to identify thirty-six prospects. Notice I said prospects, not suspects. Prospects are real buyers. Suspects are on your radar screen but only as potential buyers. Don't be in denial about what's a qualified prospect versus a tire-kicking suspect unless you really want to waste time. Now, if we assume that our normal sales cycle takes five sales calls-a reasonable average for most industries-we will require 180 days to work our prospect base (36 x 5=180). Subtract this from our selling days, and we have 36 days remaining. These 36 days represent our prospecting days. That is all we get. Thirty six lousy days to fill our sales pipeline, our lifeblood.

Mind you, we've only made quota. We get to keep our job. My salespeople were required to present a two-hundred-percent plan. They would look at me as if I was crazy.

"No way, Mike. I can't find enough hours in a day to pull that off," they'd say.

"Yes, you can. You'll just have to look harder," I'd counter. And then I'd just smile.

So the question is: How can we leverage our days to create breakaway performance? Judging by the above example, if we waste any time at all, we are in jeopardy of missing quota. To be two hundred percent of quota, we have to do things differently.

For starters, we need to shorten the sales cycle from five days to four-in some cases, three. We must improve our closing ratio from thirty-three to fifty percent, go to the meetings that we are required to go to (don't become a doughnut eater!), and yes, we'd better work a few weekends. I used Sunday afternoons to do my paperwork and plan the next week. This gave me an additional sixty hours a year-and that alone could be worth two new accounts.

Let's look at the math now. To be two hundred percent, we need twenty-four new accounts. At an average of four calls per new account and a close ratio of fifty percent, we need 192 selling days to pull this off, giving us twenty-four days remaining (216-192). Easy, right? Wrong! This is easier said than done, and not everyone is willing to make the sacrifices to be the best. Not everyone has the gifts to be the best. That's just the way it is. So as a sales manager or owner/operator of your new business, it's your responsibility to evaluate the members of your sales team and determine how to move them all forward, regardless of their talent. No sales team is made up of all two-hundred-percent performers. Salespeople form themselves into the pyramids that we see in all areas of human talent. At the base are the bad ones. Above them is a group that is slightly smaller. These are the competent ones, the ones making a living. The next level is much smaller. These are the really good salespeople. Above them-above almost all of us-are the Phil Waldreps, Harvey Kinzelbergs, Glen Arnolds, and Alex Strazzantis. They are the masters, the supernatural, talented in a way that is beyond our ability to grasp let alone attain.

So I approach salespeople with two thoughts. First, good selling consists of mastering the fundamentals (front wheel, back wheel, etc.) and knowing how to manage time. Second, while it is impossible to make a competent salesperson out of a bad one and equally impossible to make a superstar out of a good one, it *is* possible to make a good salesperson out of a merely competent one. But only if he or she commits months of hard work. That's why you need a great sales manager and lots of training for your reps.

Making a Dream List

We now have a better perspective about how limited our time is. And we need time for other things in life besides selling. I divide my life into six parts: spiritual, family, career, mental, financial, and physical. All of these six areas need some of my time if I'm going to be balanced. When I sit down to plan a new year, the planning process encompasses every area of my life.

I begin with my dream list, my ideal situation. I set the bar high, not worrying for the moment about bridling my enthusiasm. After contemplating the list for awhile, I begin to pare it down, but not too much. At this point I would rather overshoot then undershoot. I can now allocate time to these six areas of my life; once again I'm not worried about overallocating, assigning more time than I have. In fact, I look for the conflicts so I can search for solutions. This calls for creativity, thinking outside the box. Eventually I'll land on a set of goals that are realistic, measurable, and, most important, achievable. My dream list, now distilled, becomes my personal mission statement for the year-a balanced global charter, allowing me to apply time, talent, effort, and resources to its execution.

Time management techniques are available in many forms. My-Tyme has an excellent system as does Franklin Covey. Business stores have many terrific devices to help you manage time, like Palm Pilots or Microsoft laptop products. I don't care what you use, and I'm not going to spend time teaching you about time-management systems except to say: Use one. It must become a habit, and it must support your goals.

Without a system, you will fall victim to the tyranny of the urgent, with most of your time going to manage crisis. You become a fire fighter, trying to hold off the day's flames.

With a proactive time-management system, not only do you prevent crisis, but you also find solutions to deal with urgent matters that fit your plan's framework. Your life and in particular your sales time become integrated into your plan, which is driven by your goals and converted into tactics or action items (execution). You will be able to hold on to your big-picture goals while focusing on the details of the task at hand, knowing full well that you're headed in the right direction. If you don't have a destination (goal), any road will take you there.

Territory Management

Territory management is different from time management. What is a territory? It's your business, which could be a physical territory, for example. At IBM our sales territories were divided into zip codes. Everything inside those zip codes was your business and no one else's -except, of course, your competitors. A territory can be a specific set of accounts, an install base, a specific industry, a state, or a combination of these.

Territories are usually defined by your industry or your products. If you sell horizontal products, like computers, a geographic territory works well. If you sell a vertical product, an account-driven or industry-driven territory is more effective. But in all companies-big or little, complex or simple, horizontal or vertical-you must have territories for your sales force. How else do you define, let alone penetrate, your market?

If you tell your sales force to just get out there and sell something, without any thought about what's in their market, they will waste time, and you will never really learn what's there. Without territories, your reps will eventually have disputes. Most salespeople tend to "cherry pick" the big accounts. They're elephant hunters, and it's just a matter of time before they start stalking the same elephant. That's all you need-two salespeople sitting in your office, fighting over the same account. Now, *there's* a good use of your time.

I believe in territories. In fact, I had territory agreements with my reps, contracts that said this is yours, not to be interfered with. To keep it, you had to make quota, adhere to company policies, and be accountable via regular reviews as to what was in your territory. In other words, manage it, and focus on opportunity.

I expected the reps to evaluate all aspects of their territory. *First*, they had to identify and gather all research materials defining their territory (market data and statistics). *Second*, they had to identify and rank the greatest opportunity by industry and by account (opportunity analysis). *Third*, they had to segment the opportunity by company size, year-over-year growth, and location, all within industry (market segmentation). *Fourth*, they had to classify and prioritize their opportunity (attack plan). *Fifth*, they had to plot the geographic concentration of all of their prospects (leverage locations). *Sixth*, they had to identify their competitors and ways to beat them (competitive analysis). *Lastly*, they had to present a precise set of action steps to be performed over the first sixty days of a new year to help them achieve two hundred percent of quota-their fast-start plan. Seem tedious? The first time through, maybe. But after quality time in their territory, salespeople find this process to be much easier, and their productivity soars.

Taking a Beachhead

Now you have a chance of penetrating a market. I call it taking a beachhead, a specific point of control in your territory where you dominate. That's the whole idea of the fast-start plan: a full-scale attack on a high-potential segment of your territory, where the competitors pack up and leave because they know it's your beachhead and you will defend it to the death. Once you take a beachhead, you can begin planning your next attack. Over time, if you plan your work and work your plan, you will take multiple beachheads and become the dominant market maker. That's when things get really fun.

When I first took over my territory as a new salesman at IBM, I had to do all of these things for my manager. Every rep did. Planning was the easy part; execution was a different story. I knew of one street in Harwood Heights that had two excellent IBM System/3 customers-great references and terrific people. I was puzzled that none of the other thirty companies in the industrial park had bought an IBM system. They were all manufacturers like our customers, and they were similar in size, at least physically. My fast-start plan was to attack the entire industrial park. That would be my first beachhead.

I went to the IBM install base rep who handled these two clients and asked if he would introduce me to them. He made the appointments, and I met George Carstens, the president of Carstens Manufacturing. I asked George everything about his business and his relationship with IBM. Why did he buy the system? How did Carstens use it? How did they justify it? I asked him if he knew any of the presidents of the other companies in the area. Not only did he know them, he knew their businesses and in some cases how they felt about IBM and, for that matter, computers in general. I told him that my plan was to put an IBM computer in every company on his street, and I wanted him to help me.

"How can I help? I don't know anything about computers," he said.

"That's even better George. Most people are afraid of them because they don't know anything about them," I said. (Remember, this was 1975.) "All I want you to do is tell your story about how your IBM system helped your business." (It was a great story, too.)

"Well fine. And maybe there are a few things IBM can do for me," George said.

As part of my fast-start plan, I negotiated some additional resources for Carstens Manufacturing. George and I developed a great relationship. He hosted most of my client visits, on-site demonstrations, and provided countless references for me. This support, combined with the power of the newly announced System/32, was the reason I made Rookie of the Year. I sold twelve systems in nine months. Eight of them were on the same street as Carstens. I took the beachhead. By the time I left IBM, I had installed twenty-three systems in that industrial park, nearly eighty percent of the companies.

This example demonstrates the importance of planning a territory, managing your attack strategy, segmenting a market, and total focus. That's how you dominate. If you throw the universe to your reps and say, "Have at it," you will come up short, and you will never fully understand your marketplace.

Have No Biases

When your reps receive a new territory, it's important that they have no biases. Don't let the prior rep talk them out of anything. Just because he couldn't crack a certain account doesn't mean someone else can't. Some of my best accounts at IBM came from lost causes.

One story to illustrate my point:

Denny Bowland and I decided to prospect together one day, his patch in the morning, mine in the afternoon. Teaming up made the day more fun. At that time we were still going door to door. We called it smokestacking. The idea was that any company that needed a smokestack was probably big enough to afford a computer. After lunch-a Coney dog at the Plush Pup-we decided to drive over to Schiller Park. We parked at the end of Charles Street, a one-mile strip of perfectly groomed manufacturing companies with green lawns and American flags. We were feeling prosperous on that beautiful summer afternoon.

We began attacking vestibules. One hour later we came to the famous Charles Paper Company, for which the street had been named. No IBMer had *ever* gotten in the door, let alone made a sale. They wouldn't even buy our typewriters, which at that time were the best in the world. Instead, their office was filled with Remington Rand keyboards, Xerox copiers, and a Boroughs bookkeeping machine. They hated IBM.

"We are not going in there," Denny said. "I wouldn't give them the time of day."

"Aw, c'mon, let's have a little fun. Maybe we can get thrown out," I quipped. I walked briskly to the door. Denny followed, looking agitated.

We had this thing where we would flip a coin before walking in to see who would start the call. It kept us on our toes. Denny lost the toss.

The front door led to a small vestibule that had a linoleum floor, concrete block walls, two plastic chairs, and a dead plant. That's it. No pictures, no nothing. To the left was a sliding-glass window built into a wall, similar to those in a dentist's office, behind which sat a receptionist who looked worse than the potted plant. She wore cat's-eye glasses attached to a gaudy rhinestone chain that hung around her neck. She dropped the glasses to her chest as we approached the window.

Denny held out his business card. But she merely glared at him as if to say, "Don't touch my window."

Undeterred, Denny said, "Good afternoon, miss. My name is Dennis Bowland from the IBM Company. We would like to see Mr. Charles."

The woman's mouth looked as if it needed a hook in it -the lipstick line doubled the size of her lips. "Do you have an appointment?" she asked in an impatient tone.

"No, I'm sorry, we don't. But we have some marvelous news for him, and it would be great if we could see him for a few minutes." Denny could be very charming when he wanted to.

The receptionist looked at the card, stood up, and disappeared around the corner, muttering disapprovals.

Denny rolled his eyes, and I started to laugh.

"God, what a bitch!" I said. "She's too lazy to water the damn plant let alone receive somebody properly."

Moments later, a very stern-looking woman came into the

vestibule. She was in her midfifties and a victim of a bad face-lift. And she was buried in makeup, the powdery kind that smells like your grandmother and leaves orange stains on the collar.

"Mr. Charles doesn't see anyone without an appointment," she said. Although her name was Glinda, like the good witch in the Wizard of Oz, I was waiting for a house to fall on her, too. "So you will have to call to make an appointment. That's our policy."

I could tell Denny was fading.

"Why would we do that when we can make an appointment right now?" I asked.

She stammered, not prepared for my question. Finally she gave us some stupid reason, like she didn't have his appointment book or he might be going out of town or something.

Denny rebounded and decided to press. "Look . . . Glinda . . . we really do have some exciting news, and we're only asking for five minutes. I know he's busy. So are we. We've been coming here for a long time and have never been granted an appointment. Five minutes is all we're asking for. Will you *please* try to get us in-now?"

With arms folded, she took a long, hard look at Denny and in high disgust walked back into the office.

"This is unbelievable. Where do they get these people?" Denny muttered.

Meanwhile, the receptionist was rubbernecking behind the glass, trying to read our lips. Denny stared her down.

We waited for what seemed like an eternity, and then through the sliding window we saw Glinda pointing to Denny's card on the desk. Next, a pair of what were clearly old hands picked up the card, held it for a second, then tore it into about ten pieces. The wall had blocked our view, so we couldn't see who it was, but it had to have been Old Man Charles. We pretended not to see what had happened.

"Watch this," Denny whispered to me, pissed off now, as Glinda returned to the vestibule and announced more forcefully that Mr. Charles wouldn't be seeing anybody. "I see . . .well . . . that's very disappointing. Say . . . uh . . . Glinda, we have one more stop to make right across the street before calling it a day, and I just realized that I gave you my last business card. Do you think I could have it back? I can send one in the mail later if you'd like." Denny couldn't have said it more sweetly. I was about to offer mine when he stepped on my foot.

Looking stricken, Glinda walked back into the reception office a second time. We again averted our eyes as she scraped the pieces off the desk. The receptionist was now grinning behind her hand. She was on to us.

"You don't think she's going to hand us those pieces, do you?" I asked Denny incredulous.

"We'll see," he replied.

We waited what seemed another eternity until the door opened. Glinda handed Denny his card, meticulously Scotch taped back together. The tear marks were almost imperceptible.

"And here is a quarter for the damage. Mr. Charles insisted that we pay for it," she said. Just then Denny whipped out another card and handed it to her.

"Here, keep both of them. And tell Mr. Charles they're two for a quarter." He winked, flipped the coin into the air, and we headed out the door. Behind us, we could hear the receptionist howling.

We laughed all the way back to the car, picturing her taping together that stupid business card. "Did she actually think we were going to use it?" I asked.

Back at the office, we picked up our messages. We were standing at the reception desk, telling Glen Arnold the story, as Denny leafed through his messages. He abruptly stopped.

"Oh, shit! Old Man Charles called," Denny said, handing me the message.

"Holy crap, you guys are in trouble," Glen said, wiping tears of laughter from his eyes.

Denny stared at me. "It's your territory. What do you want me to do?"

"Call him up. We haven't done anything wrong . . . have we?" I asked.

"Hey, call from my desk," Glen offered, eager to hear the outcome.

Denny dialed, keeping his face vacant while he was connected. A moment later he said, "Mr. Charles, Denny Bowland from IBM, returning your call."

He listened silently to Old Man Charles for a minute. Then he slowly hung up the phone and gave us blank stare.

"Well?" I asked impatiently.

"We're in!" he hooted.

I was stunned. "*What?!*"

Denny laughed. "He told me that he called to let me know that he surrenders. His exact words were: 'I figure anybody with balls the size of yours deserves a little of my time. You and your colleague can come in next Tuesday at eight o'clock. We've given you one hour. Don't be late.'"

Three months later we installed a brand new System/32 at Charles Paper Company. Bob Charles became a friend and one of my best references. He loved telling everyone about the stupid business card.

The point of the story is to have absolutely no biases about any account, regardless of history. And to get in the door, sometimes you have to be outrageous.

Summary

Time management is actually a misnomer because we all have the same amount. But some salespeople accomplish twice or three times as much as others in the same allotted time. Therefore, I prefer to use the term "self-management," which suggests that we manage ourselves, not the clock. We first make our habits, then our habits make us-or break us.

Breakaway performers are opportunity minded, not problem minded, managing their time and territory toward victory and employing strategies to prevent problems. They also don't ignore problems, they just see them differently. For them, solving a problem is just another opportunity. It's a mindset.

Above all, they have an acute sense of the ticking of the clock. So they set priorities. And their goals are clear, measurable, and most of all, attainable. Then they organize and execute around them. They cut their time into powerful, productive slots, where each completed slot has a doubling effect against their goal.

Nothing is wasted.

Breakaway Performers

Every year a couple of sales reps blow away the numbers-and they tend to do it year after year. What do they do that makes them so different? Why does the leader board jump from one 116 percent to 230 percent, with no one in between? How do they make it look so easy? Why are they the ones who start their own businesses?

Breakaway performers have an edge over everyone else. They have something inside them that burns, that generates tremendous drive and a desire to be the best. Usually this drive can be traced to an event or series of events in their life that changed them, forever. How do I know this? I've talked to hundreds of them. The stories are all the same. Somewhere in the past they faced overwhelming challenges or severe adversity. Most of them learned how to work hard at a young age to escape being broke. They were always competitive, whether in sports or shooting pool or playing cards, it didn't matter.

This powerful drive seems to have three origins: fear of failure, a need to prove something, and anger. That's why the top achievers always shoot for two hundred percent-fear of failure. Then if they miss, they're still at one hundred fifty percent. Perhaps they had a disapproving father or a coach who didn't believe in them, or maybe they were abandoned, either physically or emotionally, so they have something to prove. Or they have anger. Of course, exceptions do exist. Not every high achiever has faced adversity or lost a parent or was shown disapproval in some way. But they are rare.

Tom Watson Jr., one of the greatest executives of the twentieth century, was driven by a need to prove something. His father, Tom Watson Sr., the founder of IBM, handed down quite a legacy to his son. Although Watson Jr. was groomed for the job from day one, many people doubted he could continue his father's legacy. The shoes were just too big to fill.

Or take Lee Iacocca, the sales genius who convinced the federal government to lend money to Chrysler Motor Company, which at the time was at death's door, and completely turned that company's fortunes around. Iacocca had suffered the worst defeat of his life when he was kicked out of Ford by Henry Ford, who was jealous of Iacocca's success with the Mustang and his rising popularity within the company. Iacocca had left Ford disgraced and humiliated.

Something burned inside these two men. They had something to prove.

I offer this theory of adversity as the driver for high achievement because in my heart of hearts I really believe it is true. The Pollyanna approach that advises work extra hard, sharpen the saw, design a personal mission statement, and do all the right things leaves a lot of people disillusioned when they come up short. Once again the focus is on the mechanics when instead the focus should be on what drives you, what makes you passionate. Mechanics are important, but they are never enough.

Finding Top Salespeople

One of the most difficult jobs you will face is finding top salespeople for your company. It's the number one complaint from every business owner I've ever known. "Where the hell are all the good ones?" they would say to me.

I was always blessed with great salespeople for two reasons. I knew what to look for in the interview, and I put a ton of time into their training and personal development. Take your time interviewing salespeople. Often we are so desperate to get someone on board that we lower our guard and hire the first person with a great smile and a nice tie. Don't be in a hurry. Hold out for the best. If you don't, it will cost you dearly in salary and training expenses as well as in millions of sales dollars that you will never see. So get to know them as people, not merely as producers. What makes them tick? What are they passionate about? Find out about their troubles, their failures. What did they learn from this experience? How has it made them a better person, a better salesperson?

A top performer is not a fraud. He is the real thing. All you have to do in the interview to reveal a fraud-the one who claims to be a top performer-is ask him how he did it. You know what? He can't tell you because he's never done it. I'm not trying to be simplistic here. I am convinced that this is the most important question you can ask: "Tell me in minute detail everything that you did in your territory and within your company that made you successful, allowed you to achieve these extraordinary numbers that you claim to have, and made you a better person." If he's the real thing, you'll get the answer. If he's a fraud, he won't have a clue. End the interview, and go to the next candidate. As for the real ones, give them what they want-within reason. You'll never regret it.

Finally, if salespeople are struggling, don't ignore them. Help them-immediately. Treat them with care and understanding. You don't need to remind them that if they don't produce, they're out. They already know that. Diagnose the problem, develop an improvement plan that's measurable, gain their commitment to the plan, and give them at least four months to recover. If they're not back on track after that, fire them. This approach sends a message to everyone that the organization will not tolerate lack of performance. It also says that the organization will not abandon them-you are showing them a way back, a way to be successful. How many times have you seen a below-average sales performer whom you fired end up prospering at one of your competitors? Always try to save an employee. It protects your culture, builds loyalty, and it's cheaper than having to start all over again.

Selling is the most gratifying profession that I know. And I promise you, if you apply the principles that I have outlined here, you will not only prosper financially, you will also derive tremendous personal satisfaction and a lifetime of enjoyment.

Summary

Track a breakaway performance back to its origin, and you'll find that it begins with a salesperson who has a sincere desire to help people. A stunning performance is a by-product of that sentiment, that spirit. Making big numbers and commission checks is only part of the equation.

The long-held view is that top salespeople are a bunch of egotistical, blood-thirsty, back-stabbing, narcissistic bastards. They will do anything to win-lie, cheat, steal. Yes, there are unfortunately a few out there like that. But they don't last.

Remember, breakaway performers perform year after year. And they get better each year. You can't do that by putting yourself first all the time or by mistreating the staff. The real stars, the authentic ones, put the customer first and win trust. Yes, they are hard to find. So when you do, grab them, quickly.

Planning Tools

Tool #5

Tubby's Planning Model

You have to play this game right. You have to think right. You've got to take it one game at a time, one hitter at a time. You've got to go on doing the things you've talked about and agreed about before- hand. You can't get three outs at a time or five runs at a time. You've got to concentrate on each play, each hitter, each pitch. All this makes the game much slower and much clearer. It breaks it down to its smallest part. If you take the game like that-one pitch, one hitter, one inning at a time, and then one game at a time-the next thing you know, you look up and you've won.
-Rick Dempsey, 1988 Los Angeles Dodgers

I love baseball. But you already know that. So I thought I would share those important words with you. I believe they convey the essence of why we plan.

Below is a detailed outline of Tubby's planning model along with a few interpretive comments to improve your understanding of the model and how to apply it to your business. If you use this model along with the discussion material in chapter 14, you'll have everything you need to perform effective planning.

One last thing: Don't overengineer your planning process. Strategic planning is an art, not a science, with many ways to do it. But to be suc- cessful, planning requires a creative blending of vision, goal setting, active manager involvement, a functional organization, proper delega- tion, unflagging commitment, and a willingness to take risks. To assist with this blending, I recommend that you use a professional facilitator. Many CEOs depend on a skilled, objective strategic-planning facilitator to jump start and shepherd the process, particularly during the early years of a business.

The facilitator helps the company install the planning and review process, trains the planning team, leads the mechanics of the process, intervenes when issues become tangled, and exits once the team is self-sustaining. I used a facilitator for three straight years to help with the software business planning. After that I brought him back for an occasional "tune-up." The American Management Association and the *Inc.* 500 Council are great resources for finding and learning about facilitators, and they will help you to define the skills that you'll require.

Tubby's Five-Step Planning Formula:

Step 1. Planning Foundation-Where are we today?
Step 2. Expected Results-Where do we want to go?
Step 3. Method-How are we going to get there?
Step 4. Implementation-Who will do what?
Step 5. Progress Review-How are we doing?

The planning base has four categories, designed to answer the initial question: *Where are we today?* To go anywhere in business, you need to know the point you are starting from. You will be amazed at what these categories reveal about where your company is at.

I. PLANNING FOUNDATION
A. Internal Assessment. This examination outlines the *strengths and weaknesses* of your company. What do you do best and where do you need to improve?

B. External Assessment. Here you identify the *opportunities and threats* that lie ahead. This exercise groups and pinpoints the specific markets that you will enter, the products you will offer, and the obstacles you will face.

C. Assumptions. Every plan is supported by a set of *requirements or prerequisites* that must be in place to achieve a goal. Your job is to identify them here.

D. Priorities. You are likely to develop far more strengths, weaknesses, opportunities, and threats (SWOT) than you can address effectively, profitably, and with available resources. Therefore, prioritize your SWOT list to no more than five *critical success* factors that you must confront and overcome to achieve business success. These are the nonnegotiable factors. If you make these happen, everything else will fall into place.

Each manager-including you, the boss-is expected to do these things. This is not just for sales, it's for every department: operations, finance, customer service, and so on. They must all establish their base, which is eventually boiled down to their five critical success factors. Once this is completed, you'll begin to see duplication of effort, tradeoffs, and synthesis between departments. This process boils down tasks to their absolute requirements and optimizes the action items and time to complete them. This will build speed into your plans.

Once this phase is completed, you must determine what results you want: *Where do you want to go?*

II. EXPECTED RESULTS

A. Vision/Mission. Most companies face a big challenge in getting their people centered on a vision or strategy. One of the best ways I know of to bring about this vision is by creating a *mission statement.* Not just something that you whip together during planning but one built through input and effort from every level of the organization. It needs to be a *living constitution* that holds your values and beliefs and acts like a *compass*, a reminder of where you are going.

B. Goals & Objectives. I provide each manager with a *goal worksheet*, outlining in broad strokes what I want the company to accomplish. Some examples are: sales revenue, gross-margin percent, return on assets, return on invested capital, capital expenditures, debt to equity, average A/R collection, marketing expectations, and headcount. This is a rough list, but it gives you an idea. The important thing for you, the boss, is *you* have to set the *big* goals. Now each manager must figure out how they will deliver their part. This is an iterative, collaborative, and negotiated process.

A tip for the boss-Set the big goals in rather broad strokes, and request that each department align their individual plans to meet these goals. You must remain flexible, negotiating and melding their plans into one final cohesive plan. It's a process that has to run its course.

Okay, so we now know *where we are today* and *where we want to go*. Now we have to figure out *how to get there*.

III. METHOD

A. Business Strategies. Strategies are the means, ways, and hows, combined with detailed methods by which you can achieve your goals. Strategy is about being different, engendering *formidable competitive advantage*. It is no longer just a set of carefully linked activities designed to leverage your core competency. Competitive advantage is to fleeting-today's markets are too unstable. Who knows how long a market will last? But in complicated, fast-moving markets, the opportunity exists for significant growth and wealth. Therefore, the most salient feature of competitive advantage today is not *sustainability* but *unpredictability*. So you must manage as if it could all end tomorrow, and you'd better have your next idea ready to go, or at least started. So define your competitive advantage: cost, value, differentiation, price, speed. Think through the external strategy to thwart your competition, and win market share. Design inside processes to support these activities. Decide whether to grow, hold, milk, or get out of a market. Think through acquisition, divestiture, development, and restructuring. That's the stuff of which strategy is made. Keep it simple, clear, and easy to communicate. But always, always, always *be alert*. Markets can dry up instantly when you least expect it.

One last point on strategy. While the tactics are important, they are less important than the strategic direction of the firm. The inference is obvious: You can tolerate some mistakes in tactics provided that your overall strategy is sound.

B. Organization Model. By definition an organization is a group of people working together toward a common goal under a single leader. You must now organize a team to get the work done, establishing and agreeing on the goals as well as strategies for achieving them. Your team will be effective only when it can answer the following questions:

1. What is the goal?

2. What part do they play in attaining the goal?
3. What part do the other teams play in attaining the goal?
4. What part does the leader play in attaining the goal?

Now all you have to do is put together an organization chart and position descriptions. The organization chart is needed to delineate the leaders and team members, and the position descriptions are needed so that you can function properly. And if possible, you should put the individual's goals for the year within the position description itself, such as the one given below for Tubby's regional sales managers.

Regional Manager Position Description

· *Your goal is to sell and install seventy System/36s this year.*
· *You have a budget of $125,000 for expenses other than salaries and a budget of $200,000 for marketing programs.*
· *You must achieve an average gross margin of forty percent.*
· *You have full discretion on pricing but must not go below eighty percent of list price without approval from the vice president of sales.*
· *You are to have no more than seven sales people to accomplish this goal.*
· *Your sales territory is protected and consists of five states.*
· *You have final authority on all sales hires.*

By incorporating annual goals into the person's basic position description, you will flesh it out and transform it into something precise, measurable, and fully owned. Put another way, the closer that accountability approaches the doer, the better the performance. Thousands of relatively small transactions per day are what ultimately dictate a firm's performance. I like to post the results in some way. Inspection of an individual's results by one's peers is one of the most effective prods that I know of. Peer surveillance works.

C. Marketing Programs. This is the stuff that breathes life into your strategy. You must develop a marketing mix. It starts with good collateral material to *show off* your company. Don't scrimp on this. Each sales manager must utilize some or all of the mix, whether it's mass mailing, advertising, telemarketing, blitz days, seminars, partnering, or whatever. Cover your territory with a clear and consistent message. That's your goal. Don't worry about budgets right now; that will come later. Just identify all the programs first.

The next important question is: *Who will do the work, and exactly what do you want them to do?* The effort has to be coordinated. Let me show you.

IV. IMPLEMENTATION

A. Delegate Objectives and Programs. Your goals and organization have been established. Now you must delegate these objectives and the supporting programs to your team. This is called *decentralization*: the delegation of authority and responsibility down the line in your organization to the point where every decision is made at the lowest possible level, to where the clearest information exists for making it. If you don't delegate, you die. This is where the work is done. Make sure the accountable individual presents you with a complete and detailed plan of implementation and achievement. This will answer the question *Who will do what?* You gain leverage and maximize performance through the sum of thousands of small transactions done every day. It's a beautiful thing to watch when you have capable people who understand their job and how it fits into the big picture. The productivity explodes.

Some of the objectives are staff assignments, programs structures designed to support sales or customers. These are not direct profit assignments. People with direct profit and loss responsibility (which I believe is the ultimate goal of decentralization) have a different charter. For them to succeed, they must have control over-or at least access to-sales, shop functions, personnel, finance, and legal. If you don't give this to them, they are handicapped, unable to control their destiny.

Finally, to eliminate vulnerability during implementation, it's better to miss the plan completion date then to prematurely launch a set of actions without an adequate map, thus missing the mark.

B. Compensation and Incentives. Money is clearly the prime motivator, especially for salespeople. We all know that the cost curve in the business tends to be flat, while the profit curve, once you are beyond break-even, is steep. My advice is to pay less for the early sales dollars and much more (in fact, accelerate commissions) for the later sales dollars. This formula drives early sales to cover costs and rewards the rep handsomely once the company achieves profitability.

Whatever system you choose, it must contain group incentives. And not just sales groups-all department compensation must be aligned with the goals of the organization. You want to encourage and reward individual initiative; but, more important, you must encourage teamwork. So when the team wins, everyone should be rewarded.

And that brings us to the last component of planning: *How are we doing?*

V. PROGRESS REVIEW

A. Progress Reports. This is really about *controlling* your organization. Delegation without control is abdication. Progress reports that deliver the results of a manager's effort must be distributed at regular checkpoints up and down the organization. Strong initial control will assert your management prerogatives, and you'll be respected for it. Subsequent loosening will be interpreted as a gesture of faith in and respect for your subordinate. Your reporting system is your feeder for control. You also need a control cycle. This is the time it takes to conceive, document, approve, implement, and assess the results of a decision. These should be short intervals, say, every quarter.

In summary, your company is properly controlled when your team is selected and trained; they know what to do, when to do it, how to do it, and what's expected. They follow company policy and track their progress against accurate reports to spot potential problems early, while there is still time to do something about it.

B. Meetings. Meetings are for one purpose: to enhance the prospects of achieving the company's goals and objectives. This is done by identifying problems and fixing them. You need a meeting schedule for the management team. There is a set agenda, you identify who's to be there, and it lasts one hour. Get in and get out. If there is a significant problem or event to deal with that will go over the allotted time, take it off the table, and put a different set of resources behind it. Don't be bogged down by staff meetings with tangents or wild goose chases. Stick to the agenda. Everyone is assigned a subject to present. Meetings are for contributors, not audiences. All participants are expected to show up with completed staff work, reports, presentations, whatever. And if they're not on time, lock the door. No exceptions. Better never than late.

For special meetings, the practice is to publish an agenda two days in advance, identify the participants, request staff work if needed, set a time and a place, and come prepared.

Emergencies are different. I call these *red alerts*. Anyone on the management team can call one. The meeting will be held within four hours of the alert. All senior managers are expected to respond either in person or by teleconference; again, no exceptions. These are rare meetings-something has to be really wrong for these to occur.

C. Early Warning System. I manage the business from one piece of paper, and I insist my managers do the same. This is the best way to communicate what's happening in the business. There are just a few facts that count in every business. When these things are going right, everything else falls into place and the business is healthy. *If something goes awry, this one piece of paper becomes your early warning system.*

What counts most for me are sales dollars, sales orders, shipments, gross margin, gross margin percentage, number of inbound sales calls, number of outbound sales proposals, payroll expense, headcount (adds/deletes), customer credits and returns, six key variable expense items, A/R balance, inventory balance, debt to equity, and capital expenditures. I distribute this to all managers. These indicators become our focus. Never squander your time on matters that at best generate marginal return. Go after the big ones. When one of these indicators is off we have our early warning. My managers can now investigate and solve the problem. It works.

D. Accountability. You must aggressively and consistently understand where the company is at and where it's going. The only way to know this is to review the milestone results. These must be quantitative at first.

Have your CFO give you the adjectives and adverbs later, summarizing the information and providing a prognosis for good or ill. Next is accountability, which presumes that your Management By Objectives program is in place and understood. If so, your managers can now perform at their best only if they are regularly, formally, and objectively measured. This is the essence of accountability. Harsh though it may seem, managers either deliver on what they sign up for, or they have to move over and let someone else try. Which brings me to my last point: The emphasis has to be on results. To achieve excellent results, you, the leader, must perform excellently in your job. Your people will see this and identify you with an expectation of a high level of performance.

Tubby's Planning Model

1. Planning Foundation *Where are we today?*	Internal Assessment *Strengths & Weaknesses*	External Assessment *Opportunities & Threats*	*Assumptions*	*Priorities*
	Critical Success Factors			

2. Expected Results *Where do we want to go?*	*Vision/Mission Statements*	*Goals and Objectives (Revenue/Quota)*

3. Method *How will we get there?*	*Business Strategies (Competitive Advantage)*	*Organization Model*	*Programs (Marketing, Coverage)*

4. Implementation *Who will do what?*	*Delegated Objectives (Quota Assigned)*	*Compensation Incentives*	*Delegated Programs (Who?)*

5. Progress Review *How are we doing?*	*Progress Reports (What, when, who)*	*Meetings (Staff & Executive)*	*Measure (Early Warnings)*	*Accountability*

Tool #6

Plan Your Planning

We're not done yet. Now you have to *plan your planning*. That might sound strange, but believe me it's not. I take my entire team off sight for our *first* meeting, usually someplace relaxing and functional, with plenty of white boards, flip-chart paper, markers, and an overhead projector. I make sure there are snacks and soft drinks, and I always have a working lunch brought in.

At the first meeting I present the "big goals" and the rationale behind them. To this, I invite the teams' comments and reactions. This discussion will be more lively than efficient, and you should expect to catch a lot of chaff with the wheat. Some will embrace your ideas, some will push back, but all must listen. The quality of the meeting lies in the participation and a chance for everyone to contribute. Eventually the goals are sorted out, and they are no longer mine but the teams'. They can now go away and build individual plans using the planning model.

Quick story on individual plans:

Former Secretary of State Dr. Henry Kissinger was known for, among many other things, his insistence on excellence in planning documentation. An aide who had submitted a plan to him several days prior asked Dr. Kissinger what he thought of it. Dr. Kissinger mildly asked, "Is this the best plan you can devise?"

"Well," the aide hesitated, "I'm sure with a little more work it would be better."

Dr. Kissinger thereupon returned the plan to him.

After almost two more weeks of effort, the aide resubmitted the improved plan. Several days later Dr. Kissinger called the aide into his office. "Is this really the best plan you recommend?"

Taken slightly aback, the aide mumbled that "perhaps a point or two could be better defined, perhaps more direct accountability. . . ." Once again the aide left the office, revised plan under his arm, determined that he would develop a plan that anyone, even Henry Kissinger, would recognize as perfect.

The aide worked day and night for the next three weeks, on occasion even sleeping in his office. Finally finished, he proudly strode into Dr. Kissinger's office, handed the plan to the Secretary, and braced himself for the inevitable.

"Is this really the very best plan that you can come up with?"

"Yes, sir, Mr. Secretary!" the aide exclaimed.

"Good," said Dr. Kissinger, "in that case, I'll read it."

The lesson is obvious: Your managers will devise better plans if they believe you expect them to. Mediocrity is not acceptable. Don't let them bother you with plans that aren't excellent. This is a signal to the entire organization that only excellence and thoroughness of planning is acceptable.

All right, back to where we left off. At the next meeting, the team members present their departmental plans. Once again they are subject to evaluation and negotiation, with the aim of pinning them down. This meeting may take two full days. Next, the CFO or vice president of operations review and consolidate these plans, then assign capital and create procedures to support them. This is what I call the smell test: Do we have the resources to pull these plans off? In our final meeting, we adjust the plans to align with the constraints of our resources; then we inaugurate them and publish them. After that we communicate the plan to everyone in the organization, and then we go do it. So you see, we must plan our planning.

Tool #7

Decision Making

Let's talk a moment about decision making. *Decisions* are your prerogative. You're the boss. Move fast on the decisions you can reverse, less fast on the ones you can't. For example, if you make an organizational change and don't get the desired results, you can change your decision, and restore things as they were. If you fire somebody, that decision is permanent. So make sure you differentiate between reversible and irreversible decisions. When you move fast with something reversible, make sure you tell those affected that it is reversible if you don't get a certain result in a specific time frame. This way you will get a one hundred percent effort. If your people think it's a permanent decision, they might hold back. But for the big decisions, the ones you can't change, take your time. You've got to be right on those.

Tool #8

Who Looks After You?

Lastly, you must take care of yourself. A lot is riding on your shoulders. Your job is to see to it that your team gets what they need to do their job. But who looks after you? How do you stay sharp? Try this: The American Management Association has something called the Presidents Association. Every year, usually in the winter, I attend a one-week Presidents retreat, where I'm locked up with twenty men and women who are there to learn. We cover subjects ranging from human resources, marketing, and data processing to management skills, and customer service. You name it, it's covered. A few years ago for example, we were required to develop our own "management creed" to be taken back and shared with our teams. This creed was an expression of our most sacred values and a comprehensible guide as to how we will run our business. Each of us was assigned a development partner to assist with the process. We then presented our creed to the group, which provided the principal benefit. It was a marvelous experience, and I returned to the office fired up. The point is that you must treat yourself to this kind of continuing education. Staying sharp requires staying current. Read everything, listen to tapes, go to seminars, join your industry association, participate in the Inc. 500 Council, and make friends with worthy competitors. I have developed many lasting relationships through the American Management Association (AMA,) and when I needed some advice, they were always there ready to help. Whether it's the AMA, the Young Presidents Organization (YPO), The Executive Committee (TEC), the Inc. 500 Council, the Rotary Club, or the Masters Forum, join one and get involved.

Management Tools

My Management Creed

The following is the Management Creed that I created during my week at the AMA Presidents Association. This creed was distributed through a memo that I wrote to all of my executives and first-line managers. Over time, it became a management lighthouse-providing immovability and illumination. I've kept it in its original form. I hope you find it useful.

MEMORANDUM

TO: All NCC Managers
FROM: Mike Kerrison
DATE: January 20, 1997
RE: Straight Talk about the Business

Not long ago I developed a "Management Creed" to equip our management team with a road map on how to operate within the business, both day-to-day and strategically for the long haul. I've modified this creed to better reflect the needs of NCC. I hope you find it useful because it truly captures the essence of what I want our company and our managers to be.

I want to talk about three matters: commitments, operating policies, and ground rules for managers. These thoughts will govern us now and in the future, so they are to be taken seriously.

Commitments:

As managers, whether we are a public or private company, we have two inviolate *commitments*: (1) Earn an attractive return on money invested, and (2) provide meaningful work opportunities for our employees. This means that NCC must provide a better return on investment for its shareholders than would otherwise be earned through comparable situations. It also means that we have a commitment to ensure that all employees are treated fairly and given opportunities for personal growth matching their interests and capabilities.

To meet these commitments, we must sustain an average growth in earnings per share of twenty percent and a return on equity of thirty percent. This is more easily achieved in a fast-growth start-up situation like we have today, but it will become more difficult as we grow and mature. At the same time we must strive to maintain a stable earnings pattern, even during economic decline. This will aid forecasting and allow us to meet our financial obligations to employees and vendors. Achieving a stable pattern will require each business unit to do the same. This means that each manager should take responsibility

for the performance of his or her unit. We will determine and track the net profitability and return on capital invested (after all allocations) for each business
unit. Any time a business unit does not meet our profit goals, it will be regarded as a drain on the corporation which will not be tolerated.

Operating Policies and Guidelines:

The business will be governed through a few basic *operating policies*. We will
run our business by developing and approving plans, then achieving planned
results. All business-unit managers are expected to develop and implement an
annual operating and strategic plan for each important segment of their business. I know we have all worked hard on these plans over the last few weeks,
and I'm anxious to inaugurate them at our final planning session. These plans
will be challenged vigorously in our session. Do not take this personally. We
are simply guarding against the enormous problems that come from misguid-
ed and unsupported strategies.

Once plans are approved, managers will have all the authority they need to
operate with minimal interference from me, provided they are achieving the
planned results. When managers depart significantly from planned results,
they should expect prompt senior-management action.

When results are falling short of plan, each manager involved is expected to
identify the underlying reasons for the shortfall and initiate the corrective
actions required to get back on track within ninety days. If the original plan
proves to be faulty, the manager must restructure and create an alternative
plan that will meet our growth and profit objectives.

As a rule, failure to meet planned results means that either the plan was faulty
to begin with or its execution was poor. Thus I intend to judge a manager's
performance on how effectively they develop good plans and then achieve
their planned results. Managers who cannot create high quality plans or who
fail to overcome the operating or competitive obstacles that inevitably appear,
will be moved aside to give others who have these capabilities a chance.

We intend to improve profits by continually improving productivity, both for ourselves and our clients. We must create real and measurable gains for our
clients through the productive use of our products and services. We should
avoid or even reject sales opportunities if we don't believe we can help clients
realize these gains.

By the same token, we should achieve annual productivity improvements in
our own operations that offset the increasing costs of health care, labor,
recruiting, and training. These accomplishments will allow us to stay competitive and attract and maintain quality employees without losing money. We are
in the technology business. We must practice what we preach.

Let's turn our attention to our employees. We will adhere to four primary operating policies:

> 1. *We will always pay above-average wages for above-average perform-
> ance, and we will monitor the wage structure in each market so we
> don't fall behind.*

2. *Our fringe benefits will remain comparable to our top competitors, and we will improve benefits when profits allow.*

3. *We will agreeably try to accommodate individual preferences for work assignments and schedules. If employees are performing well in their current position, we will never penalize them for turning down new assignments. Nor will we penalize employees who decline working overtime because of personal considerations.*

4. *We will encourage open communication with employees and always respond to their recommendations and criticisms in a professional, sensitive, and intelligent way.*

Employees should be encouraged further to tell us when we are not following these policies. If they feel they cannot, dissatisfaction and distrust will develop, and they will ultimately seek by whatever means a better situation for themselves.

We must make some promises if we are going to operate effectively. We will never act unfairly or lack integrity. Admittedly, this sounds like an impossible request because people do make mistakes. What I am really referring to is our actions, not our talk. In a company that is growing like ours, effective communication is difficult, and the chances for different interpretations of policy and situations are great. Therefore, we need to work hard to do what is right.

We want our actions and decisions to be based on logic, facts, and fair play. What we don't want are shaded opinions or distorted facts used to justify any of our actions or decisions. Nor do we want facts or opinions covered up that might make a situation look different than what it really is.

Solid profit can come only from giving our clients genuine value more effectively than the competition does and by controlling costs. Profit growth should never come from taking unfair advantage of any supplier, employee, customer, or business partner. Nor should it be achieved by aggressive accounting or business decisions that inflate the profit picture or overstate results to the detriment of the long term. We also must be consistent and avoid having to "throw the long ball" to win the profit game. And we don't want anybody on our team who doesn't play the game fairly.

Fairness and integrity are full-time principles that cannot be turned on and off to suit monetary desires or needs. Sometimes we will have to sacrifice sales and earnings in order to make these principles stick. But we know we cannot compromise them and remain the kind of company that we want to be.

We will squeeze corporate staff down to a minimum. This does not mean that we intend to operate at a deficit. Operating management should continually challenge all staff activities, to determine whether they are essential for contributing results. We must guard against ideas and programs that seem important but put an unbalanced cost burden on the operating units, which pay the freight.

All corporate staff functions will be expected to present annual operating plans for review and approval in the same way business units do. These staff plans should outline the major activities during the period ahead and justify the costs associated with them. Staff plans and reports will be brief and straight-forward. Reports will be limited to what is done, not what is interesting. And we will not have a secretary for each officer when one is enough for three.

Ground Rules for Managers

To perform well and get good results, managers must abide by certain ground rules. None of these are difficult to agree to. The difficulty is following them. Moreover, doing them will never win a manager a popularity contest. But a manager who does not follow these ground rules will fail, regardless of how brilliant or well trained he or she is.

I believe three elements represent the core responsibilities of every manager: (1) organization and staffing, (2) planning and execution, and (3) people development (including the managers themselves). If you're not getting better than by definition you're falling behind. Below are the ground rules for each of these responsibilities.

Organization and Staffing

Ground Rule #1: People, not structure, make or break any organization. Blindly following organizational concepts or principles simply because they appear theoretically correct or because they have been proven successful for someone else is a sure route to wasted talent, wasted effort, and poor results. Organizational models alone answer nothing. Dedicated people can make almost any structure work. Conversely, ineffective people will render any organization a failure.

This does not mean that organization is not important or that we shouldn't consider changing them. Change often leads to better use of our talent, improved planning and control, and reduced costs. But tinkering with a sound organizational model is usually a means of escaping or putting off fundamental problems in the organization that are difficult or uncomfortable to deal with. So we won't tinker; we will manage.

Ground Rule #2: All managers should have back-up people who are potentially as well qualified for their job as they are themselves. No manager has the right to feel he or she has done a good job if a logical successor is not clearly visible at all times. A manager who concludes that no one has this potential must give top priority to bringing in someone who does. This does not mean the staff has to be enlarged; it means that one or two people in the organization who don't have the qualifications or potential to move up should be replaced with someone who does.

Ground Rule #3: Every manager must make certain that individuals in the organization know what is expected of them, how their assignments fit into the whole, and that their performance will be measured. Each individual should have a precise set of goals and deadlines to meet so that no misunderstanding arises about what must be done. These become the standards for measuring that person's performance. Our whole system of rewards and penalties must reinforce this concept. The payoff should always be for achieving results, not for making the effort. Those who perform well should be recognized and rewarded. Those who don't should expect limited rewards, lesser responsibility, and even dismissal.

Ground Rule #4: Be alert for organizational misfits. No matter how carefully we recruit and screen, misfits will show up. Quick, decisive action is needed to weed them out. People in the organization always know who the misfits are and draw negative conclusions about the managers who permit them to remain.

Ground Rule #5: Suspect committees. A committee may be useful in situations where a cross-functional review is essential to ensure coordination on major projects or a new product development committee or where an oversight function would be too much for one person to handle, like a compensation or audit committee or an open house committee. But on the main street of business management, there is simply no place for committees. They never make decisions, and they are impossible to hold accountable for anything.

Planning and Execution

Ground Rule #1: Establishing a solid strategic direction for any business is critical to formulating a good business plan. Good planning leads to good results. Too often our annual and multiple-year plans are developed as extrapolations of the immediate past, with little thought given to the fundamental mission or to market realities. As a result, time and effort are misspent chasing goals that, even if achieved, won't advance the business purpose or contribute to the future of the enterprise. Therefore, a prime responsibility of our management team is to maintain strategic focus of the business.

Ground Rule #2: The business plan must be in writing. If it is not, it has no value. The discipline of committing a plan to paper exposes the holes and vagaries that are bound to crop up when it is only talked about. Regardless of its complexity, a good plan properly thought through can be put down in a few paragraphs and pages, not books and volumes. There is an old saying: The reason we write long, complicated business plans is because we don't have time to write short, precise ones.
The smart manager knows that eighty percent of the benefits from planning usually stems from the first twenty percent of the effort. The rest just feels good-as though you're being thorough and professional. Take the first 20 percent and run.

Ground Rule #3: Fact-based decisions are crucial to good planning at all levels. The word "fact" is supposed to convey certainty, but no word is more loosely used, especially in business planning. What are presented as facts frequently turn out to be merely:

- Apparent facts
- Assumed facts

· Reported facts
· Hoped-for facts
· Half-true facts

The distinction between facts that are real and facts that are not real may not be very important in some matters. But in business the distinction is vitally important. When a manager accepts or submits a fact that is unreal, painful chains of events and decisions are put into motion, sending large parts of the business in the wrong direction.

A solid manager is able to sort real facts from all others. He is absolutely bold in questioning colleagues to be sure that what they are presenting as unchallengeable facts do not turn out to be unreal stories.

Ground Rule #4: Keep priorities straight. This is one of the toughest managerial obligations. It is easy to duck unpleasant problems or issues by shifting thought to longer-range problems or opportunities. To avoid this, managers should always follow these priorities:

·Forecast surprises by staying on top of day-to-day activities. Keep officers informed of all developments, good and bad. Phone mail, E-mail, and short memos are perfect to keep communication flowing.

·At a minimum reach your planned goals for the current quarter. Otherwise you are relying on the long pass again. This is not only risky and uncomfortable, it also cripples cash flow.

·Then and only then are you free to move on to your other responsibility of charting your course for future growth and development.

Managers always have more to do than they can possibly get done. Slotting tasks according to these priorities is the only way to make sure of doing first things first.

Ground Rule #5: Active managers seek to make things happen according to plan. They don't get caught off base and then scramble to salvage the situation that could have been averted by staying on top of the operations activities. They never drift into decisions or actions or permit actions to be taken by default. They always know what is going on and what they are doing.

Active managers must know the details. They cannot do this by sitting in the office or allowing themselves to be cut off from the front line activities by rigid organizational lines. They cut across or through these lines and talk to anyone without advise or permission, but they do not interfere with lines of authority or the decision making process. They simply recognize that this is the only way to find out what is truly going on.

Managers who don't know the details are bound to be superficial. Not knowing enough to take action until a crisis develops, they can only be reactive. There is no way this kind of manager can succeed. One crisis will lead to another, and the entire company will slowly drift out of control.

Ground Rule #6: No manager should ever grab the credit for success. The whole team deserves the credit. Good results flow from the team's efforts, not the leader's alone. No jockey ever crossed the finish line ahead of the horse. Conversely, every manager must shoulder the responsibility for results and commitments that have gone sour. Shortfall or outright failure occurs when the manager has done a poor job of fulfilling the core responsibilities of planning, staffing, organizing and assuring implementation (control).

People Development

Ground Rule #1: A healthy environment permits people to work effectively, develop themselves, and achieve their aspirations. The good manager places emphasis on creating this kind of environment (culture). I do not mean trying to make everybody happy or making work easier for them; I mean fostering a work environment that has these four characteristics:

1. Absolute honesty and integrity in what everyone says and does. Everyone should feel free to say what he or she really thinks. They have the right and the responsibility to be open and constructively critical of whatever is wrong or needing improvement.

2. A genuine desire to get problems on the table and correct them, rather than worrying about pinpointing blame or scurrying to keep shirttails clean.

3. A willingness by our managers to listen to other people and a willingness to admit to being wrong when the facts and logic prove so.

4. Recognition of accomplishment through smart and hard work. Nothing beats the excitement of being on a winning team or a team that handles adversity with spirit and confidence.

Unless this kind of corporate culture exists, good people will leave, and the mediocre will remain. An organization staffed with mediocrity is a certain loser.

Ground Rule #2: Put a limit on tolerance of marginal or poor performers. Most managers kid themselves into thinking that by allowing these individuals to continue, listening oversympathetically to their excuses and frustrations, they are being fair and that somehow time will correct the situation. That's wrong. Basic personality flaws or skill deficiencies simply don't get corrected with time.
It should never take more than one year to determine if someone can do the job. The real job. The capable manager is a tough-minded performance evaluator. An early decision on who can and who cannot perform may seem ruthless, but it is necessary. Fairness and compassion are also necessary. The manager must help the person preserve both dignity and employability.

<u>Ground Rule #3:</u> Ensure that people in the organization know exactly where they stand and what their career outlooks are at all times-even if it hurts. This doesn't mean they should expect to have their career paths mapped out for them or be promised certain promotions. But it does mean that people should know how they are performing and whether they are regarded as having growth and leadership potential.

There is nothing kind about glossing over weaknesses that could be corrected if the individual were aware of them. Nor is there anything kind about deluding someone into thinking he or she is doing well or has great opportunity when this isn't the case. Failure to be completely honest can hurt someone's chances of becoming an effective contributor. And it will jeopardize the person's career. No manager has the right to do that. And if the manager can't get up the nerve or confidence to talk straight about this, he will be taken out of his job.

<u>Ground Rule #4:</u> Personal characteristics have nothing to do with individual effectiveness. A manager should never notice a person's nationality, race, religious preference, gender, sexual orientation, political inclination, educational affiliation, or preference as to recreation, friends, or things of this nature. Not to notice takes effort, but it is part of a manager's job. Rather, the manager must concentrate on what really counts:

- *Who faces problems squarely? Who has the guts to tell it like it is? Who does not? Who commands the respect and commitment of others?*
- *Who contributes to the team regularly? Who does not?*
- *Who articulates good ideas and stimulates good ideas in others? Who tears down good ideas?*
- *Who produces consistent results? Who makes their commitments? Who does not?*

Managers who get hung up on personal characteristics and do not give sufficient consideration to the things that really count are going to lose. Competition and the whole world will pass them by, led by people who have a broader perspective on what it takes to produce results.

There is nothing new or even sophisticated about these guidelines and principles. But they truly represent my values and the values I want for our organization. A couple of years ago I made a commitment to nineteen other CEOs that I would create this management creed and share it with my team. I wish I could say that in my eighteen years of leading a company I have always met these standards. I haven't. But it is with renewed vigor that I enter 1997 and the years to come.

I see great things for NCC. I see stability, innovation, and growth within our industry. I see opportunity for people. I see a legitimate force in the marketplace, where competitors pack their bags and leave. I see loyal clients, happy families, and a rich heritage. Let's make it happen-together. With God's help we can.

Index

A

Accounting, 191
Accounting System, 95, 103
Accounts Payable, 194
Action, 97
Adversity, 44
Advertising Firms, 115
Angels, 97
Anvil of Prosperity, 75
Approach, 166
Abdication, 170
Assessment External, 164
Assessment Internal, 164
Assumptions, 164
Attitude, 125

B

Balance Sheet, 106
Banker, 97, 202
Baseball, 23, 266

Behavior, 206
Beachhead, 256
Bureaucracy, 212
Best Practices, 120
Biases, 257
Black Monday, 136
Blitz Days, 168
Breakaway Performances, 262
Bulwarks, 194
    Characteristics of, 194
Business, 24
    Bootstrap, 105
    Life Cycles, 105, 216
    Monthly, 105,
    Planning & Control System, 193
    Planning Needed, 162
    Starting, 97, 103, 162
    Strategy, 203
Buying Behavior, 244

C

Cancer, 31, 123

Career Path, 202

Cash Flow, 105, 117

Center of Excellence, 205

Champion, 205

Change, 191

Change, Pain of, 191

Committees, 168

City Business, 216

Client Satisfaction, 214

Collaborative Discussion, 203

Columbus, Christopher, 162

Commodity, 182

Compensation System, 170, 205, 214

Competition, 116

Competitive Advantage, 116, 119, 166, 213

Computer Options Inc., 93

Computerworld, 98

Control Cycle, 171

Control System, 184

Control Unnecessary, 212

Corporate Culture, 128

Counterclaim, 148

Critical Success Factors, 164

Cross The Chasm, 97

Culture, 79, 132, 212

Culture, Rudiments Of, 211

Customer-Intimate Approach, 213

Cost Cutting, 149

Customer Services, 116, 127

D

Datacomp, 156

Decentralization, 169

Crossover within, 169

Decision Data, 153

Decisions, 127

Irreversible, 278

Reversible, 278

Dempsey, Rick, 266

Denial, 28, 126

Diagnostic Tool, 194

Differentiate, 105

Distortion Within, 176

Dream, Tyranny of, 152

Dreams, 66, 104, 254

Drinking, 127

Drive, 66

Drive, Origins of, 262

Due Diligence, 155, 198

E

Eagle Award, 69

Early Warning System, 171

E-Commerce, 209

Entrepreneur, 17, 125

Excellence, 132

F

Failure, ix

Family, 44, 105

Fast Growth, 179

Fast Start Plan, 256

Fear, 33

Filters and Funnels, 176
Franklin Covey, 254
Fiduciary Responsibility, 148
Financial Responsibility, 148
Financing Mezzanine, 214
Financing Bank Debt, 214
Financing Venture Capital, 214
Forecast, 117
Founder, 105

G

Giftedness, 75
Gino & Gorgetti's, 164
Goals, Corporate, 202, 205
    Individual, 167, 202
    Misalignment, 206
    Worksheet, 165
Golden Handcuffs, 128
Grace, 176
Grief, 28, 33
Growth, 104
    Problems, 104, 129
    Skills for, 133

H

Heiman, Stephen (Strategic Sales),
    227
Hierarchy, 176
High Achievers, 210
Hiring, 105
Holden, Jim (Power Base Selling),
    227
Hopkins, Tom (How to Master the
    Art of Selling), 227

I

Iacocca, Lee, 263
IBM, 34
    Channel Strategy, 174
    Hundred Percent Club, 65, 160
    Values Add Program, 156
Implementation, 164, 169
Inc. Magazine, 107, 149
Incentive Stock Option, 198
Industrial Psychologist, 73
Industry Standards, 119
Infrastructure, 104, 127
Insure Clients, 104
Intimacy, 207, 213
ItelCorporation, 77

J

Jesus Christ, 145

K

Kick Off Meeting, 203, 212
Kissenger, Henry, 276

L

Last Look, 179
Launch Plan, 97, 129, 131
Law Suits, 148, 149
Lawyer, 93, 139
Leader/Planner, 103
Leader/Visionary, 194
Leadership, 104, 172
    Chapter 17, 201
    Conditions of, 104

Essence of, 171
Within Markets, 203
Levinson, Daniel, 152
Life Cycle, 155
Of a Company, 191
Restarting the Cycle, 191
Lifestyle, 114
Lift, 103
Line of Credit, 117
Liquidation Problems, 104

M

MacKay, Harvey, 131
Malice, nor pity, 105
Maintenance Innovators, 119
Management Creed, 283
Management Reporting, 117
from one piece of paper, 171
Manager/Builder, 103, 194
Market Back Mentality, 162
Marketing, 115
4x of Postcards, 115
Brochure, 94
Find Leads, 116
Four P's, 8
Integrated, 116
Repetition, 115
Strategic, 115
Telemarketing, 116
Mix, 168
Mediocrity, 132
Message, 168

Microsoft, 108
Midsize, 133
5 obstacles to reaching, 133
Minority Shareholder, 91
Miracle, 97
Misfits, 131
Mission, 103, 165, 254
Mistakes, xvi
Money, borrow, 89, 90
Motivational Climate, 204

N

North Central Consulting, 198
Norwest Bank, 202

O

Objection Handling, 106
Obsession, 69
Obstacles, 191
Overcoming, 191
Offices, 106
Office Hotel, 211
Ohio University, 41
Opportunities, 164
Optimization, 180
Ordinary People, 81
Organization, 193
Learning, 193
Model for, 116, 167
Orientation, 212
Owens, Tom, 159
Owner/Operator, 103, 194

P

Partnering, 168
Passion, 104
Padua Franciscan High School, 40
People, 117
    Assessment of, 117
    Malice nor pity, 105
    Managing, 105
Performance, 206
    Balanced, 206
Phased Bid Methodology, 213
Pity, 105
Planning Base, Four Categories,
164, 166
Planning, 105
    90 days, 105
    Five steps of, 163, 267
    Model, 127, 275
    Plan your plan, 276
Policies, 117
Politics, 129, 132, 213
Position Description, 168
Power, 130
President's Club, 116
    In the club, at the club, 116
Price Low-balling, 179
Price Perception, 179
Principles, 203
    Guiding, 203
Priorities, 164
Procedures, 117, 127
Professional Days, 178

Professional Services, 198
Promoting from within, 128
Prosperity, 44
Provincial, 113

Q

Queens, N.Y., 45
Quota, 116

R

Rackham, Neil (Spin Selling), 227
Radio Advertising, 120
Receptionist, 107
Reception Area, 212
Recognition program, 212
Results, 163, 166
Review, 164, 169
Risk, 128, 212
Roundtable discussions, 178

S

Safe Harbor, 130
Sales, 227
    Amalgamation, 227
    Axiom, 226
    Culture, 105
    Cycle, 61
    Finding sales reps, 263
    Interview Reps, 263
    Model, 56, 242
    Quota, 116
    Salesman, 56

Structure, 62, 229

System, 226

Territory, 62, 251, 254

Training, 62

Mechanics of, 65

SBA, 97

Schuller, Robert, ix

Search Ministry, 144

Security and Exchange

Commission, 198

Self Directed Work Teams, 176

Self Management, 261

Self-Esteem, 69

Seminars, 119, 154, 168

Shareholders, Internal, 215

Sorbus, 152

Spaghetti, 42

Spin-offs, 127

Spiritual Life, 143

SSA North Central, 195

Stock Unit, 216

Stock-for-Stock Purchase, 198

Strategy, 166

Strength in weakness, 150

Strengths & Weaknesses, 117, 164

Success, xvi

Secrets of, 221

Sustainability, 166

Synergy, 203

T

Telemarketing, 116, 120, 168

Territory, 251

Beachhead, 255

Management of, 252, 254

Time Management, 252

Systems, 254

Toolkit, xvii, 162, 223

Trade Show, 168

Training, 106

Transformational Thinkers, 213

Trauma Center, 149

Two-Hundred Percent Plan, 90

U

Unmanageable, 129

Unpredictability, 166

V

Values, 44, 104

Venture Capital, 97

Vision, 104, 201

Visionary, 117

Vulnerability, 104

W

Watson, Tom Jr., 262

Watson, Tom Sr., 262

Weakness, 26

Notes